UNDER THE RED EAGLE

First edition, published in 2004 by

WOODFIELD PUBLISHING
Woodfield House, Babsham Lane, Bognor Regis
West Sussex PO21 5EL, England
www.woodfieldpublishing.com

© Dr F.T. Pearce, 2004

All rights reserved.
No part of this publication may be reproduced
or transmitted in any form or by any means,
electronic or mechanical, nor may it be stored
in any information storage and retrieval system,
without prior permission from the publisher.

The right of Dr F.T. Pearce
to be identified as Author of this work
has been asserted by him in accordance with
the Copyright, Designs and Patents Act 1988

ISBN 1-903953-34-0

Under the Red Eagle

A Tour Overseas with 239 Wing Desert Air Force 1942–1945

FRANK PEARCE

Woodfield

To my wife Joan who, during the writing of this book, regularly lost me in the study.

Also to my daughters Daryl and Gale
and my four grandchildren
Oliver, Zoe, Sarah and Fergal

marked the conclusion of a highly successful raid in the late stages of the campaign.

The following signal was sent to 239 and other Wings from A.O.C. Desert Air Force:

"FULL PHOTOGRAPHIC COVER HAS NOW BEEN RECEIVED OF THE RESULTS OF THE ATTACK AGAINST VENICE HARBOUR INSTALLATIONS ON 21/3.

THE RESULTS ACHIEVED ARE EXCELLENT AND THE MAXIMUM AMOUNT OF MILITARY DAMAGE HAS BEEN DONE BY A COMPARATIVELY SMALL FORCE. BOMBING WAS .MOST ACCURATE AND NO APPARENT DAMAGE HAS BEEN DONE TO ANY OF THE CULTURAL MONUMENTS IN CLOSE PROXIMITY TO THE TARGET.

THE ANTI FLAK ATTACKS WERE WELL TIMED AND ACCURATELY DELIVERED.

THANKS TO THIS AND THE EFFICIENCY OF THE A/S/R MEASURES, WE DID NOT LOSE A SINGLE PILOT IN THIS MOST SUCCESSFUL OPERATION.

MY BEST CONGRATULATIONS TO ALL THOSE WHO TOOK PART IN THIS NEATLY EXECUTED OPERATION."

George H. Westlake
Wing Commander Ops. (Flying)
239 Wing Desert Air Force,
Later Group Captain

ABOUT THE AUTHOR

Frank Pearce was born in the Midlands and educated at Kings Norton and the University of Birmingham, where he obtained first and higher degrees and two fellowships. He had obtained an entrance to the University by an earlier matriculation, an Air Ministry grant, and an interview carried out at his station (Bridgnorth) by an RAF psychological team. When he actually got to the University he found that on the male side it was much like an Officers' Mess with so many out of the Services and pretty well every rank present.

At the start of his service he joined the RAF after the toss of a coin, and as a teenager. He then served as a Gunner at RAF Waddington in Lincolnshire, in what was later to become the RAF Regiment. Then, posted overseas, he embarked at Liverpool on the very inauspicious date and time of Friday 13th February at 13.00 hours, in 1942.

His troopship – the *Duchess of Richmond* (X5) managed to avoid the "wolf packs" of the North Atlantic, although her sister ship *Duchess of York* did not. He found himself at the start of a journey which was to take him round the world through a dozen countries, before finally entering the Reich. On the way, in Italy, 239 Wing, to which he was attached, gave "Close Support" (its motto) to the Eighth and Fifth Armies and *inter alia,* as it turned out, the redoubtable Harry Secombe and Spike Milligan.

INTRODUCTION

This is a record of a 'tour overseas' as experienced by many airmen in the World War of all ranks up to "Air". Many sailed the North Atlantic on a journey to far places, in violent storms and under constant threat from the German Navy, the Luftwaffe, and the submarine "wolf packs".

Many had no idea where their posting was intended to end. It could be the Gulf, India, Burma, the Far Pacific, or elsewhere. They would become familiar with many eastern languages and not least with "RAF-ese", a service lingo with mysterious references to "shooting a line" (exaggerating one's endeavours), "take a dim" (regard something unfavourably), "collect the gen" (acquire sound information), "put up a black" (do something incorrectly). In the last case you were liable to be called a "Prune" which implied someone incapable or who had "bent" (crashed) an aircraft. There were hundreds more of these expressions, to which Arabic, Urdu, Hindi, Persian and other tongues made a contribution.

The book draws on personal experience as seen by an observer of sufficient rank to have access to all messes. The first part of the book deals with the work of Wireless Units in Iraq, Persia and Egypt. These were sophisticated observer units equipped with radio and directly in touch with Command if necessary. They watched for enemy aircraft and performed guard duties such as those over the oil pipelines serving the Eighth Army. In Iraq the unit faced a possible German assault through Turkey, to take over the oilfields. In Persia it was much the same, although this time facing the Germans advancing through the Caucasus to the Persian oilfields. Had these been successful it would have opened the way to India for Hitler. In the event, it was not successful because the enemy was halted at Stalingrad. So the unit was transferred to Egypt to back up the Eighth Army before Alamein. It was of this Army that Churchill said: "If you are asked what you did in the World War, it will be enough to say 'I marched with the Eighth Army'"

The second part of the book deals with our observer's posting to "Air Headquarters, Western Desert". This brought him through the murderous Mediterranean under the escort of the Royal Navy into Tripoli, losing three troopers on the way. When he finally arrived at "Air Headquarters" he was shunted on to "239 Wing". Looking back, if any posting in wartime can be said to be lucky, this one was. It was the most famous Wing of the Desert Air Force, flying Kittybombers,

It had fought its way from Cairo to Kairouan and, moreover, was a Commonwealth Wing which included British, Australians, South Africans, New Zealanders, Rhodesians, Canadians, and in due time, after their capitulation, was even joined by Italians. "It would not surprise me," said the Adjutant at the time, "if we got members of the Luftwaffe posted in."

Then the Wing moved into an Italian orbit and found itself groping its way towards the north. Most people in the UK think of the "invasion" being the one into Normandy in 1944. In fact, the Wing found itself supporting no less than three invasions – into Sicily, into Italy and into Southern France. It even reached the first capital on the Continent to fall – Rome – two days before the troops embarked for Normandy.

The battle up Italy in support of the Eighth Army, and at times the American Fifth Army on the west coast, was, to say the least, tough. The soldiers had to fight their way over scores of rivers which lay in their path. The Desert Air Force had the advantage of flying over these but complemented the ground forces over the hell of Cassino, the striking attack on the Pescara Dam and by being called down by the troops below them to act as flying artillery over Firenze, Bologna and Venezia (the operations of 'Rover David'). Often, the Wing flew from landing strips under the German guns. In the case of Venezia it was such a sensitive target that it was ordered to be carried out without a bomb falling into the city: otherwise senior airmen were liable to be "bowler hatted" (ie. retired from the Service).

~ Under the Red Eagle ~

The whole campaign – as Herculean as any of the war – came to a halt at Campoformido Airfield in northern Italy when battlefront pilots, more used to attack, performed a remarkable display of ceremonial flying. It was executed in impeccable style and the Air Officer Commanding gave a compelled salute.

Thus it was all over, and to quote a bit of "Bless 'em All", the famous Hughes and Lake song of 1940, the Wing was:

'Heavily laden with time expired men,
Bound for the land they adore…'

~ Under the Red Eagle ~

Air Officer Commanding, Desert Air Force briefing 239 Flight and Squadron commanders in the early days of the Italian invasion.

to find that, even in the estuary, he was static in his hammock but the whole vessel rolled around him like a pendulum, side to side, in a deep gloom. Below decks, sleep was barely possible, even for the dog-tired.

The following day the convoy sorted itself out into lines and began to move up the Irish Sea. We were not zig-zagging as yet, since this was not necessary until we were past Northern Ireland. We were, in effect, passing through the narrow neck of a funnel with the Isle of Man to port and Barrow to starboard. The huge hulks of the troopers, and the smaller merchantmen, slid through grey-green water in the slight mist of a February afternoon. Near the Clyde the convoy was closed by some very heavy guns – a battleship, a battle cruiser, two aircraft carriers and two cruisers to add to a screen of some twelve destroyers. The log of one of the carriers, HMS *Formidable*, states that she passed through the boom and sighted the convoy, when she reduced to twelve knots and stationed herself on the beam of the Commodore. Later she recorded being joined by HMS *Eagle* and HMS *Newcastle*.

A weak yellow sun broke through the overcast and bathed the convoy in a strange light as it slid over the grey sea. A speech from Churchill was relayed and claimed stunned attention. It contained the shocking news that Singapore had fallen to the Japanese. Clearly, the Far East was unlikely to be our destination; more likely the Middle East or India.

We were now well into the North Atlantic, somewhere above Ireland. The swell intensified and the *Duchess* was rolling and pitching as we had been warned. Seasickness passed over those lacking "sea legs" and at mealtimes there was food to spare. Everyone slept fully clothed and lifejackets were shouldered at all times. "Darken ship" was piped at sunset each day, when no glimpse of light had to show to attract U-Boat attention.

During the day the destroyers raced around the convoy doing their "greyhounds of the sea" bit, each with its creaming bow wave. They were lean, fast, powerful, and theatrically dramatic, with screws flailing the waves as they charged about at any alarm – or none – going round or through the convoy like sabres, at thirty-five knots. The larger looked more like cruisers and whether or not they had managed to sink a U-Boat was not always certain, since the undersea enemy had different ways of confusing the issue. One was the Submarine Bubble Target, which was ejected from the submerged boat and created a gas bubble under water, which passed for gas emerging from torn plates. These bubbles echoed on the asdic of the destroyers and could hide the German or encourage the hunter onto a false trail. Another ploy was to eject oil, clothes and other junk from the torpedo tubes to simulate a sinking U-Boat.

The first indication of a U-Boat presence would be from the asdic ratings, who would pick up a 'contact' and warn the Officer of the Watch, who would then sound 'action stations'. The asdic tracked the course of the contact by the "ping" and "pong", the time difference indicating the range of the contact. When the two noises were simultaneous the destroyers were, in theory, right over the top of the contact and depth-charges would arc over the stern. If set shallowly the explosion would send the spray high and almost lift the ship upwards, then drop it. Alternatively, a deep explosion would produce a low curve and an effect like lightning glancing across the surface of the water in a shimmer of light, even in the day. If survivors surfaced after an attack they faced an extremely cold Atlantic even in the best times of the year and their chance of fighting another day were remote – as was the case for the Merchant Navy.

I acquired some information about the "undersea boats" from an old officer in the crew, much bearded. The latest versions were captained by an Oberleutnant or occasionally Kapitanleutnent. The typical version was 770 tons, 74 metres long, 6 metres in diameter, and carried 14 torpedoes. Twin diesels gave it 19 hours on the surface and charged the batteries at the same time – which it generally had to do every 24 hours. If submerged, this reduced to a maximum of 9 knots for an hour, after which the batteries were virtually flat: or they could chug along at a knot or two for 3 days, by which time the air was almost unbreathable.

The Battle of the Atlantic in which we were now engaged was one between convoys and U-Boats – or surface raiders, if they appeared. We stared out over the ocean and thought of those back in the UK, who were short on rations and long on bombs. This battle had to be won ultimately because we knew that families were within a short time of starving. But at present the Germans were sinking more ships than could be built, so we were losing.

Then came the storm... The wind rose and low scudding clouds swept low over the masts. X5 began to demonstrate why she was called the "Drunken Duchess". She pointed her bows to the sky, then threw them down to the sea bottom. She rolled 40 degrees and more from the vertical, pitching and tossing through a world of grey – grey sky, grey-green sea, grey vessels ... and many grey faces.

Great rolling walls of ocean chased towards the stern, then along either side of the ship, looming scores of feet above the rails and heaving up the vessel as though in a giant lift. We were in the northern passage somewhere in the triangle of Iceland, Greenland and Newfoundland which, according to the US official history published in later years, is:

> *"...the roughest part of the Western Ocean. Winds of gale force, mountainous seas, biting cold, body-piercing fog and blinding snow squalls were the rule rather than the exception; U-Boats could escape this by submerging but the escorts had to face it."*

The waves curled over the stern, flying dreadful white manes like gigantic sea creatures. Salt spray whipped across the decks in cutting and stinging sheets and worked its way into sore necks and down shivering backs, despite the thick greatcoats. Boots slipped on decks running with water from the solid tons of sea crashing onto the upper decks. The destroyers in the distance bobbed like corks. In such conditions there was a danger that Officers of the Watch had so great a problem of potential collision that they could not concentrate fully on their main job of detecting and destroying U-Boats.

Unwieldy merchant ships could veer out of position or break down. Asdics were interfered with by numerous underwater sounds and ship transmissions. Radar was cluttered by the many ships and spurious echoes. In short, there were complex distractions from every angle and this reduced the likelihood of U-Boat detection.

But there was an advantage from this abominable weather. If the convoy could survive, it might perhaps worry less about U-Boats, who were doubtless keeping their heads well down below the wild surface. Torpedoes could not follow an accurate track across such turbulent waters.

The heavy warships around us sank their bows into the tumultuous seas and then lifted them again, slowly and wearily, as green water cascaded back as far as the bridge, and then poured away over the sides like waterfalls.

The Commodore had his work cut out. The control of X5, as of the whole convoy, rested with him. These men were frequently retired Flag Officers who had re-engaged. They were elderly and grizzled, bearing a blaze of ribbons on the chest and the look of command. By day they would use visual signalling if the weather permitted and some of the messages could be pretty trenchant. In calm, clear weather, all could be relatively orderly, but nevertheless dangerous. The fact was that much could be seen from a conning tower a few feet above the sea and on such days the smoke of a big convoy might be seen fifty miles away. Otherwise, at night, a conning tower in a mid-Atlantic swell was, to all intents and purposes, invisible. The convoy might disintegrate and a weary Commodore had to pull it together again by sheer seamanship and long experience. There were few times when he could rest easily on the bridge.

It was now the 23rd February and we were ten days out. Talking to a Naval Lieutenant I found that we were roughly in the area where, nine months ago, the pocket battleship *Bismark* and the heavy cruiser *Prinz Eugan* broke out into the Atlantic to attack the convoys. *Bismarck* sank the HMS *Hood* and was later sunk in turn.

The Lieutenant relayed the story of a vicious action, having been on a bridge struck by a shell. HMS *Hood* was the first to open fire at a range of 25,000 yards. The *Bismarck* replied. What exactly caused the loss of the *Hood* the Lieutenant did not know. It could have been a shell penetrating the aft magazine. At all events there was a tremendous explosion with jets of flame and the ship was literally torn in two. Over 1,400 men were lost. *Bismarck* took hits from the *Prince of Wales* and from a torpedo released by a Swordfish aircraft – the beloved "string-bag" – flying from the *Ark Royal*. The torpedo jammed the *Bismarck's* rudders and it could merely circle.

The British shot off a considerable amount of ammunition, firing over 1,500 rounds. In the end it was again torpedoes, this time from the *Dorsetshire*, that sank the *Bismarck* and over 1,800 of its seamen. I heard all this from him in some quiet. He had obviously been badly affected psychologically, apart from facial injuries and this probably explained his presence on a troopship. The implications were clear: if the two German warships had achieved what they set out to do and been joined by the *Scharnhorst* and *Gneisnau* – which had already sunk 22 ships twelve months before – then the four raiders together could have massacred the convoys. That would have included this one...

At night the scene could become like one from Hades, when an escort fired a flare. This was capable of lighting the sea miles around and intended to discover any submarine on the surface. Its blinding light hung over the waves and was a valuable action from time to time, since U-Boats had a habit of resting below the surface during the day and at night using their better speed to follow and choose targets.

Then the storm passed its peak. No gale of that force could last long. The weather started to improve. The wind sang on a high note in the rigging but it had lost its malignancy. The great clear grass-green walls still curled on either side of the X5 but their height was less. During the day the sun penetrated the clouds for the first time for a week and touched the water with gold. It warmed our uniforms and raised a drift of steam from the drying decks.

The Tannoy broke the silence. "I do not doubt," said the Captain, "that my crew has been telling you that we passed through a mild flurry. In fact, that was as rough as I have seen in thirty years on the Atlantic." A thin cheer greeted this information, and a song was sung to the tune of the Crusader hymn "Blessed Assurance":

> *"This is my story,*
> *This is my song,*
> *We've been in this Airworks,*
> *Too bloody long,*
> *So roll on the Nelson, the Rodney, Renown,*
> *This two-funnelled bastard,*
> *Is getting me down."*

The cyclone ebbed even more in the next few days and the air became noticeably warmer. On the deck, in the black hours before dawn, the sky became brilliant with coruscating points of light. The Pole Star had already dropped some way towards the northern horizon. Below was a peculiar phosphorescent light where marine insects flushed and glowed among the dark billows. I stood on the deck and watched this unexpected performance. Foam curled away past the ship's sides and a moon hung over, in its first quarter. The dawn tinted the eastern sky and the grey warships plodded on around the X5, reduced to convoy speed.

Later in the morning the carriers started to spew aircraft, presumably to probe for any dark shapes below the surface of the sea. At the same time a number of amateur navigators were encouraged to try their skill with pencils and thrown shadows. Where were these aircraft likely to be heading? The best guess was that the ship was somewhere off the eastern coast of Florida, known to be a haunt of U-Boats. Then we were reminded that this, in truth, was a dangerous place…

Kerumph! Kerumph! A double explosion surged over us from a vessel on the outside of the convoy. An evil flare of orange swept along its deck and a tall branching plume of black smoke rose thickly into the sky. The funnel began to tip forward over a broken back and a thousand silver bubbles broke the surface of the sea in a whitish-green collar around the sinking ship. The ship slowly turned over, capsizing into the water as though some enormous anemone was swallowing it. The internal pressure hurled hatches and parts of the deck into the air like a handful of straw thrown into the wind. Oil spilled across the surrounding sea – which was devastating for anyone in the water who would gulp it into mouth and stomach. They were unlikely to survive. Even with scrambling nets from a destroyer hazarding its chances, the oil soaked figures climbing up scrambling nets were difficult for intending rescuers to grip.

A destroyer headed in quickly then halted and pointed its bows across an apparently empty sea. Its sister came racing across the nose, with a black flag hoisted, and canisters curved through the air and dropped eight fathoms below. The spouts of sea, tall and white, climbed into the sky and fell back in a great sluice of water. Distantly and subdued, there was a series of dull explosions.

The siren of the moving destroyer blasted twice. It was a triumphant sound.

Churchill said the Battle of the Atlantic was "a war of groping and drowning, of ambuscade and stratagem, of science and seamanship." In another comment the First Sea Lord wrote of the early months of 1942 that they were amongst the most anxious of the war. If we lost the battle at sea, we lost the war. His opposite number Dönitz never faltered in his assessment of this fierce North Atlantic campaign as "the veritable heartbeat of the war".

The X5 was now in the sound of this heartbeat. Before it lay the Caribbean. Because of the presence of U-Boats and bombers on the French Atlantic coast, convoys such as this one had been routed at the greatest possible distance from those bases, which extended the length of the passage and meant that we would cross the Atlantic twice over – once to the North American coast, and then back to West Africa. But this implied that we could not escape the Caribbean, which was almost as lively an attack area as the mid-Atlantic. Even at Freetown we could still encounter unexpected attack, while Cape Town held out a promise for both German and Japanese submarines.

Any severe mauling of a convoy like this was the equivalent of a lost battle on land. Reducing the conflict to its bare essentials, if U-Boats could sink merchant ships faster than they could be built, then we would lose. By February 1942 over 2,000 ships had perished and spirits in the convoys were low. The balance of annihilations was clearly against the Allies.

At this time a new factor entered the situation. Formerly the Admiralty Tracking Room had been able to read U-Boat communications by breaking codes of their 'Enigma' machines. But this intelligence was lost when they adopted the new four-wheel 'Enigma' two weeks before we sailed. The ATR was now unable to read the new cipher and could not guide the convoys. So, we were in effect ploughing through danger zones lacking information and air cover and relying wholly on our escort and uncertain direction-finding by shore stations. The troops and airmen were not, of course, aware of this and gloom did not descend. Only the senior naval staff aboard calculated the odds with unease. Ignorance was, perhaps, bliss.

The convoys were symmetrical and balanced, most of the time. They wove patterns in the warp and weft of the seas. The ships in the centre column, where the X5 sailed, had varied spacing as they straggled or moved ahead, until a vexed and succinct signal from the Commodore corrected their station. Around this central core raced a screen of destroyers, corvettes, or frigates, like a grey garland. They swept around port and starboard and then snapped back as though pulled by elastic, hunting and enduring. All eyes on deck, bridge, and mast, scanned to the horizon, asdic listened for the enemy, and the radar probed. On dark nights, from the X5 deck, a few black merchantmen shapes could be seen but only the radar could check on the flock.

At dawn the same ships, in roughly the same place, could be seen if we had been lucky, ploughing on day by day over 220 sea miles, each ship with characteristic stack and bow wave.

This morning there was a particularly bright star in the southeast, luminous enough to glow through a small cloud which had passed before it, and cast a radiance. The gale through which we had steamed now lay far behind in time and nimbus, cumulus, and cirrus were present in a sky nine-tenths clouded. When the sun did get through it was distinctly warm: we were a long way south.

The Red Ensign was hoisted. We had been sailing without flags so far so we were presumably out of the main danger zone. The area of the Atlantic through which we had passed twice had seen grievous losses this year. This would clearly be a long voyage around half the world, with threats all the way. With the Mediterranean more or less closed, all supplies and reinforcements to the Far and Middle East would have to make the long trip round the Cape. "Pukka gen" from the crew was that the next port was Freetown.

Ultimately the Services issued a ribbon for service in the Battle of the Atlantic – the "Atlantic Star" – designed for those who had convoyed, escorted, or had run independently. It was a watered ribbon, shaded in blue, white and sea-green, and a very honourable award.

Victory in the Atlantic would be an essential precondition to any D-Day assault across the Channel.

2. Cancer and Capricorn

"It brings back a night of tropical splendour
It brings back a memory ever green."
Cole Porter

What would happen, wondered Harris, if one of his more careless colleagues fell over the side of this trooper? It would be easy enough to do, especially if the weather were heavy enough to roll the X5 at 40 degree angles. Harris had read the instructions on the boat deck. The liner did not, apparently, stop for anyone disappearing behind in its wake. As always, for everything, there was a service procedure:

"The person observing the occurrence is to call loudly "man overboard" and report to the nearest MP, who will throw a lifebuoy and report to the Captain."

Well, that was clear enough. The only problem would be finding this MP. The NAAFI or the Bar might be useful places to look. Say half-an-hour to find this buoy-throwing authority? By that time the unfortunate might perhaps be seven miles back…

A principal game for the bored was "Housey, Housey". While gambling with cards was expressly forbidden, this method of losing money seemed to be acceptable, so "schools" proliferated around the deck to enliven the day. One paid one's money and a card was thrust into the hand. On this discs were placed according to the cries of the caller, which was not simplified by the custom of substituting "Clickety Click", "Kelly's Eye" (our own Kelly always raised a cry of approval at this one), "A Couple of Ducks", or "MO's Delight" – otherwise 66, 1, 22 and 9. There were also versions quite unmentionable in polite society. The fact that gambling was forbidden did not, naturally, preclude it – therefore Poker, Vingt-et-Un, Brag and others were commonplace recreations.

The sun began to assume an even more southern character. Harris and an "oppo" sat on one of the numerous chunks of machinery near the fore hold, playing pocket chess. Around them lay many prone figures, all in various states of undress. Once the crew started operating again with hoses, which was frequently, they would have scant regard for these recumbents. Swoosh! What jolly fun!

The atmosphere had become very clear and we could see all the vessels behind us, since the "Duchess" was leading the convoy. This had been reduced to one carrier and some destroyers: no battleships or cruisers were in sight. Rumour had it that they had switched to Gibraltar, so that probably meant that we were now off the Western tip of Africa.

The colours around us had changed – the sea from Wehrmacht grey to Reckitt's Blue and the warships from dun to a light dove grey.

The wind was fresh and alleviated the heat. The clouds rode high in "Mares' Tails" and the sea creamed back from many prows behind us. On the trooper to our starboard a score of tiny figures in PT vests and blue shorts bounced up and down like marionettes. From further away sharp cracking reports reached us from a vessel testing ack-ack and cannon. This was not a pleasure cruise.

It was not always blazing sun in these equatorial regions. The sky could be overcast but since the sun itself was higher in the sky and stronger behind the clouds there was a luminous, even milky, effect. But the greater warmth was undeniable and we were now glorious in khaki drill: The blue eagles were replaced with red.

The order to change became effective as we had crossed the Tropic of Cancer at four o'clock in the morning. The normal outfit had become drill bush jackets, shorts, long stockings, and plimsolls, still with the blue side cap although we still had the heavy pith helmets lumbering up the kit we had to carry. Khaki drill, it appeared, meant Near, Middle, or Far East locations. Army dress differed in having epaulettes on the shoulders, carrying any officer rank, and trousers which buttoned up into shorts, allegedly referred to as "Bermuda Shorts." In our case we had separate long trousers against the mosquito – which we have yet to encounter. We shall need to get this lot tailored to improve the fit, as soon as we can.

Preparations were in hand to rig awnings over the open decks, and a boxing ring had appeared over the middle hold. Stalwarts battered each other about to thunderous applause, with the Duty Medical Officer in attendance.

Minor excitement was provided by Fairey Swordfish flying from the aircraft carrier *Illustrious*, exercising themselves with feigned bombing and strafing of the convoy, amidst sarcastic jeers and reversed "V-type" gestures. Some X5 gunners had been recruited from our unit and practised a little deflection. Up, down, circle, dive, bank; and again and again.

Suddenly a grimmer episode intruded. This was on aircraft carrier *Formidable*. Fighters flew and returned to it with great panache, skidding to a standstill like ducks on water, when one would have thought they had little chance of being grabbed and halted in time.

The point was that one aircraft was not grabbed. About noon a solitary fighter came in close over the water. As it touched down it undershot and tipped sideways, plunging under the waves at the side of the carrier. This shocked our trooper into a stygian gloom. The sun appeared to darken. It was a certainty that there was little chance of a survivor, which inhibited any casual discussion of the loss. Violent death by accident on land was something airmen were used to. The same on a sunlit sea was quite another matter, and one which those leaning over the rail, had not seen. Silence reigned.

The log of the *Formidable* was laconic in its entry:

> "28.2.42. 12.00. Lat. 09.00.5 Long. 17.15.7 Lifebuoy dropped for pilot of crashed aircraft and not recovered."

Not even a record of the pilot's name?

Another loss did not even have the credit of being death "in action". Flags in the convoy were lowered to half-mast – or, more strictly, lowered entirely and then raised again to half-mast. The flag of death was considered to fly above the Union Flag.

It appeared that some wit on the *Empress of Bermuda*, sailing on our beam, cut into the supporting strands of a colleague's hammock. What a joke, he would fall out with his feet striking the floor in a highly comical fashion! Unfortunately, on this night, the colleague boarded his hammock the other way round. It was not his feet that struck the floor, but his head. He broke his neck and was buried at sea the following night. It was presumably nothing more than an odd coincidence that the triangular fins of sharks appeared round the convoy for the first time, the following day... or was it?

The temperature dropped this morning and the sea looked untrustworthy. The X5 pushed through grey-green waters again. When we stood on the stern the foam twisting away in the ship's wake did so through "white horses". The wind had risen, shouted its way through the rigging, and was canorous in the two funnels. It started to drizzle – a mist obscured bows from stern and the few uniformed men on the deck could be distinguished only as drab outlines. But we could see the surface and found that sharks had been replaced by more friendly dolphins. Close to the bows, they curved gracefully in and out of the water, matching our speed with ease.

Distant firing from guns to port. The dolphins departed.

The muffled thuds suggested a heavy exchange over the horizon, but we had not the slightest idea what this portended, if anything. There was a rapid flurry of signal flags, and blasts on the siren. We swung from a southerly course to north-westerly. Each vessel dropped smoke floats and a dense white cloud rolled over the surface of the sea. Despite the brilliantly clear day, this screen was so effective as to eclipse the convoy completely. We zigged and zagged for some hours until resuming a south-southeast heading. The firing faded into the distance. A Sunderland flying boat circled the convoy and flashed an Aldis lamp. It then levelled out and disappeared towards the unseen coast to the east while the sun dropped below the western horizon in a blaze of fire.

What was all that about? A surface raider? Otherwise it could have been a sally by U-Boats since we know at least two were around this West African sector of the Atlantic. One, the U-36 under Commander Karl Marten, had left Lorient two days before we departed from Liverpool and had been successfully sinking British vessels.

Washing Day. Daily Routine Orders announced:

> "The co-operation of all ranks in conserving water makes it possible for fresh water to be available for washing clothes between 10.00 and 12.00"

The basins were fully manned at 10.00 prompt and the slightly off-white and khaki wear was pummelled and twisted.

Having only carbolic I borrowed some 'Lux' from an aesthete. The results of this energy were now draped all over the ship, which looked as though it had been dressed overall for some weird review. Calculated not to assist this washing drill was an "action" alarm. The washers nonchalantly assumed their "Water Wings" and went on washing. After all, even if the enemy was about, not too much time was available for their wash. The Order of the Day then became siesta and a thousand or so recumbent bodies lay prone under the flapping washing. Zzzzz…

I leant over the bows and looked down at the swiftly moving water creaming away around the prow. What appeared to be large dragonflies drove away from the sharp edge and dropped back into the water. They were not insects but flying fish, small, about the length of a finger, with steely coloured bodies flashing like silver as their almost transparent "wings" lifted them through the air for six feet or so before they fell back, sent a small curve of water forward, and vanished below the surface like miniature torpedoes.

Land at last! As dawn broke, a range of grey hills lifted above the horizon. Behind them, the sun came up as a huge ball of fire and flung a path of scarlet light towards us. We were in a great, almost landlocked, bay.

This was the 'Dark Continent'. It was quite different from one's imagining. As the sun altered into full light the country became green and hilly with colours as vivid as a Technicolor film.

X5 proceeded to its dock with a pronounced list. MPs desperately trying to shift the crowd from port to starboard. They were clustered and looking with some interest at "the most soul- and energy-destroying place in the world." It was to be not only foully hot and humid but had the reputation of giving those who served here for any length of time a yellowy-brown and pallid tan. Further, from November to March, Freetown often had to endure the dry dusty wind from the Sahara known as the "Harmattan". Luckily, we missed this.

Then the lads of the town arrived. Young men and boys surrounded the ship in frail boats and coracles carved with skill and handled with aplomb. Some did a roaring trade with fruit, which was tempting, although probably not all that wise to eat. Others dived for "Glasgee tanner, Johnnie?" This was an invitation to fling overboard any spare small silver and the dark brown bodies curved over in a dive, twisting and turning through the water. It was an impressive swimming display and they rarely failed to grasp the treasure.

Since the troops were British, it was not long before assorted wits found a way of precipitating a display at less cost. Pennies were covered with cigarette tinfoil and looked like half-crowns as they fell towards the water. In went the divers again. Then their heads emerged with a flood of fruity English:

"Not silver money. You *?!* me!"

There was a roar of unsympathetic laughter.

Two squaddies were leaning over the bow rail.

"Freetown? Funny name for the place. I'm told that the only things free here are sweat and syph!"

Unable to sleep, I was striding the deck in the small hours. Failing to see a deck fitting, I cracked an instep on it. Later the ankle ballooned badly and became painful. The MO, apparently an enthusiast for X-Rays, sent me ashore for hospital treatment. Maybe I was "injured on active service"? I and two other damaged airmen boarded an RAF motor launch and plunged coastward through spray and wind, which was an exhilarating contrast from the stinkard "Duchess". Onshore, we bowled through a native quarter that was a riot of colour and ramshackle houses. Black women were picturesque in rainbow cottons, and bore bundles or baskets on the head in a graceful and poised walk. A few had tiny picaninnies safely slung in a cloth tied around the mother's middle. The men were less colourful and varied from sporting cheap double-breasted white cotton suits, topped with a gaudy tie, and even, on occasions, a trilby hat, to smocks and skull caps for the elderly.

We shot into "34th General Hospital, RAMC" according to the large roadside notice. We presented papers and I found myself in well-worn blue pyjamas and bed, with little delay.

One quickly got used to the hierarchy of a tropical military hospital. The black orderlies considered themselves a cut above the black "soldier boys", who were in turn superior to the native townsfolk, who themselves were a scatter of class and tribe which defied categorisation. Rising through the higher hierarchy black orderlies carried out the domestic chores, white orderlies the dressings, and the whole bowed to the authority of Sisters and Matron. The clients – that was us – were addressed as "Saar."

An Army MO appeared and announced that I was to be 'plastered' with some kind of splint. This was executed by his smartly mixing a brew in a rather unmedical petrol tin and then slapping it artistically around ankle and leg. He had the crown and the pip of Lieutenant Colonel I noticed, so might well have been the hospital CO. I was quickly returned to bed by two black orderlies.

The hospital seethed like some Grand Hotel. The service was impeccable and the food far superior to the shipboard ration. A tall mosquito net swept down over the bed and open windows blazed light into the black night. A thousand insects intoned sonorous sounds as they hissed and chirruped in the darkness.

Later, an unexpected benefit arose from my having a leg in a cast. I invited myself to have daily baths in the Sick Quarters of the ship, assisted by attractive Queen Alexandra nurses. This unique state was admired by all.

"Fancy," they said, "being scrubbed down by nurses. How lucky can you get?"

As the sun went down two nights later, after we were on south from Freetown, I limped round the fore deck of the ship.

~ Under the Red Eagle ~

The sun dropped westwards as a globe of orange in far mist. A group of khaki figures surrounded a gramophone, doing its best with a rumba. The tropics seemed to spring to life. Sundown was about 19.30 and in twenty minutes it was near dark. The moon came up in a brilliant crescent. We had left far behind the grey seas and skies of winter in the north and by day they were replaced by the virtual purple of the deep ocean, under an arc of blue sky. The nights were luminous with millions of stars and the Milky Way – an artist's wash of light – swept across the sky.

Rising early again the following morning I wandered along the deck under the still presence of the galaxy. The moon had set now but had been replaced by a scintillating eastern star which seemed to increase in brightness each night. Far to the north the Great Bear stood on its tail, pointing to a Pole Star that was barely visible, being only a few degrees above the horizon. The southern hemisphere was taking over from the northern. A new constellation to us, the Southern Cross, had risen above the horizon – a thin cluster of four stars formed in near perfect symmetry.

Peculiar creatures passed the ship now and again – about the size of a jellyfish, but having a 'sail' hoisted. A steely-blue body floated under the surface and was a kind of transparent sac, ribbed over its centre with a bright pink line. It resembled an exotic flower. More grimly, a posse of sharks swirled around the "gash" as the cook flung galley remnants over the side.

Some of the more scientific among us surrounded a bath. Which way round would the water circle the waste pipe before disappearing? It appeared to be anti-clockwise. What would it do after we had crossed the Equator? A further test was planned in a day or two, and the scientific retired to the bar to discuss the matter.

We 'crossed the line' and Neptunus Rex, otherwise a crew member named Truelove, turned up attended by bears and Jarvis, the "Dolphinious High Clerk". Neptune sported an ankle-length blue gown and his long coarse hair strongly resembled coconut fibre. Court was held on the after hatch, an immense crush peering intently to see what was happening.

The bears proceeded to shave anyone on whom they could lay paws, and then hosed down the victims with best South Atlantic. Enthused, they then ran amok on the deck, found a hose, and drenched everyone until the tap was closed by a dripping airman and the bears were restrained.

'Crossing the Line' certificates were produced a few days later by the onboard printing press. "All," the certificate announced, "have been duly initiated into the Ancient and Mystic Rites of our realm and exempted from further homage."

The convoy had now resumed two parallel lines and was escorted by only two destroyers and a cruiser. The latter was an impressive sight as she sped along with a large concave arc of foam sweeping back from her bows. She was one of the new aeroplane-carrying class, and the aircraft could be seen perched between the funnels.

She also towed two drogues on occasions, one airborne and one seaborne, to offer gun practice since a number of us had taken over gun-crew duties as a relief and needed practice. As the cruiser shot past all guns came to bear in the crackle of machine guns, the bark of cannon, and the characteristic stammer of the Bofors. Black puffs of shrapnel also appeared around the airborne drogue and the one being dragged through the waves was bracketed by a froth of white plumes.

Coconuts all round, it appeared.

We had not seen much night firing but when the guns were fired in the blackness, it had a stunning effect – a violent explosion heightened by the quiet of the night, and a long tongue of flame which dazzled the eye.

Something dangerous was about in the dog watches as we drew another smokescreen behind us and zigged and zagged. The "gen" was that a ship had been torpedoed off Simonstown. U-Boats were known to have penetrated far into the South Atlantic. They worked in widely-spaced groups rather than packs and had struck many blows at unprotected ships on these distant shipping lanes. The Cape was a particularly good killing ground for them. The Japanese were also about ahead of the X5. There was news that an enemy fleet including four aircraft carriers and four battleships were heading towards India. Heavy enough guns.

The Commodore's ship gave one long blast and ran up three masthead lights – two red, one green. This time the smoke was black so presumably was from oil or chemicals thrown onto the fires. The screen lay behind the convoy, on the sea surface, in a black shroud, intensifying the night.

One of the smoke floats also being used was lit on the deck before being heaved overboard. An unfortunate had pitched his hammock on the rails in the line of heave and came to life suddenly enveloped by choking smoke. With superb disgust and some nonchalance he hauled a blanket over his head and stayed put.

Two hours later the alarm had faded. It became obvious that it was to be succeeded by a magnificent and theatrical sun-up. I leaned over the rail and looked east. In the half-light between dawn and sunrise the clouds were layered over a third of a vault, in which stars were fast fading. Low on the eastern horizon was an elongated strip of nimbus cloud and below it a clear window of light. As the sun came up this strip reddened and the sky over my head assumed a pale blue-green tint; the red, far off, transmuted into orange and then flaming yellow as the tip of the sun appeared. The edges of the clouds above blushed violet and pink and the whole scene became one of lambent harmony centred on the eastern splendour. A Capricorn sunrise.

With Wordsworth: "The sunshine is a glorious birth."

Lifebelts we hauled around with us continuously. They were a kapok-filled bulk which was more nuisance than insurance, like home gasmasks. They had their virtues as pillows, seats, and backrests, but were constantly mislaid – producing panic amongst the dilatory when the Captain ordered an emergency boat drill. On such occasion, we assembled at our station in groups. I carried a Smith and Wesson and had to ensure that the lifebelts were secure. Otherwise they could throttle the wearer in the water. Down went the lifeboats to sea level accompanied by cheers from the assembled warriors.

It had dawned on the more thoughtful just how vulnerable we were to attack. Both ship and thousands of troops could be lost in minutes. We were moving into a raiding area so the threat was intensifying. So the dilatory changed their view about their lifebelts and kept them handy.

A newcomer joined the convoy – an expensive yacht with rakish bows, a single low funnel Monaco style, and wholly distinguished from the rest of the convoy by being a pale mauve. Another newcomer was in complete contrast – red with rust and very much the battered traveller on the seven seas. A real tramp.

We were now in the area of the "Cape Rollers", which were larger than average waves corrugating the expanse of ocean around us and vastly increasing the swell.

Durban at last, and the X5 docked at 10.00. The mob had already assembled on the decks and looked out across blue water and the variegated assortment of small vessels clustered together in a marina. Avenues of tall white buildings, American style, and groves of brilliant trees were silhouetted against the green hills. In the far distance lay the Drakensburg mountains.

We were to encounter apparent warriors on rickshaw duty, gorgeously feathered and with painted feet substituting for socks. Otherwise there were not too many Africans about: the shopkeepers were Indian, as were the waiters.

South Africa appeared to be a cosmopolitan place and very multiracial. English and Afrikaans were official but there were many African languages including Xhosa, Zulu, and Sesotho and the Indian Urdu and Hindi. The climate was sub-tropical and rainfall much as in England – about 40 inches a year in Durban.

There was a long line of cars on the docks, plus the rickshaws. Many cars were driven by attractive young ladies, or families, offering hospitality. These were quickly boarded by the first off the X5 and disappeared into the town. The later, or more lethargic, found the dockside bare, and marched stolidly into town, unaware that the city transport was free to them.

~ Under the Red Eagle ~

The town confirmed the distinctly American impression that we had received when entering the harbour, although the higher buildings did not reach skyscraper dimensions. There was no blackout – or not at least one which we recognised as such. Apart from the more scattered lights of Freetown, we were light-starved and had not seen such incandescence as Durban showed, for some years. Hotel and house windows streamed light onto a thousand palms and an amphitheatre on the beach was one huge glare as uniforms swirled and dresses swished under the glow of light, and the stars.

I did not get into town immediately as I still had an X-Ray to complete and did so at the local hospital. Walking into the main door I noticed that the building was surrounded by a shallow ditch which appeared to be running with warm water, judging by the steam drifting into the warm air. What on earth…? I obtained the answer from a nurse. Snakes! My plaster was finally stripped away from a leg which was noticeably thinner.

So I finally got into town. Another RAF man asked whether I would like to join his friends for dinner. Of course, and I finally found myself on a high ridge behind Durban – the Berea – sitting on a colonial veranda, below which the land dropped away into a black velvet night to the blaze of the town and a sea touched with a silver pathway from the moon. Insects hummed and whirred around us.

But there was also death in this garden – the black and green mamba and puff adders were present. Weeding needed care!

As we travelled back to town to meet our midnight curfew, a train whistled and in front of the car were alternating red lights. An open railway line crossed straight over the road lacking the barriers that would have been present at home. The flashing lights were the only warning. Round the bend came the engine and carriages, with a staring spotlight below the funnel and light from the firebox streaming away over the canes and trees. A two-tone whistle blared harmoniously and the train shot away through the trees to Durban.

Snake-charming is a fact, it appeared! A group attended the snake park on the shore and found the reptiles both in open and closed cages. In one closed cage was a black mamba, dozing on a small tree at the centre of the cage. I whistled idly in a high note and was astonished to have the snake stretch out his considerable length, swaying and flicking a long tongue. With interest, and some apprehension, I retreated. Perhaps these snakes spat…

Compared with "Saar" in Freetown, here it was "Bwana", which means "Master" or "Sir". It was Swahili – another language – from the Arabic *abuna*, also meaning "father".

"All leave," ordered the ship's notice, "expires at midnight." So that was that. Our more civilised existence was over and we were back to the hard tack. Goodbye Durban, for some time at least…

The following morning we were sung away by the "Lady in White" otherwise Perla Gibson – well known, it appeared, to all troopers touching at Durban. She emerged from a dockside building carrying a large red straw hat, but otherwise dressed in white. She was a lone but substantial figure and walked forward to the edge of the quay under a blazing sun, with drifts of smoke about her. She had a surprisingly powerful, operatic, voice and sang a number of patriotic or well-known airs, concluding with "Auld Lang Syne", which was taken up by many thousands of male voices on the trooper. The white figure dwindled to a dot, and vanished.

The main job of Perla Siedle Gibson was running the dockside canteen. It was on 16 April 1940 that she first responded to a request by a lad on a convoy leaving the harbour who had been entertained by her family. She sang "Land of Hope and Glory." In 1944 she lost her eldest son Roy but on that day sang out a leaving troop ship and continued to do so to the end of the war and beyond.

It was something of a coincidence that I was to meet Perla Gibson myself. Our own hosts knew her well and we were invited to join her for a trip and lunch, out to the Valley of a Thousand Hills behind Durban. It was an entertaining day.

When we left, for some of us, Perla's song must have been one of permanent farewell.

We now entered the magical world of the Indian Ocean. The heat increased to a scarifying level and lightning flashed continuously. The ocean was mirror-like in its calm and so clear that we could see deep marine life. Porpoises sported around us at night, under a huge hunter's moon, and shoals of flying fish accompanied us like a flock of damascene birds, rising and dipping round our bows. They were much bigger than their Atlantic brothers but much the same in colour except for one exotic version which had a blue body and fins with a yellow leading edge and a brown trailing edge. It looked like an iridescent tropical bird.

The humidity heightened and we were bathed in perspiration from dawn to dusk and on into the night. It was hard to recall that we had been in deep snow only a few weeks back. Now, we also endured regular downpours – one in the mid-afternoon and another in the early hours. The sea disappeared under a heavy mist of falling rain.

More deaths at sea, now four. Ensigns flew at half-mast as the shrouded corpses were slid overboard from under a Union Flag and three shots were fired. X5 picked up speed again.

Having parted from HMS *Newcastle* at Durban we now had another cruiser with us of the same class. We had also been joined by an auxiliary cruiser flying the White Ensign, similar to the *Rawalpindi*, which went down in heroic conditions.

We continued with our attack practice, this time with the new cruiser assaulting the *Duchess of York*. The former was presumed to have fired a torpedo, hitting the liner behind her aft funnel – the hit being marked by a shower of sparks. We, now the Commodore's ship, steamed away fast, laid smoke screens, and generally built up our greatest speed – 25 knots – since leaving England.

Somewhere in front of us was the onslaught from the Japanese cruisers and battleships which we had heard about earlier. They were heading for Ceylon and its naval bases and this could have been one of the most dangerous moments of the war – a threat to the whole Indian sub-continent.

The *Malda* – recently fitted out as a troopship of 9,000 tons and the convoy commodore's ship – was bombed by aircraft and shelled by cruisers. She flared into a holocaust and became a blazing horror with many of the crew suffering terrible injuries and jumping overboard. This occurred a relatively few miles ahead of us.

Presumably, since we were heading north-east, the Southern Cross would drop lower. At first, the four stars (or was it five?) were rather disappointing. However, all the stars glittered like gems at night and the moon became a huge disc of silver. It was quite easy to read by its light.

A Scot brought up his bagpipes and marched around to Scottish airs such as 'Scotland the Brave' and 'Flowers of the Forest'. The Scots were wildly enthusiastic about this, but the English and Welsh less so.

The Indian Ocean remained like one great sheet of glass, completely unruffled except for our wake.

One morning, looking idly over the side from my hammock slung on deck, I looked down and was surprised to see that the sea had turned almost apple green. Raising an eye, I saw that we were close inshore with mist-shrouded hills on the horizon. We were at anchor in Bombay harbour and within the Raj.

It was the rattle of chains and the hooting of sirens that had awakened me. X5 had entered the bay in the dog watch through an archipelago of small islands to anchor with a dawn view of a palm-fringed shore and the mountains of the Western Ghats on the horizon. In the city rose the great commercial and municipal buildings etched against the skyline by the rising sun.

The troops hung over the rails with nothing to do and gazed across the city. While it appeared to be a peaceful scene where we were in the docks, the violence of the East intruded suddenly. A body, face down in the water, with a knife in its back, floated past the ship's side with dhoti swirling about its loins. The idle chat died away into silence.

We finally obtained some shore leave. Bombay was very different to Freetown. While it appeared to have the same crushing poverty, it also had the smell of opportunity – the temple of the rupee. We were exhorted to be photographed, to buy artefacts, postcards of the ladies of the town, have our fortunes told and even to have our ears probed and cleaned. We declined the last offer, having some doubt about it, and forced our way through a hundred beggars. We had now become "Sahib" as a mark of respect, literally "friend" in Urdu.

~ Under the Red Eagle ~

Snarled-up traffic, street sleepers, shanty-towns Indian style, peculiar advertising on huge hoardings, and posters of strange films and actors, decorated the streets. More grimly, the "Towers of Silence" rose above us, where the Parsees exposed their dead and bone-picking vultures winged their way into the high cylindrical structures: eyries of the lifeless. They literally "gave up the ghost" and "went aloft".

As the evening approached the light seemed to turn thick and golden, and the oppressive heat of the day faded. This was the time when a sea breeze stirred, and we were reminded that Bombay had always been a gateway into India for ocean travellers. Indian police strolled around, resplendent in blue and yellow tunics and calf-length cotton breeches. They wore a pill-box hat reminiscent of the old Victorian militia. Slung on the left hip was a formidable truncheon. They brooked no argument, disorder, theft, or disrespect.

I could have used their services. Entering a craftwork shop I thoughtlessly put down my camera on the counter to study some ivory. Ten seconds later – no camera. I assumed a rage, which did not need much assuming, and demanded that the camera be produced again instantly, otherwise a number of airmen would be visiting the shop with intent to "sort out" the occupants. This was sufficient and with some hesitation one of the assistants lifted a cloth on the counter and revealed the camera. "I was," he explained, "keeping it safe for the sahib."

"Oh, yes?" I grabbed the camera, glared ferociously, and exited. Outside, and out of sight, we were in high good humour and slapped one another on the back. The threat to "spifflicate" them did the trick!

We left the X5 on the morning of 13 April and hauled our kit on to the next wharf under an intense sun. It was only half a mile or so but enough to make us glowing and wet. A complete change was necessary. The new ship – the *Neuralia* – was far smaller than the *Duchess of Richmond* at 9,200 tons but was a proper troopship, built for the job, and with correct fittings and fixtures, ventilation, galleys, and ablutions. We should have come all the way on this vessel. Another advantage was that she had space for a proper Orderly Room, and we took it over. 24 WU was detailed for many jobs –sentries, orderlies, galley, and many more including the guns. The ship thrummed with action.[1]

We moved away from Bombay towards the North-West. This time we were not in convoy and ran alone. The ship was probably fast enough for this, and could outrun submarines.

We headed into the narrow strait separating the Gulf of Oman from the Persian Gulf. The Arabian Sea itself teemed with life and again one could look down into the sea for a fathom or so through the unbroken surface. Jellyfish, flying fish, sharks, dolphins and turtles abounded and there was a strange button-like creature which floated on the surface. Arabia as such was exactly what we film-buffs expected – dusty, scorched and with brown hills rising straight from the sea, backed by high jagged peaks.

A cruiser cut across our bows with a "heave to". It dropped a boat manned by white topee'd, lifebelted and bronzed marines, with an impossibly young Sub Lieutenant. Much chaff from the troops lining the rails, which the Navy grinned and bore. Mail and orders came aboard. The cruiser recalled its boat, did its "off like a shot" bit back towards the south-east, and rapidly vanished over the horizon.

Two days later we slid up the estuary of the Tigris and Euphrates with Persia to starboard and Iraq to port. We were in the Shatt El Arab, which flowed swiftly past us down to the Gulf. An old man in a dingy passed us softly chanting one of the unending Arab folk songs. His friend did the rowing, clad in a cloth of striped cotton and an old khaki tunic. His head was stately in the *keffiyah*, which we were to come to know well, and sometimes wore ourselves. This was the Arab kerchief held in place by the black silk *agal* with its trailing tassels. These were Marsh Arabs, and this was the first and last time that we were to see them. Abadan loomed into sight, with a cluster of off-white scorched buildings and the forest of tall chimneys which identified the refinery. Then, our voyage concluded, we disembarked and

---

[1] Much later in the war, in April 1945, we were to learn that the *Neuralia* had been sunk by mines outside Taranto, with a loss of 280 passengers and crew.

sat on our kit in the platform-less station to await the train north to Baghdad.

We had been at sea 66 days and were lucky to have got through unscarred – relatively so, anyway. Not all troops and airmen had been so fortunate.

3. First Blast of the Desert Steppe

> *"He found him in a desert land,*
> *and in the waste howling wilderness."*
> **Deuteronomy ch.32 v.10**

24 Wireless Unit was now on its way into the northern desert, and travelling by a very basic train. Iraq would prove to be a fair-sized country, about 80% bigger than the UK, but with only a quarter of the population.

"You know," said Harris, "these trains aren't quite what I expected. The stations don't appear to have platforms; every time we stop in the middle of the desert Arabs appear out of nowhere; and I have doubts about the engine driver. Twice I've seen him drunk and fighting the fireman. Hardly Great Western, is it?"

This observation was received with interest. Its truth was evident. However, the greater concern at the moment was being shaken to the back teeth, bottoms on hard wooden seats, and with clattering and draughty shutters to the windows quite incapable of keeping out the impending sandstorm. A world of sand stretched from horizon to horizon and Harris was right about the Arabs – they did seem to be expert in legerdemain and appeared unexpectedly at each stop with the inevitable "*Baksheesh, Sahib, baksheesh.*" Occasionally they traded and from one handsome fellow in full Arab dress I bought a wicked looking scimitar-like knife and scabbard. That would complement the monkey-fur and tasselled dagger I acquired in Freetown. They could go on a wall somewhere, sometime.

As the sun dropped the sky began to darken in front and it became obvious, even to us newcomers that something ominous was brewing. Brew it did, and a long sloping edge of whirling sand, perhaps two thousand feet high, enveloped the train. Shutters were slammed closed, with little relief, and the train came to a halt. On this occasion we were lucky, for the sandstorm was just about to blow itself out as it reached us, and within the hour we recommenced our journey north.

Soon the desert was completely dark and without a glimmer, anywhere, of light. Feet were propped on the seats and shadowy bodies dozed in a score of different positions. Harris, always the inventive, had an illuminating idea – create a candle out of Vaseline scraped into a tin, with a piece of string as wick. It was a poor and fitful flicker but helped light our tea-making at 3am with the aid of boiling water drawn from the engine. We noted in passing that Harris seemed to have the right of it – the driver certainly had a black eye and the sullen fireman a cut on the cheek.

Hillah was on the way north and near the site of Babylon. It was a lively and bustling town with a maze of bazaars and dark alleyways, lying on the Euphrates. Babylon was approached either along the river or over a stretch of scrub- covered country. From a low hill there was a panoramic view of the ancient citadel and what remained of the inner and outer walls. They were little more than broken ridges, hardly separable from the drab landscape. Time had dragged slowly here and still did. The present war was a minor event in the many Babylonian centuries which had passed since the perfume from one of the seven wonders of the ancient world – the hanging gardens of Babylon – drifted through the air here.

Reaching Baghdad by midday, a weary unit stepped out onto a sanded platform sweltering under the torrid sun. Even the ubiquitous sparrows fluttered lethargically under the heat, beaks open and gasping. An Arab who had lost both legs came trundling along on a small trolley trying to sell "marmalade". What he intended, we soon realised, was "lemonade".

We saw little of Baghdad that day, being too concerned with boarding the lorries and finding the Damascus road – the way of so much history, ambush and blood. Speeding along the road mirages of water shimmered where the sky touched the horizon and produced the false watery coolness that was to become for me a regular deceit of the desert. The mirages were not only of water: to our surprise, miles down the road, the minarets and domes of a distant Baghdad refracted against a sky veiled in heat-haze.

After some fifty miles or so we rattled over the Fallujah bridge and into ranks of square tents formally known as "Egyptian Pattern, Indian Patent" or 'EPIPs' as we came to know them. They were to be our accommodation in extremes of climate. This group of tents was a "Personnel Transit Centre" (or PTC) on the periphery of RAF Habbaniya. So we were now fully "on active service" and according to the local RAF-erected signpost, London was 3,287 miles to the west and Baghdad 55 miles to the east.

The background to this aerodrome was that Iraq was formerly a Turkish province. It became a kingdom under British mandate in 1921 with Emir Feisal as its first monarch. He died in 1930, was succeeded by his son who was killed in a car crash nine years later and then succeeded by the infant son Feisal II when the country became a regency. By treaty, the UK was accorded certain rights and one of these was Habbaniya.

"You know," said Harris, holding on grimly to the overhead bars of a three-tonner, "I was in some stores in Blighty where there were cases marked for Habbaniya. I asked the store-basher where it was and he said 'at the end of the earth: don't get posted there at any cost…' So here I am, at the world's backside!"

Habbaniya was what the Indian Command would have called a cantonment, or military post. It lay just south of the Euphrates, which put it a mile from Mesopotamia, a name well known in the Great War and on the northern extreme of T.E. Lawrence's (Lawrence of Arabia) stamping ground. There was a belief amidst Army and Air Force that this posting was so tough that anyone who served here was entitled to wear scarlet shorts – but I think that must have been completely apocryphal. Nobody suggested that we should draw such monstrosities from the stores, anyway. "Red shorts in the sunset?"

South of the airfield was a low plateau, about 200 feet high. More of that in a moment…

~ Under the Red Eagle ~

Habbaniya was a paradoxical place. Tree-lined roads with English names and English garden flowers challenged the open desert just around the corner. The CO had a carefully tended grass plot outside his office, cultivated and watered assiduously by the *jankah-wallahs* (those who had been "charged" for some misdemeanour). The whole aerodrome lay inside a seven-mile fence beyond which the hyenas yelped.

We were about a year late for the last fracas here. Early in 1941 a pro-Nazi clique overthrew the government and Iraqi troops attacked Habbaniya under Raschid Ali. Troops appeared on the southern plateau – about 9,000 men and 50 guns. Down in Habbaniya were some 2,200 fighting men and about four times as many civilians. When fighting began the training squadrons and embryo pilots strafed and bombed. Finally the Iraqis withdrew and the rebellion was crushed. Beating off the attack was a minor epic of the wartime RAF, since the planes used were a motley collection of old training aircraft. The gallant success preserved British dominance in Iraq.

On record in Germany was the statement that the war in Iraq was won by the RAF, who mopped up the Iraqi army, then their air force, and finally the German forces who participated. A bunch of unseasoned pilots, under training, with the wrong aircraft, fought a horrendous battle and won. What might have happened hardly bears thinking about. With Rommel in the Western Desert approaching Cairo and then Iraq, he would have secured the vital oil. The whole Middle East would have split, Hitler would have been on the way to India, and there would have been no way to produce the massive build-up which led to El Alemein.

Stories of the fracas still abounded. One was about the two brass cannon that stood outside the Officers' Mess. These were packed with nails and brought into use. Another was that the Iraqi gunners fled their weapons under RAF attack. A third was that the animal and other bones still littering the plateau were the last vestiges of the aggression. Raschid Ali himself had bolted to Iran.

Well, Hitler could have reached out a long arm to India. But we supposed that he could still do that because the Germans were even now pushing their way into Russia and towards the Caucasus. Perhaps we would be involved in a second run of the Habbaniya story?

We remained in the P.T.C. which could have been classed as "rough" in comparison with the camp proper, but at least we had equal access to the swimming pool, cinema, shops, clubs and churches. Our tented camp was patrolled by locally recruited "Levies" who were mostly loyal and disciplined Assyrians who hated the Arab with a deep passion. They were also good shots, which Harris found out to his cost. In the dark hours one of these Levies spotted a dark shape crawling across the desert between the tents. He challenged – no answer – so he shot it, then shot it again twice more. The object continued to crawl, which was too much for the Levi who knew perfectly well that he had hit the object. He yelled and fled, not being enamoured of ghosts or spirits. The following day all was revealed. The dark shape had been a kitbag. Local thieves had a habit of attaching a long piece of twine to any kit seen below the tent flap during the day. Then they laid out the twine in the desert and returned at night to haul in the booty. It was this moving kitbag that the Levi had shot. He had done well, since there were three holes in it and various apertures through Harris's underwear. Harris was not at all pleased.

Another night event involved me. I was up in the small hours of a moonless night and had draped a blanket over my shoulders, then proceeding to search for a 'desert rose'. Why they were called this I never found out – they were merely urinals, one petrol tin perched on top of another buried in the sand. Later I was to hear that the next sleeper to me had woken up and jumped to the conclusion that a thieving wog was in the tent. At that moment, another sleeper groaned in a nightmare. Strewth! Someone has been knifed. He yelled blue murder, which promptly woke up the rest of the tent. I returned to scenes of chaos. The funny side was seen only in the light of day.

The same morning one of the unit made his way to the latrines. These were open, canvas-shielded, and no more than a large hole spanned by the usual pole. They were disinfected, daily, by one of the P.T.C Iraqis. The airman concerned entered the latrine and a minute passed. Then there was an explosion and the airman reappeared, shorts round the ankles, yelling "Who did that?"

It transpired that the disinfecting Iraqi had been short of the usual chemicals so had the bright idea of using petrol. It was unfortunate that the airman was a smoker and his nose was not of the best. Sitting reflectively on the pole he had lit his cigarette and tossed the match downward. Poooof…! His story lost nothing in the telling and reduced his tent colleagues to near hysteria.

In truth, it was not unusual for the sanitary squad to use petrol to burn out the latrine – but not, as the Iraqi did, to be too generous with the petrol and fail to light it.

Now the night was calm and a cool desert wind billowed through the camp. The moon rode high. This was very different to what we encountered earlier in the day.

We were out for a dip in Lake Habbaniya, on the plateau. Glancing to the horizon I saw that the sky had darkened again and the wind was rising. We had been in the country long enough now to know what this meant. Soon the loose surface of the sand whipped into our faces with stinging force. We bent forward steeply against the blow. Before us, a mile away, rose the long swirling edge of the *simoom* – the strong suffocating sand-laden wind of the desert. The edge was some hundreds of feet above the land surface and howling towards us. Everything became the colour of sand – sky, ground, air. The heat was intense and we perspired freely as the wall of sand swept over us like a gigantic wave which nothing could halt. We were engulfed in its embrace and stuffed handkerchiefs and towels round mouth and nose. Even the chin strap of the topee hardly held it on our heads and eyeshields were of little protection. Our teeth gritted with sand. The sun was obscured and the day became leaden.

By this time we had lost the road altogether and regained it only by seeing the flash of lorry headlamps. We got a lift and were dropped near the camp. The storm was now in full blast and the sand whirled so thickly that we could hardly see individual tents. They loomed as indistinct shapes, billowing out against strumming guy ropes and ripping pegs from the ground – which were being desperately hammered back in by grey figures. Sand, sand, everywhere. We dived under blankets and sweltered, with more towels and scarves around our heads. A real ordeal might have just begun, because local lore was that these 'blows' could last for three or four days. We just lay there, sweating it out, with occasional sips from a water-bottle. The hours passed as a torment with little sleep and no food. The cookhouse could not cope.

Suddenly, however, it was all over. We were not to have the three-day bluster. Men emerged from the tents dazed and plastered with a shroud of dirt and sand. One would not have thought that a *simoom* of that ferocity could melt away so quickly.

Some days later I found myself in the camp proper – specifically, in the hospital. Dysentery was the cause, and I graduated slowly from a water diet to food over two weeks. Luckily I had the less vicious version. Our Queen Alexandra nurses were handsome in scarlet and grey or the tropical white drill frock with scarlet and white epaulettes. Again I found myself in rather threadbare white shirt and blue trousers, some inches short. Freetown again. The ward was certainly cooler than the Transit Camp with fans circulating air very much fresher than the desert variety. Tiled floors and coolly coloured walls were also a relief. Weighed, I was set aback to find that about twelve stones had become nine. To where did all that flesh go?

The nurses allowed only the near-dead a measure of tolerance. The other patients had stints and jobs to do, and we even "lay to attention" on ward rounds. Sheet tight over the chest, arms by the side, feet extended. Absurd!

It was all a more comfortable existence than the PTC but after a fortnight I was glad to be back with the unit…

"Hello, where've you been?"

A movement order arrived. We were destined to drive south of Mosul in the deep desert. So we crossed between different ethnic groups – urban Arab and Levi to nomad Bedouin and Kurd. Religiously, too, they differed, Between Basra and Baghdad we passed through Shi'ite country; to the far west, where we were headed, they were Sunni. Sunnis regard Shi'ites as a sect of wealth and privilege.

~ Under the Red Eagle ~

Our lorry allocation, one for each of fifteen posts and some for HQ, were Ford and Crossley. The former were in good desert camouflage of sand and green, the latter were a non-committal field-grey. They looked, in fact, like Wehrmacht trucks, and we hoped our airborne colleagues could distinguish them as friendly.

Day followed day with skies of intense blue and reeking with heat. There was a fair amount of air movement and we had been visited by 'sand spouts' or 'dust devils'. These were tall, thin whirlwinds which towered hundreds of feet high, were some 20-30 feet wide, and picked up all kinds of loose material. They could even rip up tents.

The movement day came and we packed and headed north from Habbaniya, our last outpost of civilisation, into the wilder desert. The convoy inevitably swirled up clouds of sand and dust and the trailing vehicles greyed rapidly. The fitters' vehicle, last in line, suffered most of all. The trucks jolted and jolted again, rattling our teeth. The metal of the bodywork became far too hot to touch and was easily capable of frying eggs, which we did, just to prove it.

Radiators boiled and boiled again. The first mishap occurred when Kildare, our Irish MT driver, behind the wheel of one of the big Crossleys, trailing a full water bowser, skidded off the tarmac on a patch of wet tar. The Crossley slipped down the roadside dip and ponderously turned over on its side. The bowser, luckily, stayed upright. "Whoa, the convoy!" We halted and rushed over to rescue a mangled Kildare and mate but Irish luck had held and both crawled out of the roof with barely a scratch but stinking with the petrol and oil that had cascaded over them. With some luck, energetic shovelling, and tow chains from two lorries acting as desert tugs we hauled the Crossley back onto its wheels with a thud: no damage at all apparently. The convoy reformed and departed.

We left the macadam behind, what there had been of it, and headed into the full desert, up and down *wadi* after *wadi*. These were desert watercourses, dry except in the rainy season. Striking across a range of hills the going got really severe. The vehicles bounded every way, left the ground, yawed, tossed up their tailboards, and generally tested every nut and bolt. We strained up hills in auxiliary gear, drummed our way down the far side into dry wadis, holding on grimly, and wondering how long even these military vehicles could withstand this kind of battering, what was going to fall on us next, and how long this was all going to last.

Tiffin was a relief from the pounding, and taken under the walls of Hit, a typical desert town clinging round a hill. The town was alleged to have more thieves than any other place in Iraq, so we kept a close eye on our kit and lorries as the local Arabs swarmed round us. It was clear that the inhabitants of Hit did not hold with foreigners – British or any other, particularly airmen. They glowered. We scowled back.

The unit laagered for the night in the dry course of a large wadi. It was a picturesque scene with the dark shapes of the wagons silhouetted against moonlit hills and the flames of cooking fires flickering against drawn skins. Guards were posted and we lay back under a velvet-black sky peppered with stars. The following morning, breasting another ridge, silver oil tanks appeared on the far horizon. This was K3, our destination. After four months HQ 24 WU would at last be in position. A small forest of tents sprang up.

4. Getting Our Knees Brown

> *"They that dwell in the wilderness shall kneel before him."*
> **Psalm 72 v.8**

> *"...for in the wilderness shall waters break out, and streams in the desert."*
> **Isiah 35 v.6**

"Getting your knees brown" was RAF slang for the process of acquiring experience in the far-flung outposts of empire. One who had brown knees was no longer a 'rookie' but an 'old hand'.

24 WU did not take all that long to become used to the desert. Air Ministry Regulations tended to get rather modified, however. Discipline was not lost but dress became more informal. Sun helmets of the old style, wide-brimmed and high-crowned with flashes, were discarded – the RAF was the first to do so – as were the myths about the "noonday sun" that the Empire's Englishmen had had enshrined in dress regulations for a hundred years. The heavy helmet gave place to the lightweight, low-crowned, topee, if Stores could be persuaded to issue one, or the simple forage cap if not. The old version had marked arrivals as new to the eastern scene as soon as they stepped off the gangplank.

We did, of course, need some protection from the fierce overhead star, otherwise sunstroke or heatstroke could strike. By mid-morning stones and sand were fully heated and the air went limp as its essence was frazzled out of it. Breathing became a chore. By mid-afternoon the sun was still radiating a formidable barrage of heat and light and the shade temperature could be up to 130 degrees or more. We were "flattened on the anvil of the desert" as Lawrence said of the Nafud of Saudi Arabia. In the evening the battering relaxed, the heat lessened and it became easier to breathe again.

Eastern suns are fiery. They beat down on wide deserts and remote, uninhabited, places lacking shade. There is the ever-present threat of sun blindness. If one looks at the sun for too long it literally "puts out the eyes", either partially or fully. Fools who have tried to "stare out the sun" have been known to be returned to England for a blind discharge. Under the sun there is colour on the face of the desert – but not bright colour. It is quieter, more pastel, and ever-changing. After dawn, when the Bedouin is able to distinguish a white thread from a black, the sand dunes and cliff faces are red, the drifts ochrous and the far mountains empurpled. As the sun rises during the day the intensity of its white light fades the sharper colour and the glare is so strong as to require dark glasses – which we all wore.

At night the whole scene becomes a silver-touched monochrome as the moon rides high against the pale swathe of the Milky Way. Photographers judge the moonlit scene to be one-six-hundred-thousandth of the sunlit scene. It may be less here. To most of the unit, the full desert came as something of a shock. There were extremes of heat, then temperatures bordering on the cold, perpetual shortage of water, and considerable distances to be covered. The bare landscape, which stretched from horizon to horizon, imposed its own psychological strain.

The posts each had a lorry and moved from time to time. This imposed a routine that was overlooked at their peril. Tyres had to be checked to expel air, otherwise they burst with the heat. Tread was lost from time to time. Was there sand in the carburettor? Then there were all the "POW" checks that one would carry out in the UK and in the wilder places one should adjust the compass and check over the weapons.

The routine of the sun continued day after day, month after month. It was a continuous "flaming June", except for sandstorms and the occasional downpour which vanished quite rapidly. So far, we were not subject to the mosquito, which had no still water in which to lurk. In general, as someone remarked, "Both the desert and the Ritz are clean and comfortable: it is only in the transition between them that the filth and squalor appear." Well perhaps, but the desert is hardly antiseptic.

A new British Command was created, which included us – "Persia and Iraq Force" – shortened to "Paiforce". The old name "Persia" was adopted rather than "Iran" because of its similarity to "Iraq" and the possibility of confusion. The Command was initiated because of the real risk of the Germans to our north breaking through the Russian defences round Stalingrad and in the Caucasus. That could open the way to the Middle East and to India, probably through northern Iraq. The rich oilfields of Persia and Iraq would be overrun on the way. Those who thought about the matter realised that if the worst happened, Panzer divisions could sweep down from the north with a victorious Rommel coming in from the west. With our ancient rifles and light arms we would be an expendable force.

Some far away in Burma called themselves the "Forgotten Men". We thought we were a "Forgotten Army". But Paiforce should have been large enough to be remembered, with a territory of some 850,000 square miles, about seven times as large as the British Isles. There was a probably apocryphal story about three men left in this Command a bit too long: they were all right when recalled, except for having their names mixed up…

The troops in Persia had kept non-stop delivery going between the Gulf and Russia, which was about the longest delivery road in the world. They were also lonely – no papers, no radio, little communication with others. Iraq is a wild country where our posts are marooned. By road from Baghdad to Damascus, just to the south of us, was 500 miles across a desert so bleak and scarified that even the camel-thorn wilted under the sun. It was much the same north to Mosul. With perspiration dripping from us, the wind from the desert was as if someone had opened furnace doors. The sunlight was blazing white. There was an initial order that "tropical hours" should be worked – i.e. not in the afternoon – so our day was about 5.00 to 9.00 and then 17.00 to 20.00 in the evening. Even the local sparrows, as we saw at Baghdad station, simply flopped on the ground in the afternoon with wings spread and beaks gasping.

How did we stand it? Not too badly, but with heat-stroke, sand-fly fever, dysentery and scorpion stings all raging. Even so, we looked fitter than any home football crowd and were remarkably accommodating. The place was alive with scorpions. We had syndicates of airmen with fighting insects, pitted against one another, or placed in a ring of petrol fire – whereupon they thrust their sting down their throat and lanced themselves to death. There are also insects called "scorpion spiders". If put into combat with scorpions they could demolish numbers and eat them all at one go. The scorpions themselves were green or black with a sting strong enough to drive through leather. The former could give one a nasty jab but weren't fatal. The black were more dangerous and could kill if the victim were not in good health. We had such a case when one of our labourers encountered a scorpion under the tent flap, where they lay in ambush. His yell was fierce and although the medicals did what they could his leg turned black and he died in the hospital at Habbaniya. We were now very wary with flaps, blankets, and mosquito nets after a number of these sudden discoveries. Scorpions live – if not in our tents – in moist shady places under rocks. The fat-tailed species emerged at night. Its venom was again strong enough to kill. I was not sure whether there was an anti-venom or not. Among Iraqi tribes a *sulaimaniyeh* (cat's eye) stone was supposed to counter all pain and poison but we had yet to establish this as true.

Blood sports on a larger scale consisted of gazelle hunts by the posts, to supplement their rations. They chased the animals in the lorry, bumping and boring round the dunes, and loosed off with rifles.

What, exactly, were we doing in this wasteland? That seemed to be pretty obvious, although no-one had explained why. Away to the north was the Tigris, and next to us the Euphrates. Between the two was "Mesopotamia" or "land between the rivers" The name "Iraq" meant "cliff", which was characteristic of the landscape. An oil pipeline came down from Mosul beyond the Tigris with pumping stations every so often. They were identified by letter – K2 was furthest north, where our end post, number 15, was located. K3 was next to HQ and the posts ran away to the south-west where H2 was next to our other end post – number 1.

A triple pipeline carried the oil across Mesopotamia, through the Syrian desert, where we were, down through pro-British Jordan, to an outlet at Haifa on the Mediterranean. It was the equivalent of the convoy system across the Atlantic, and what was going on in the desert, both here and beyond Cairo, was analogous to a naval war, which accounted for its repetitious quality. Nomadic tribes inhabited the region and had fought barbarous skirmishes with Lee Enfield and Turkish rifles left over from World War I. They would have had regular affrays now had it not been for our inhibiting presence on their desert.

Access to Iraqi and Persian oil was clearly a primary necessity for the Allies. Navy, Army and Air Force were all dependent on it. Any threat to Iraq would endanger output, interrupt the flow of oil to the waiting tankers at Haifa and could ultimately silence the roar of aircraft, tanks and lorries in the Western Desert. Again, the road to India lay through Persia and Iraq and down the Gulf, where Hitler could potentially join up with his Japanese allies. We could face an attack through Turkey, north of us. Here at Haditha the pipeline forked, one branch to Haifa and the other north to Tripoli. Great Britain largely depended for the maintenance of the war effort on the oil we were guarding.

The desert was not like any other war zone. I guessed that London hadn't much idea of the conditions here, although well enough aware of the potential threat. That was why we were here. They probably thought it was all golden sand warmed by the sun, across which drifted the shade of T.E. Lawrence. Golden sand it isn't – mainly dust, grit and flies, bits of dead animals and wind.

Oh that wind! I shall always remember it. We were on a high windswept plateau with the pipeline and K3 only a hundred yards away. Apart from the river village of Haditha we were well into the open desert and had exchanged the flattish country around Habbaniya for a scorched and wild steppe-desert in a hilly region. "Digging in" had been a problem; we had bent four picks already in the process. Explosive was what we really needed.

We saw animals occasionally – mainly camel, jackal, fox, lizard and gazelle. In former times the lion was not uncommon but was now extinct. In the deep desert, occasionally, there were feral cats, jerboa, wolves, hyena, gerbils, hares, tortoise, geckoes, and assorted poisonous snakes. Much more rarely there were a few wild asses and ostriches.

The desert to the west of the Tigris, in which our posts stretched down 150 or so miles to H2, was part of the Syrian Desert – a wide stony plain with rare sandy stretches. It was filled with wadis up to 250 miles long; dry most of the year they could carry torrential floods during the winter rains. The Euphrates was in flood between March and May, as much as forty times its winter level.

I mentioned the wind already. I should have added that it is the *Sharqi*, a dry dusty wind from the south which can gust up to 80 mph between April and early June and last several days, often accompanied by violent dust storms rising to several thousand feet. This is reversed from mid-June onwards by the *Shamal* from the north – a steady wind which drops only occasionally.

To return to our function… it was that of an advanced observer system which can be used on any battlefront. Here, it would give warning of the approach of hostile aircraft heading for the pipeline or anywhere across our front. It is a chain of wireless posts, each manned by five or six airman with a wireless-telegraphy set, stationed at intervals of ten or twenty miles. The men relied on vision or hearing to detect aircraft and to pass back reports to HQ and thence to Command. There is also a pipeline guard function.

HQ contained all the administration, CO, Adjutant, cooks, signallers, and a medical unit manned by orderlies.

A final word about our domestic life. It was pretty Spartan. We shaved and washed on perhaps a pint of water. Washing clothes was generally considered wasteful. Alternatively, we scrounged some petrol in a largish tin, threw in shirts and shorts, and then laid them on the sand. In a few minutes we could wear them again. Surprisingly, they had no smell.

So far as food and drink is concerned, tea is regarded as an essential and this is true also for the Arabs, who trade with us "eggis for char". It certainly keeps up morale and I understand that the government has undertaken to buy the world's crop. There was next to nothing to drink otherwise; alcohol was not available except on unusual or medical occasions and tea was more refreshing anyway.

The cooks struggled with the food – largely bully beef, tinned meat, and vegetables, dehydrated potatoes, and herrings. So this means stew in nine cases out of ten. A few tablespoonfuls of curry may be heaved into the pot and biscuits – RAF version – were on the table for those with strong teeth. We were truly "out in the blue".

The song we sang was "Desert Blues":

"I'm just tired of seeing Eastern moons,
Bright red sunsets and shining sand dunes,
Must get away,
I've got the desert blues.

Miles of sand whichever way I look,
Swell but only in a fairy tale book,
All I can say,
I've got the desert blues.

Camels galore, goats by the score,
Must go before it gets me down,
I never knew it could be so blue,
Just take me to a respectable town.

I'm just tired of domes and minarets
Eastern sunshine and the silhouettes,
Tired of it all,
I've got the desert blues,

~ Under the Red Eagle ~

I don't want to be an airman,
I don't want to go to war,
I'd sooner hang around,
Piccadilly Underground,
Living on the earnings of a high-born lady.

I looked at my knees. They were brown and getting browner. At Habbaniya it appeared that we were already becoming old hands.

5. Deep Mesopotamia

> *"Oh! that the desert were my dwelling place"*
> **Byron**
> *"To the man who knows it, the desert is a fortress*
> *To him who does not, it is a grave."*
> **Old Arab saying**

It was my birthday and I celebrated it in the Indian hospital with an inflamed and swollen ankle. "Oedema" was diagnosed by the medical orderly (later I found out that this is merely an unexplained swelling). So I sat there with one leg on a petrol tin. This was certainly windy corner. There was a steady blow from the north which varied little from day to day although tending to drop at night. The tents lifted and undulated uneasily as the evening wind caught them between inner and outer roof.

Apart from my leg, I noticed that the desert thinned the blood. On a slight cut it looked like red ink. On a more severe wound we needed to bind it well, since it could become septic very quickly.

Both sides of the tent were open. Through one door stretched long topaz rays from the setting sun and a golden haze hung between me and the horizon, caused by many motes of dust. A camel train wound its way against the western glow and it was profoundly quiet except for the splutter of the Signals charging engine and laughter from the medical tent where the orderlies were preparing supper with liberal draughts of 'medicinal' scotch. At the other side of the tent were the floodlit silver storage tanks of K3, while overhead swept the Milky Way, which was very distinct at this latitude in the absence of light pollution. A soft breeze, lacking its strength of the day, swung the hurricane lamp gently.

However, there was more to the scene. The golden haze westwards was churned up less by the camel train than a brigade of the 10th Indian Army, whose convoys had been swirling along for days. Sikhs, Ghurkas, Hindus and Europeans passed in all kinds of transport. For several nights they encircled our own small encampment and surrounded us with a hundred flickering fires.

The desert saturates consciousness and numbs the mind. There would be little for eye and ear when the Army departed – no real structure in the landscape to attract or rest the eye. Even the food had been tasting insipid of late… The smoke from my Senior Service cigarette drifted upwards slowly in the still air. Cigarettes were a free issue but they were horrible throat-rasping atrocities going under the brand name of "V". This letter, we believed was for "Victory" but their contents were universally claimed to be made from dry camel dung and had been donated by an Indian prince as his contribution to the war effort. "Whose war effort?" we were inclined to ask, "Hitler's?"

Eventually even the hardened smokers rejected them and abandoned this particular weed entirely.

The Flight Sergeant "Discip" wandered through the tents and spotted a card game in progress in the lee of a tent. I watched, interested to see what he would do. Six men squatted around a blanket, tossing money into the middle. He loomed over this brag school. "Don't give a toss for Air Force Regulations, do you?" he enquired, "the only game of chance you are permitted is 'Housey Housey' and then only when I organise it. You're all on a charge."

No one spoke. The finer points of Air Force law were not considered to apply in the blue. They knew that, the Flight Sergeant knew it, and they knew that he knew. He changed step, "You're idle, all of you. Give me a rifle Corporal, I intend to shoot these men."

This was regarded as wit of a high order and the group smirked uneasily. "Flighty is a one, isn't he?"

They were saved by the bell. The cookhouse was on fire. Yells for the extinguishers. The brag school hurriedly dropped its cards and headed for the fire equipment, led by Flight. "Grab these you men; aim at the base of the flame…"

~ Under the Red Eagle ~

It was of little use. The cookhouse tent flared into a torch as petrol gushed from the cookers, and its canvas became a pillar of fire, threatening the other tents. The poles caught, cracked, and down came the tent; black shreds of canvas blew in the evening wind, and distorted metal pots and pans blackened. The dinner, well roasted in the dixies, was lost. But was it? An enquiring mind thought to taste the meat and pronounced it "great". We all departed for our "tools". We would think about another cookhouse tomorrow, which was another day, as Scarlett O'Hara had famously announced.

As a result of this loss, most of the rations perished as well, so the Sergeant Cook was despatched to Habbaniya to collect replacements. Later, we gathered that something like this conversation ensued:

SERGEANT	"Replacement rations for 24 WU please. Cookhouse burned down."
STOREMAN	"Who are you, exactly?"
SERGEANT	"I said. 24 Wireless Unit, at Haditha on the Euphrates."
STOREMAN	"R.A.F? What are you doing with this chit. It's for Indian rations."
SERGEANT	"Indian rations? What does that mean?"
STOREMAN	"You are indenting for curries, unwashed potatoes, mutton, rice and so on."
SERGEANT	"I thought the curries were desert rations?"
STOREMAN	"Not in this Command they aren't, except for Indian troops. Here you are, rations for 120 men for a month. Indent properly next time".

The Sergeant Cook reported back to the C.O.
"Cigarettes, jams and tinned meats, you say?"
"Yessir! we've been eating the wrong rations for two months."
The unit looked at its next meal with astonishment.

~ Under the Red Eagle ~

"They've gone puggle at Base!" ("Puggle" was, of course, barmy.) No wonder the food had been tasting insipid.

I watched an airman polishing his brass buttons over his buffing stick in anticipation of Pay Parade. They had been abraded like this so often that the eagles were down to a blur. The buttons must have been shifted from an old uniform and sewn on the khaki drill. He was a regular, and buttons like this said even more than medals. They had seen considerable service.

Who was it who said: *"How much it is to be regretted that the British should ever sit down contented to polish when they are candidates for eternity."* Hannah More, I think it was, late 18th century.

"Eternity, eh!"

It was time to visit our posts, which we did every two weeks or so, and head out across hundreds of miles of desert. We went north: Adjutant, Flight Sergeant Discip, Kildare as driver and myself. We were fully armed. First down to the ferry across the Euphrates and then into Mesopotamia proper. The crossing lay just below K3 and both river banks had a thin fertile strip in front of which the river flowed swiftly and water-wheels lifted water to irrigate the soil, which they had probably done for hundreds, if not thousands, of years. The ferry was a private one of the Iraq Petroleum Company but we used it regularly. The ferry was merely two rather tatty boats lashed together with a railed-in platform, rather like a pontoon bridge. It was connected by hawser and pulley to cables slung across the river and the crossing was made by adjusting the rudders and letting the river do the work. We signed the usual forms and accelerated up the slope into the desert, with pipeline telegraph poles stretching away to the horizon as excellent markers.

The first post lay off the pipeline, only just visible as a small white speck on top of a minor hill. It was Flight's practised eye which spotted the triangular tent-top and when we got there we found that the site commanded a good view of the desert in all directions and presented a neat appearance with stones cleared away and arranged to form paths. An Arab grave was quite near: Bedouin probably, and poor company for the wilds!

Number 10 post was in a state of chaos: they had dropped the tent and were just about to move, due to a misinterpretation of a signal from Base. Orders were given to put everything back again pronto and stay right where they were, which, unfortunately for them, was a flat, featureless desert, under strong wind and whipping sand. We had been keeping an eye on the tyre tracks of the ration lorry, which we knew to be ahead of us, the redoubtable "Soapy" being the driver. Why, then, did the tracks veer away from the pipeline towards the east, into remote desert? Trouble of some kind? We decided to follow and rescue the perishing, if that was required. The tracks wandered through various wadis, probably all connected to the big Wadi Tharthar, still running south- east, and on both sides we saw gazelle, birds, and one silver fox. "Aha," said Flight, "He's probably off to do a spot of hunting…" We breasted a rise after some miles and spotted the lost truck in the middle of a huddle of black tents. Bedouin? As we approached white-garbed figures, including some children, came out to meet the unusual intruders.

Flight's Arabic was up to an interrogation. "Where," he demanded, "is the driver of this truck?" Arab eyes flashed and they looked distinctly uneasy. Then, out of one of the tents came a discomposed Soapy. We finally got the full story out of him. He had encountered this tribe on an earlier trip and they had been trying to persuade him to join them – together, of course, with the truck, which was a highly valuable commodity to them. He had been offered a portion of land and one wife to start with. "Of course," he stuttered," I had no intention of deserting; it was just a laugh."

"I should think not," said Flight, "considering I remember you have a wife and two children at home. Get back to the pipeline and we'll follow. You're on a charge." The Arab children wailed as Soapy departed; he had obviously been a hit in the camp.

"What on earth…" said Flight, back in the staff car, "do I charge him with? I shall have to look up the regs."

So back to the north-east, with Soapy's lorry raising a cloud of dust ahead of us. One post followed another. Number 12 had the worst conditions so far; they had been under a sandstorm for three days, and looked it.

Still deep in the uttermost parts of Tharthar, Flight spotted a sand-coloured and tracked vehicle a mile or so away and heading towards us. It carried black crosses and seemed to be an SdKfz.9. We abandoned the pipeline and shot round the back of a sand-dune into a wadi. Crawling up the side, we peered over the top. The Germans had not seen our staff car and lorry, which is just as well, as they were better armed, with two cannon-type guns on a ring. We were confined to rifles, hand guns, and a Bren. Still, four men a side, so that was equal.

We opened fire and the half-track slewed. Our shooting was good and accounted for two. They slumped over the tail. It was much later that we realised who these Germans might have been; a special Kommando unit which had flown into Mosul with a brief to assist the Iraqis. The small action was brief if energetic. Our shots continued to be well aimed and either raised puffs of sand round the half-track or could not be seen at all – which should have meant hits. We kept our heads well down between bouts of firing and the Germans were clearly in some doubt from where the shots were coming. Then the armoured vehicle backed away and sped round the back of a dune. They kept going, and the last we saw was a small fume of dust making tracks for the horizon. We strode over and found that they had left two bodies in the sand.

The action took no more than fifteen minutes but was lively enough. We buried the two corpses in the lonely desert on top of a small hill. We had no wood, nor anything that would serve as a grave marker, so we just stabbed their rifles into the ground and balanced the helmets on top, with their dog tags looped through the trigger guards. We saluted and left.

The sun was dropping in the west so we headed for the nearest post for the night. They would be interested to know what had been about in their vicinity!

The first stars twinkled as we got to the next post, number 12, who provided us with a stove for cooking dinner and we delved into machonochie, fresh tomatoes and melon – the last being non-ration, although we had severe doubts that we should have been eating it.

We were away early the following morning as the sun rose and spotted number 14 post four miles away. Hereabouts was a sheen of what might have been grass, but it had been well scorched near death. We took time out to drink from our *chagguls*, which were slung over the door handles and on the bumpers. *Chagguls* were porous canvas bags, always wet and dripping, but with the great advantage that the water inside remained cold, however hot the outside temperature – in fact the hotter the air the colder the water. They were a great boon on long-haul desert travel.

The last post was near the buildings of K2 and the brightly reflecting aluminium well marked the pumping station position from many miles away. We found ourselves welcome guests for the night and luxuriated in cool linen and a cooler bath.

The next day we called in at Baiji on the Tigris; the Romans were alleged to have called tigers after this river, which could certainly be angry and raging. We spent some time in the open-air market – properly called a *souk* – which was thronged with Iraqis, a few Kurds, and many "chicos" – anyone, it appeared, between six and one hundred and six! An astonishing range of vegetables was on sale, including "ladies fingers", pumpkins, red water melon, cucumbers, tomatoes, onions, bajinjas, egg fruit, haricot beans, yams, and simple potatoes. We purchased some vegetables for the unit, recalling that they would need very thorough washing, preferably with some of the medical orderlies' disinfectant. We were also encouraged to buy livestock, but the staff car was not that big and to have a goat in the back would have been insupportable!

Dates were starting to appear on the palms and it was unexpected to see them growing like huge bunches of yellow grapes. The only version we had seen was in boxes at Christmas, but here they were considered overripe in that soft brown condition and were eaten long before that; the taste the Arabs preferred was a pleasing combination of nut, grape and date.

~ Under the Red Eagle ~

At dawn the following day we loaded the staff car again and swept south west from K2 on the long road back to the Euphrates, keeping a watchful eye open for any more swastikas. Behind us as we left the sharp-edged hills screened the Tigris and thrust jaggedly into the glowing eastern sky. The two sets of our former wheel tracks had scored the light sand, so there was no navigating problem even when we were out of sight of the pipeline. The road – if one could call it that – had only a graded sand surface except for short distances across the Wadi Tharthar. There it was ramped, embanked, metalled, and with culverts. Thereafter, to Haditha, there was a gypsum plain, rough on tyres and badly corrugated.

All went well in the silent desert until we approached post 12 again, when the ruffling of sand warned us that another blow was imminent. It was enough to obliterate the tracks and in consequence we lost the pipeline and moved into unfamiliar country. We plunged along the base of a canyon with the hills rising on all sides. This would not do, since we had had no hills like this on the outward trip. We checked the sun, still to be seen in the sky, although clouded with sand and turned south-west.

This proved to be the right move and after some miles the grey shadows of pipeline posts lay ahead. By evening we crossed the Euphrates again, called in at HQ and then headed out along the south western stretch of the pipeline. This was a smoother run and we were able to travel at fair speed across the flat and featureless expanse of the Syrian Desert. It looked rather similar to the horizons we saw at sea, but this was sand and rock, not water. Where the pipeline traversed broken country the track deviated to easier ground. Under traffic the soil broke into dust in the summer, and was soft after rain, but being in a relatively light staff car, and in summer, we could diverge from the track when it had become too weather-beaten. Number 4 post was in a photogenic situation, right on the lip of a canyon. We could now see for many miles over undulating sand and ridges and on the rise we could see post 5 ten miles away – and a post was only a relatively small tent and a lorry. Our eyes must have improved!

~ Under the Red Eagle ~

Post 5 had a problem. They had pitched their tent in the lee of a sand dune but the following day found the same dune on the other side of the tent. Genies, Arab-type? Flight had the answer from an exchange with Habbaniya; these dunes had the capability of moving under the desert wind, it was not the work of the Devil. The same post had another story to tell us. Their motorman/cook had stepped away into the desert that morning, with a spade, for the usual personal reasons. Squatting on the far side of another dune – this time an immobile one – he observed an interesting hole in the sloping side of a dune facing him. Regarding this orifice thoughtfully – big rats? – and with his shorts around his ankles, he was dumbfounded to see a great snout emerge followed by a black visage and large pointed ears. No rat, this... it was big, very big. The next thing his colleagues knew was to see a wild figure come scurrying back, trying to haul up his shorts at the same time.

"Wolf, wolf!" he yelled.

The unit dropped its chores and emerged to view this interesting event. What was cookie doing now? In the distance behind him, travelling rapidly away, appeared to be a jackal or some such inoffensive desert beast, retreating in a panicky minor cloud of dust. They fell about laughing. Cookie hauled up his shorts sheepishly. "Well, it looked like a wolf..." he mumbled.

By the time we arrived, the story had lost nothing in the telling and cookie was telling most of it.

A thought about the relatively few desert dwellers... There was probably under one person per square kilometre around us, according to the map, but even this was perhaps an overstatement. It was in the deep desert that one met the true Bedouin, who was nomadic. Their name actually meant "inhabitant of the desert" and they all believed that their wild spaces were peopled by *"jinns"* or spirits. Maybe they were!

The desert nights were cold and dawn came as a relief. Gradually a touch of blue then pink lightened the sky in the east and coloured the sky overhead, much as I saw at sea except that the colours were more vivid. The black and white landscape of the moon started to acquire the more flaunting tints of the day until the bright orange globe of the sun rose above the horizon and began to warm the sand and stone. Time for the lizards and cold-blooded creatures began to speed up. Slowly the desert took on the full blazon that had coloured it from the dawn of time. A clear call echoed from the black tents. This was the summons to prayer, when the men emerged from the tents to kneel together. The women did so too, within the tents. The day then started with a glass of sweet, amber tea.

The tents were not just canvas. When closed they were warm and waterproof. With the sides raised they offered shade and let any cooling breeze waft through. The tents were easily struck and moved, and were often owned by the senior woman of the family. The Bedouin had something to teach the infidel about desert clothes. What they wore was loose, flowing, and covered them from head to foot. This withstood the fierce heat of the day and insulated them from the cold of the night.

Whether veiled or not – veiled against strangers – the women used black kohl to great effect and in older age may have their faces and hands decorated with blue tattoo. They were always hungry except on special feasting occasions and had to tighten the belt under their clothes. "With some folk," says Pushkin, "custom's rule prevails" and that was certainly true of the Bedouin. They had rules of bearing, rules of treating guests, rules of dealing with enemies. To them the desert was pure and clean, like the Ritz, and they bore themselves nobly. A stranger was welcome at any tent and was sure of three days bed and board; perhaps this is the origin of the quote that "guests and fish stink after three days."

"Hurry is the devil's work," said the Bedouin and took their time over all matters. When they died in the desert they were buried before sundown in shallow graves which we had seen ourselves, marked with a stone at head and foot – except for children's graves which were distinguished by a small oval of stones.

We mostly saw the Bedouin in deep desert or when they traded in small towns, as they did at Baiji. They were elusive. The town-dwelling Iraqi was an altogether different matter. They would often ask for a written *chit* (note) to prove their loyalty to the British and to the RAF in particular. What they actually got depended on the humour of the writer: "Do not trust this loose wallah" might appear if the writer had been aggrieved; "This is a whizzo bloke" if not.

On another trip along the posts I had the superlative experience of travelling by night and by stars and compass. On this occasion, as the sun went down at the last post, we turned back to the Euphrates for a long dark run to the ferry. We rolled in a brief twilight through shallow valleys and wadis, this time well away from the pipeline and across thinly marked trails on the plateaux. Nightfall advanced across the desert from the east and a quarter of an hour was sufficient for the first pale glimmer of stars to appear. It began to be difficult to hold a course and more than once we lost the trail into uncharted wilds. Even by the official maps much was not known, which was perhaps not surprising since I had read somewhere that this area was still being explored as late as the 1930s.

Finally the sky became a blue-black vault with the Milky Way curving over in a luminous band. The swathe of beams from the headlights cut out only a small path of light. There was something sublime about the night desert; it stripped the mind of inconsequential dross. Pairs of green eyes gleamed as we swung down yet another wadi. Then a remarkable vision against the night. A silver fox was outlined on the ridge in front of us. The headlights swung across the top of the ridge and for a second the fox was bathed white in the glare, ears cocked and brush stiff. It was like a chromium mascot on a car. It was only a second before the animal was leaping away into the night. What had seemed almost a silversmith's model had gone forever, yet it was one of those seconds which can stand in the memory down the years. Then came the flick of a white tail and a gazelle fled from the wadi bottom, up over the ridge and away after the fox.

The constant motion and hum of the engine, the warm night breeze, and the million pinpoints of the constellations overhead, combined to produce a great splendour. By day, there was something austere and antiseptic about the glaring desert. By night it became haunting as the moon rose and transformed the sand and rocks into a silver tapestry of light and silence.

> "I saw Eternity in that bowl of night
> And the blackness of departed day
> Past the blaze of stars in their patterns bright
> And beyond the flare of the Milky Way."

After some hours, and far away where the sand touched the sky, we saw a faint glow of light some miles distant. We were travelling in the right direction; that would be K3. An hour later we pulled up on the river bank and blew the horn for the ferry. Some time to wait. We could hear the swish of the river against the rocky shore as the oily water raced south towards the Gulf. To the right we heard again the perpetual creak of the water wheel and the distant barking of pariahs in the village of Haditha.

But what was the ferry doing with lights all over it? Something unexpected. An English voice sang "Ol' man river". Dimly seen khaki suggested that something unusual was afoot. I recognised Harris's voice and we realised that HQ was having a night out. We rolled on board and were amazed to be offered ice-cream, food in the Iraqi fashion and whisky and soda from an improvised bar. The Iraq Petroleum personnel were entertaining the unit in high fashion. It was a magnificent climax to a tough run.

Harris's song changed to the inevitable:

"Bless 'em all, bless 'em all,
The long and the short and the tall,
Bless all the Sergeants and W.O. Ones,
Bless all the Corporals and their bastard sons,
For we're saying goodbye to them all,
As back to their billets they crawl,
You'll get no promotion, this side of the ocean,
So cheer up my lads, bless 'em all.

This was the slightly expurgated version!

~ Under the Red Eagle ~

We were too exhausted to participate long and we left them to it, in high good humour, and retreated to our tents – but not without taking some of their whisky with us.

6. Come at Four O'clock

"Keep thy foot out of brothels.;
And defy the foul fiend."
Shakespeare, *King Lear Act 3 Sc.4*

Harris wandered into the Orderly Room to see if there was any tea on the brew. The desert flamed outside, as usual, and the unit was at 130°F the shade. Most of the Arabs and animals had retired from the noonday heat into their mud houses, tents, or burrows and only the RAF showed a little life – but not much at that.

That year the summer had been hotter than usual, adding ten degrees in the shade. There was little relief and even the local population looked thin and pale, while the Indian troops were actually succumbing to heatstroke. The long dry months of the summer had also brought the regular dust and sandstorms, squadrons of flies, and dust devils. The air became so full of particles that the sun could be obliterated and the landscape, what one could see of it, looked as though a London fog had descended – but hot, not cold.

Harris found the Corporal studying a letter which looked as though a scorpion with inky feet had been wandering over it.

"Here's a rum go," said the Corporal, "We have been invited to tea at the Tigris Hotel, River Street, Baghdad, at four o'clock next Saturday."

"Who," asked Harris, "has done the inviting?"

"Dunno," said the Corporal "the signature is indecipherable, but I suppose it could be from one of the memsahibs in the British colony." His "memsahib" disclosed that he had spent all of a few days in India.

Enquiries around the unit elicited no further information. So the invitation was taken at face value and six enthusiasts, drawn by lot, set out the following Saturday to accept the inducement and see what was what. Tea was tea anyway, and this was free. These airmen had a love-hate relationship with Baghdad. They were intrigued by the shimmering vistas of an alien skyline, which they had seen as a desert mirage serried by mosque domes, minarets and date palms. Hot and pungent odours rose from rain-parched streets, coupled with a hundred ether smells from rose perfume to stench. Baghdad had the capacity to stun the Westerner with its climate or to lay him low with sandfly fever, scorpion bites, malaria, dysentery or any other of the 47 diseases to which the flesh, and all the Services, were heir.

The group of airmen straggled down the main, Al Raschid, street with its columns, blinds, and shaded shops. Immaculate men in well-tailored suits rubbed shoulders with beggars and Arabs in full traditional garb and *kaffiyeh* head-shawl. Heavily veiled women, mostly barefoot and bearing water jars or kerosene tins on their heads, with graceful strides, contrasted with other women, in western dress, displaying all the chic that one expected of Paris.

The one thing in short supply, in Baghdad or up country, was female company. In Iraq, as in most of the East, unmarried girls were either virgins or harlots. There was no middle way, and airmen had problems in coming to terms with this fact. Virginity was a delicate flower, requiring constant surveillance from relatives if it were to be maintained. The brush of a hand, a knowing look, or the flicker of an eyelid could taint a girl's honour. The net result was that celibacy was thrust onto the airman if he was wise. If he was not, and consorted with the second of the unmarried types, he was likely to be a candidate for the Medical Officer.

In the narrower streets one needed to give way to heavily laden donkeys or camels, cramming the street from side to side with their panniers and could only be avoided in a welcome doorway. Motor horns honked continually and those selling their many wares shrieked their bargains, of sweetmeats, fruit, toilet articles, doubtful postcards, jewellery and a hundred other articles borne on trays. There were altercations between chicos or between men who seemed ready to fight one another, but were in truth friends or relatives. They also had the habit of spitting on an already filthy pavement.

Finally, the six found the dark and narrow River Street, which did in fact front onto the Tigris. Here were the little open-fronted shops of the Amara silversmiths displaying their wares and skills in a wide variety of delicately-made trinkets and jewellery.

On the opposite side of the street, the river side, lay the "Tigris Hotel" which, to their disappointment, looked rather dingy. They entered a hall with a bar from which the local brews were available, ranging from gaseous beer to the extirpating *arrack* – a coarse spirit distilled from the date. Drinking it was a chargeable offence. The Medical Officer did not require his hands to be full of paralysed airmen.

They were ushered into a large room by a black-eyed small boy and met the ladies who had issued the invitation. They were not British, nor memsahibs. They were Olga, Annie, Fatima and others, dressed in many forms, in a riot of colour, and in dresses, which Harris noted, all buttoned down the front.

Some were white, sharper-featured, and with light skin. Olga had a flame of red hair. Others, including Fatima, had the black headdress and falling ringlets of the local female Baghdadi; two added huge circular ear-rings, yashmaks, and the cylindrical nose decoration of the female desert Arab. Who were these ladies? Some kind of local Womens' Institute?

Tea was the prerogative of Fatima, it appeared, a rather vivacious girl. It was obviously an important ceremony and the group had been in the country long enough to realise its consummate significance. Fatima heated her small enamel teapot on the fire until the water – into which she flung a fistful of tea – boiled over. She then filled the small tea glasses, about the size of eggcups, and emptied them back into the teapot. The brew was boiled again and the process was repeated twice more. This was going to be a long teatime. Then followed the testing, the final boil, and the amber liquid was served from a pot held two feet or so over the tea glasses. There was no spillage, and froth was considered a desirable part of Iraqi tea. Sweet cakes were served and small fingers were extended from the tea glasses in a manner that the ladies, especially the white, clearly thought fitted the occasion.

We were also served yoghurt, which we knew was often offered to guests by nomadic Arabs. Here, we were rather surprised to be offered it. It had an unusual pungent taste with an after-sapidity. We accepted it for the courtesy of the matter, but were aware of the desert fable that the effervescent process was started with a chunk of decomposing horse or ass.

The only oddity in the scene, which might nearly, but not quite, have been translated to an English vicarage, was the rather large Arab gentleman, curved blade in belt, displayed rather obviously, who sat in the corner of the room and was clearly some kind of bodyguard for the ladies. He glowered, fingered his blade, but said nothing.

By this time the group was thoroughly at home and talk flowed in broken English, some French, and fractured Arabic. A young Arab boy entered the room and squatted with a stringed instrument on his knees. The high, tinkling, sound echoed round the room and Fatima danced. She appeared to be the principal hostess. Her ear-rings trilled and her sinuous body curved and arched under a startling cascade of brightly coloured silk. Her fingers flicked in time to the music.

Harris disappeared to find the loo. He found it furnished with raised narrow bidets and other inexplicable equipment, plus row upon row of highly coloured liquids in small bottles. The rooms, he felt as he passed them, were rather over decorated with hangings of wild silks and cottons and, he noted, large mirrors suspended over the beds. Glancing into one room from which much laughter flowed, he was astonished to spot on a chair a military cap with a bright scarlet top – an MP!

Illumination dawned. Harris practically fell downstairs. He hissed to the assembly: "Chaps, this is no hotel. It's a brothel. We're probably out of bounds, and what's more there's at least one MP upstairs."

So that explained the warm invitation!

There was a scurry of feet and six airmen charged out into River Street. This was no time to hang about.

The Iraqis in the street grinned.

7. Desert to Mountain

> *"So all day long the noise of battle rolled*
> *Among the mountains by the winter sea"*
> **Tennyson**

Haditha lay below the camp on the eastern side of the Euphrates, so was truly in Mesopotamia. It was a cluster of single-storey whitened and bleached houses separated by narrow alleys.

Wandering through one of those alleys, I found the end blocked by high walls and a thick door. Under the impression that this probably led into the next alley, I pushed it open and found myself faced with a small courtyard with palms and coloured with bright flowers. Several women in black, unveiled, turned enquiring eyes towards me. The chatter ceased. Light dawned. I had entered a harem!

A large Arab squatting under a palm rose and whipped out an evil-looking curved knife. Unarmed, I considered this a time for discretion rather than valour and retreated. Halfway up the alley, moving sharply, I heard the door flung back and the large Arab appeared in the gap, waving his cutlery. Some indecipherable Arabic was yelled. I accelerated and shot round the corner. Behind, I heard a lock thwacking into place. The sanctum sanctorum was not for western eyes, especially those of the RAF!

In general, we got on well with the local Iraqis but less so with the deep desert Bedouin, whose pilfering was a way of life. Some of our posts had local nomadic encampments, from which they got visits at night. Anything of value outside the tent, even inside, would be missing by daybreak, and occasionally guards had to be mounted. We heard of another Wireless Unit where matters had become more serious. An airman woke during the night, hearing a low sound near the tent, challenged, and was shot dead. At dawn his CO led a party to the nearby encampment to find the culprit and search for lost equipment. A few Enfield rifles were discovered. The women of the tribe stood apart, lamenting. The skirts of one massive lady failed to hold the booty and knives and forks, two pairs of boots, and a variety of other RAF property fell about her feet. A female "loose wallah"! The Bedouin culture believes all is to be shared, which probably included our property as well. Perhaps this was borrowing rather than pilfering.

A minor disaster one morning. Our main latrine was a simple structure as already mentioned – a canvas screen and a large hole over which was slung a stout pole. This gave an opportunity to bunch together in the morning and exchange quips and unit gossip. Walking towards the latrine, I was near enough to hear splintering wood and muffled yells as one too many sitters precipitated all into the unmentionable depths. The unfortunates scrambled out, hitched up filthy shorts, and cursed. How they cursed!

Since we had recently filled the bowser, we were not too short of water and the morning was spent scrubbing. But they still smelt: we would have to indent for new kit from Habbaniya.

We had now been long enough in the desert to think up ideas for easier living, or adapt ourselves. Here are some examples:

TEA: Half-fill an old petrol tin with sand, pour in petrol and light. This will keep going for quite a time – certainly long enough for a 'brew'. Most desert units did exactly the same. One wonders how much of the high-octane petrol was used for this purpose and not to power tanks, aircraft and vehicles.

DRINKING GLASSES: Get an empty bottle, probably beer, and fill with oil to the required level. Light the oil. The glass will break cleanly at the surface of the oil. Bingo!

FOOD: To get some variety into the rations – boringly monotonous, especially when we were mistakenly on Indian rations – we used bully beef, biscuits and vegetables, if available. This made a passable stew. Or we would hammer the square biscuits into flour and make up some fritters. There were a good many variations of this type. Sometimes we could shoot gazelle in the desert, chasing them with lorry or 15 cwt. Improved the bully no end.

CAMOUFLAGE: If needed on the tents, use oil

TOILET: One quart of water per day had to do for personal washing, perhaps less. Shave first, then face armpits and feet, in that order. The remainder went into the lorry radiators.

URINATION: By the ever-present "desert rose" – a petrol tin sunk into the ground with another canted at an angle and fitting into the first.

BEDS: The different ways these were created had to be seen to be believed. A little wood and wire produced a quite comfortable couch. The lazy on the unit just slept on groundsheets after checking around for scorpions and snakes. Mosquito nets were provided but rarely used because there was little standing water around for them to breed. We saw them occasionally, probably from the river banks, but not often.

FLIES: We were regularly under attack from fly squadrons. The insect population. We beat off a thousand fly sorties every hour, until the evening, when they return to base. This gave rise to the anti-fly mug. Our fitters, always prepared to make anything, constructed lids for mugs, with a thumb-lever attached by which the lid could be raised, then quickly dropped. This was claimed to be proof against flies if one were a "quick sipper". Lacking a lid – not all were *persona grata* with the fitters – flies would go for a swim in the tea and need to be flicked out. Ugh!

Curly thought up a scheme for embarrassing the medical orderlies. He drilled a small hole through the thick skin on the palm of his hand and inserted a bristle from a bass broom through the hole, which projected from the other side of the hard skin, for a quarter of an inch or so. The full length of the bristle was concealed with the other hand. It looked remarkably as though he had run a splinter into his flesh. He tried this out on one or two colleagues in his tent, with some success and gratifying results, so he approached the medical tent for aid. 'Doc' Brown took one look and hunted through various boxes for his forceps. With realistic "Oohs" and "Ahs" from the patient, the splinter was withdrawn. At one inch Doc looked interested and said "hold on…" At two inches he observed "what the hell is this?"

Various Curly comrades watching the proceedings turned away in near hysteria. Curly snatched away his hand leaving Doc with a four-inch bristle still gripped in the forceps. Medical dignity was affronted:
"You bloody fool!" remarked Doc, with feeling.

Continuing the medical theme, many of us endured "prickly heat" or *miliaria*, an acute itching eruption of the skin caused by blocking of the sweat glands, usually in sensitive places. We also suffered chronic eczema, psoriasis, and 'dhobi itch', all to do with heat affecting the skin. Only by transferring the sufferer to cool conditions could these symptoms be fully alleviated; we had to take the alternative route of treatment with mild antiseptics or aniline dyes.

The country was in fact bad for transforming a slight injury into a serious one. One of the Orderly Room airmen had a small shaving rash on his chin, probably because his razor was not properly sterilised, and this was transformed into a horrible raw weeping rash from nose to throat. Muffled in bandages, he became very depressed. This was *Tinea Barbae* or "Barber's Rash." He turned into a full hospital case.

Not all found the desert a tedious and unfriendly place. A few developed an appreciation by day for its sheer space, clean air (apart from flies) and rough cliffs and crags. By night there was a mumchance peace in the sky, which became black velvet, punctuated by stars and the soft glow of the galaxy.

The question of an emblem for the unit was raised. The desert rat or jerboa having been appropriated by the 7th Armoured and the scorpion by the Long Range Desert Group, I was asked to find another animal and design a symbol, and I adopted a blue jackal's head – remembering the chap who was caught with his trousers down – against a white background with a red flash behind the head to signify the radio element of what we did. This was well received, so I cut a stencil and put the jackal on all our mobile equipment. We were now better recognisable as RAF signals.

For us, as for all Middle East servicemen, two of the most detested people were Lady Astor MP and King Farouk of Egypt. Lady Astor, it was alleged, had relieved herself of the opinion that all troops returning from the Middle East should wear a distinguishing mark to show that they were liable to have been infected with various diseases. She had only to be mentioned in any gathering of airmen to call forth a violent outburst of boos and catcalls.

I must say I had my doubts about this: it seemed doubtful that any public figure should make such an unfortunate remark. But she did have the reputation of being headstrong.

King Farouk was a different matter. His unpopularity stemmed from the widely held belief that he was anti-British and had kept guards of honour broiling in the sun to demonstrate this. This may well have happened; in any case the belief was strong. The song went:

"King Farouk, King Farouk,
Hang your b--------s on a hook,
Stanishwiya, pull your wire,
King Farouk, bardin."

If a chorus were reached, it became:

"He's the king of the wogs."

And much more, which brought in Queen Farida, camels, horses, and dogs (rhyming with wogs).

We met the Arab Legion. They were on their way south down the pipeline and paused to take a meal with us. Shades of Lawrence of Arabia! The NCO in charge wore a chequered red headdress flowing round his shoulders and his khaki uniform sported bandolier, pistols, rifle, grenades, and a businesslike knife. He was a Bedouin: the Palestinians wore yellow headdress. There was little love lost between the two. Their physical appearance was different also. The Bedouin had classic features, almost effeminate, dark bronzed skin and raven black hair. The Palestinians were whiter-skinned and almost European-looking. Their OC was, of course, Major Glubb, although he was not with them, and they patrolled extensively. After the meal they turned south, exchanging "thumbs up" and grinning delightedly.

The nights were getting cooler now and Jimmy the Adjutant came into the Orderly Room one morning with his teeth chattering. The full moon of Ramadan was failing and the Arab fasting would soon end. Nightly, the moon was exceptionally brilliant and bathed the desert in a silver light from horizon to horizon.

❖ ❖ ❖

I am writing now, shakily, in a maelstrom of wind, sand, and rain, and have occasionally to blow fine sand from the diary pages to avoid clogging the pen. The storm opened majestically. It had been cloudy all day and the sun had disappeared behind a layer of milky altostratus. In late afternoon dark clouds appeared to south west and we lost the light quickly. The wind strengthened and drove a lower nimbus across the sky. Then came a huge frontage of whirling sand, beaten up by the rain and towering a thousand feet above us, into the low cloud. A vaporous draught of hard-driven sand blew across the camp square and the full storm was upon us. Canvas billowed wildly and sand penetrated every tent corner. All we could do was lie on the campbed, talk about the next possible move, and gradually grey with dust and sand. Kildare stated, "After this lot, the only thing to shake me would be a convoy of Waafs driving into the camp for the night."

❖ ❖ ❖

We knew that German troops were pushing down towards the Caucasus and they could penetrate to the River Araxes in North Persia. This was not the only threat with which Paiforce might be concerned since there had always been a risk of a German penetration into Iraq through Anatolia, which could put them into the Gulf and on the way to India.

This River Araxes formed the border at the north west of Persia and there was open country between Kasvin, Teheran, and Hamadan. If the Germans overran this area they could bomb the Persian oilfields. It followed that our sector had to be held at all costs.

Rumour was rife of a move into Persia as part of the front line there. We have halted "digging in" here, stopped sending washing to Haditha, cleaned up the armament, and sent a thousand gallons of petrol to the posts.

~ *Under the Red Eagle* ~

We had a good idea of why we were being shifted. Throughout this summer of 1942 matters had become ominous. It was touch and go whether the 8th Army could stand at El Alamein, and the Allied position was precarious. Rommel was within fifty miles of Alexandria. Stalingrad was under attack and the Wehrmacht could then drive down to the Caucasus and beyond. We could be flung across their front but were so lightly armed and dispersed that we would be unable to halt the progress of armour and heavy troops.

The rumour about Persia proved to be true; we moved from the heat of the desert to the snow of the mountains.

First day. We hauled down the tents and bedded down over night either in the lorries or under the stars. Reveille was at 06.00 and we were away down the old rough trail to Habbaniya, where we are again accommodated in the Transit Camp. We spend an evening in the main camp roaring out all the old songs: *Bless 'em all, Desert Blues, I Don't Want to be an Airman, We're 'ere because we're 'ere, I'm Only a girl in Uniform, She'll be Comin' Round the Mountain*, etc.[2]

Second day. Into Baghdad, where we had an evening off. This time we found the bazaar, where the stench was appalling. Blind beggars, Arab women in full black with tattooed ankles and faces, old men and women weaving threads of wool, horses, donkeys, mules, meat hanging from the hook and swarming with flies. Potters turned chatties and the deep shadows in narrow streets were struck with sunlight. Over all hung the odour of the East.

We plunged deeper and entered the maze of streets at the back of the town. We were at once surrounded by scores of children not used to seeing uniform in this "out of bounds" area.

"You want my sister, Johnnie? Velly hygienic."

Back onto the main street we spotted a minaret over the roofs. An Arab produced a ladder and we clambered up a wall, and another, and emerged overlooking the courtyard of the mosque. The babble of

---

[2] For a complete collection of hundreds of the bawdy songs and recitations of the Royal Air Force and other British armed forces, see *Bawdy Ballads & Dirty Ditties*, also published by Woodfield.

the street and the honk of horns faded here. It was a quiet and beautiful place – the "Blue Mosque" – so-called from its magnificent dome of gorgeous egg-shell blue. We also visited the "Mosque Meddan" and the "Leaning Minaret" but failed with the "Golden Mosque," the very seat of the orthodox, topped in pure gold.

After dinner at the "Sinbad" – an appropriate name – the city lights flicked into life and Baghdad acquired some of the lurking romanticism which failed it by day.

The sewers of the city, we were told, held more secrets than anywhere else in the world. Looking out over the city again from a rooftop, we saw immediately in front a house being demolished, throwing its inner secrets open to all. A gaggle of black gowned workers and their donkeys scoured the rubble. Beyond were the untouched columns and arches of a two-storey building surmounted by a dozen cupolas, and in the far distance was a panorama rising above the city against a completely flat horizon with nimbus clouds. City of a thousand scenes, perfumes, and stinks in the nostril! In the evening I found myself in the open-air cinema, next to a woman in black with copper rings on her headdress. She tried to do business, but what, I could not translate. I had a good idea, though!

Third day. We set out on the road to Khanaquin on a tarmac surface which stopped short at the Iraq/Iran frontier post. In the few small villages the convoy was jammed into immobility, but we did finally move after an hour or so and the day's run finished with the foothills of the Persian mountains looming ahead.

Khanaquin had little to recommend it – narrow odorous streets and poor shops piled with vegetables and many silver ornaments. A few dwarf palms were the only greenery. Our road now lay forward, following the old caravan route from Baghdad to Teheran.

We met a few Poles, as we were to again at Hamadan, because their force did some training in the vicinity, especially in mechanised warfare. It was a body of high morale and very well disciplined, rather unlike the Polish pilots in the Battle of Britain. It was said of this Corps:

~ *Under the Red Eagle* ~

*"It was more than a military formation.
It was a crusade."
Macmillan.*

I was later to meet the same men in early 1944, when they joined the 8th Army and fought their way bitterly up the slopes of Monte Cassino.

Fourth day. The road into Persia varied from the steep to the very steep and mountains with a curious unreality rose black against the rising sun. Streamers of gold flew upwards; a striking sight.

The road passed over a sun baked plain broken by *nullahs* – streams or drains – and strewn with stones and scrub. Cranes and jackals appeared and disappeared and the road bore constant donkey traffic, loaded with humans and burdens. The Paitek Pass into Persia lay ahead.

Fifth day. We started to make heavy going of it now, up the steep inclines of the pass, and sacrificed water from the bowsers to lighten their load – which had the advantage that it helped lay the dust.

We rose about 1,400 feet in 3½ miles. The serried heights above us changed from steel grey to tints of orange, violet, red and green with the snow-capped mountains turning, as the sun set, to unearthly shades of crimson and gold.

We were now in the mighty Zagros Range between Khanaquin and Kermanshah in the steepest part of the Paitek Pass known as the Teng-i-Girrah or 'Zagros Gates', before Kerind – where we laagered for the night. I wandered down into Kerind after the evening meal but the shops were shut and the only bargaining was with the local affable blacksmith, still at work. I bought a pocket-knife of unusual workmanship and was shown one of the rifles that he had under repair. It had literally been blown apart with some obstruction in the barrel, placed there in a local feud – the blacksmith said- and anyone who had an eye behind that burst had been severely injured.

A great crag of rock towered over the village, thrown up in the ancient crumbling movement so apparent here. It was an ominous threat under which to live. The land hereabouts had few people and was desolate and uninviting. Later we found that our route was to lie through green and variegated valleys with patches of colour and shade, some wooded mountain slopes, and a running stream by the roadside. It was in sharp contrast to our scorched desert. The few people, however, were mostly ragged and thin and, although nervous of us at first, were not unfriendly.

Our convoy approached the main part of the narrow Paitek Pass and the vehicles toiled upwards, and upwards again. The Paitek was the gateway into the heart of Persia and the hugeness of the landscape bated the breath. Vast raking mountains enfolded tremendous stretches of plain carrying patches of ploughed land, crops and grass.

Finally we were brought to a night's laager beyond Kermanshah, and a visit to a local café hung with gay rugs and lit by a solitary lamp. It was more than a café, being an opium den full of heavy-eyed and somnolent figures recumbent on wooden beds. The small ball of opium was lit from a brazier and puffed witlessly. One smoker was yet sober enough to tap head and eyes and circle a finger round his temple to indicate what happened if he overdid his smoking. We did not participate.

Sixth day. Beyond Kermanshah we passed the Darius rock carvings, sculptures, and inscriptions, recording past triumphs, on the chiselled surface of the rock.

The lorries now began to show the strain of the continuous hard effort and three gave up the ghost. Fitters forward We waited for the laggards opposite a little woodland paradise where streams ran fast down the valley and there was full shade under young green trees. The waters ran into a funnel-shaped inlet and then flowed away down a small race. This drove a massive and ancient stone to grind the corn into very fine flour. The miller was an old man with one helper but found a break to talk to us. This was a timeless world.

The more sporting discovered large trout and other fish in the stream and a little thought produced a mosquito net to hold in the water while others, with barefoot racket, encouraged the fish into the net. Three were caught, despatched, cleaned, and panned. They were excellent. So we were not too concerned about the wait for our missing trucks and travelled on when they reached us. We should have been at the end of the journey today but another tough pass lay ahead.

It was by this route into Persia that the great conquerors also came in the past: Darius, Xerxes, Alexander. Through centuries this road – better, track – has borne merchants, armies, and pilgrims. We were only the latest uniforms to travel east and north into central Persia.

> "Think, in this batter'd Caravanserai,
> Whose Doorways are alternate Night and Day,
> How Sultan after Sultan with his pomp,
> Abode his hour or two, and went his way."
>
> **Omar Khayyam**

Seventh day. This was the shortest run, but the stiffest climb, up the fearful Asabad or Shah Pass. This was well over twice the height of Snowdon and ten miles or so in length. The slow climb opened out even more majestic vistas, both forward and rear, and on breasting the top we looked down and across the valley where our destination, Hamadan, lay. This pass was so steeply pitched that it made even the Paitek a minor experience. The road down was precipitous and winding, flanked by snow barriers. We reached and passed through Hamadan and set camp a short distance beyond, under the snow-capped height of Mount Elvend. We were 6,000 feet above sea level, and the mountain towered another 6,000 above us. A cool capful of wind brushed across our travel-dried skins. This was an ancient country, Hamadan being formerly ther Ecbatana of the Medes, and was buried within high mountains soaring into the sky on all sides.

We could already see that Iran, Persia, was an arid and elevated country, seven times the size of Britain. It was centred in a key battle position since it was fronted by U.S.S.R., Turkey, Iraq, Afganistan, and Baluchistan. There was much Nazi intrigue here and that was why the British forces entered Persia in 1941.

This entry allowed Russians and British to establish control over the oilfields and opened up the long supply route from the Gulf to carry war materiel in thousands of tons, into Russia. The Russians never seemed to acknowledge this help much, but it was a massive aid.

24 Wireless Unit was now in a position where it could monitor any German push south east, by land or air, through the Caucasus. If the south Russian armies had collapsed the Germans could have reached the Hamadan-Kermanshah line by Oct-Nov last year, 1942. The Chiefs of Staff, in view of this, had earmarked twenty squadrons from the Middle East proper to the protection of the Caucasus. We were sitting on a fulcrum of history.

General Auchinleck's view was to give priority to the menace to Persia if the Germans came south past the Caspian Sea. Therefore the Paiforce Command was put under General Sir Henry Maitland Wilson with directives to ensure the safety of the oil-producing regions, and the supplies to Russia. At his disposal were only three infantry divisions, a motor brigade, and a few regiments of light and armoured cars. His main problem was not a shortage of men, however, as much as getting them in position over enormous distances of thoroughly bad road, to meet the powerful threat and any minatory advances towards Persia.

It was a New York journalist who marvelled how Allied engineers had created a vast conveyor belt to carry supplies by road and rail over 1,400 miles of the toughest route to be found anywhere in the world. Iranians, Americans, invalided Russians, and British forced huge trucks from Abadan and Basra through Persia in heat up to 130 degrees and over roads so dusty that drivers had to use respirators.

Some information drifted back to us in a top secret signal. On the night of 23rd October it appeared that the 8th Army had opened up an attack at an obscure point in the western desert called El Alamein. The German and Italian panzers were caught unprepared and forced to counter the attack on ground of British choosing. They were beaten off.

Perhaps the tide had started to turn?

North of us the Germans were giving priority to the Stalingrad offensive, then aiming south east to the oil. Light German forces could attack northern Persia before the coming winter closed down operations until the spring. Russia had forces available for the Caucasus, we hoped, and could make a fighting withdrawal back towards our position.

"The north could become the decisive front" was Auchinleck's assessment. An ominous implication for us.

General Wilson took Auchinleck's judgement seriously: "I decided to fight the main defensive battle on the line of the Elburz-Mianeh mountains and at the same time to push a detachment forward to the River Araxes to deny the Tabriz area to the enemy as long as possible."

Our placing from central to northern Persia could therefore put us in some jeopardy. The immediate future could be lively.

The Germans had opened their campaign when we were in the Iraqi desert, Now they were driving towards the southern Caspian Sea. Timoshenko evacuated Rostov and withdrew the bulk of his army across the Don, leaving only a remnant to defend the Caucasus. At the same time, the battle raged around Stalingrad.

Having taken Rostov, the Germans entered Caucasia and got as far as Mosdok. They were now before the main ranges of the Caucasus where the roads led over into Trans-Caucasia.

This chapter started with a quote from Tennyson, that all day long the noise of battle rolled, among the mountains by the winter sea.

The noise of battle was certainly rolling now from North, Stalingrad, and West, the Western Desert.

8. In the High Country

> *'Tis all a Chequer-board of Nights and Days*
> *Where Destiny with Men for pieces plays:*
> *Hither and thither moves, and mates, and slays."*
> **Rubaiyat**

There was a link between the Paiforce Command and that of the Western Desert. Iraq and Persia both housed the lifeblood of oil while Persia was the only overland route by which the Allies could supply the USSR. It was a vital passage; if the Russians were successfully to resist the German pushes then they needed the Allied supplies now and the roads north needed to be kept open. That was part of our job. Were the German attack south east to reach the Gulf then they would be half way to a connection with the Japanese – at the moment held up in Burma by the 14th Army. Such a rendezvous could spell disaster.

Over two generations previously during the 1914-18 war, British soldiers led their mules along the precipices, man-handled vehicles through water crossings and over rock and created the first Persian motor road. Now the whole effort had been intensified and the Paitek-Asabad route carried traffic a hundred-fold heavier. The Army had to create its own road transport service to cope with tribesmen liable to attack for firearms and war stores, and this was initially achieved by Indian troops. Military Police set up their posts in the passes.

The UKCC – United Kingdom Commercial Corporation – came into the picture to assist the Royal Army Service Corps. Their drivers slept rough and if a vehicle broke down or was wrecked, another would tow or carry it – perhaps for 300 miles if the damaged vehicle's driver were lucky.

Until supplies from Britain destined for southern Russia could be sent through the Mediterranean, they had to be dispatched via the Cape of Good Hope to the Persian Gulf ports – the same route that we took – and then proceed overland by rail or road for more than a thousand miles. From Southampton it was over 12,200 miles – half-way round the world.

When they got here, troops and airmen were amongst the most lonely men anywhere, particularly at our own posts, scattered through the mountain passes. It was not a country in which to be marooned. But all servicemen here were extraordinarily accommodating and probably did not grouse as much as they were entitled to. If they had done this a bit more they might have got some of the air-conditioned dwellings used by the Americans in Persia.

On the other hand, of course, their function required them to live rough, and that they did.

There were two routes to take the Russian supplies north – rail and road. The former had been an astonishing feat of engineering over deserts with soft and treacherous sand, malarial bogs, and high mountains. For weather there was ice and snow, sandstorms, rainstorms, blizzards, and heat – both Iraq and Persia were among the hottest countries in the world and could reach temperatures up to 130° F, while the Persian winter was severe, with drops down to 60° F below. Alternatively, there were the roads, but these were mostly fair-weather tracks in bad repair. In the mountain passes, they were just as dangerous and we passed many trucks upside down in stream beds a hundred feet below. War supplies poured into Russia along both routes. Tanks, aircraft, heavy engineering, ammunition and every other essential for war flowed towards the battle zones.

Our own encounters with this traffic lay in guarding the mountain passes from Hamadan to Kasvin and we met UKCC drivers of many nationalities, from natives to invalided soldiers doing an alternative job. They thrust their lorries over routes rather than roads, on ways more accustomed to men on foot and the donkey. Spadefuls of earth and rock were sometimes hurled into the bigger potholes, but only rarely. The drivers might well set out with an aged chassis, faulty

~ Under the Red Eagle ~

brakes, and an uncertain engine. It called for courage, even heroism, to tackle winter ice with 2,000 foot precipices on either side. They were fierce, fast, and often careless, drivers. Meeting them on the same road was an experience.

Our HQ at Hamadan was below Mount Elvend, the 'Orantes' of the ancients. It was from here that the town got its abundant water supply and around it was a plain containing vineyards, orchards and gardens, with the reputation of being one of the finest locations in Persia. The streets of Hamadan were narrow and filthy and it had some 20,000 inhabitants. The bazaars were well-built and, apart from the usual trade in trinkets and food, sold copperware, leather and wines. There was a resident group of some 2,000 Jews, for whom the town had always been a sacred spot, due to the alleged tombs of Esther and Mordecai, of Old Testament fame, in a holy place in the town centre. This was a famous objective for Hebrew and Moslem pilgrims. More about it later…

We needed to go to Teheran so Jimmy and I took the 15 cwt and travelled north and east to the capital, some 250 miles away. Turning east from Kasvin, we approached at speed what were obviously staff cars parked at the roadside. A cloud of dust rolled in our wake. An officer stepped into the road, waved us down, leaned casually on the door, and observed in an Oxford accent:

"I say, old man, just thought I would suggest that you don't cover the General with too much dust."

"General? What General?"

"Maitland Wilson, old boy."

We blinked at one another in astonishment.

"Our apologies. Slowly it is."

We had just been about to smother the C-in-C in the grit of his own Command!

❖ ❖ ❖

Teheran was an eye-opener. Even in war it had open cinemas, cabarets, restaurants and generally was a strange mixture of Occident and Orient. There were long avenues, many trees, and the unusual addition of running water along channels cut at the roadside. Being December, it was cold and the poverty of Teheran made itself known. A small boy in rags, carrying a hand brazier for warmth, accosted me for alms. I could do no less than pass over some rials. His face lit up.

We passed the German Legation with its eagles – "I say, shouldn't we heave a brick or something?" – into streets thronged with a kaleidoscope of familiar British and foreign uniforms. As RAF we appeared to be unique. The Persians, probably cavalry, wore long swinging greatcoats with flared trousers of a peculiar mustard colour. They tended to hold hands and to smile warmly at one another. We noted this with some humour; not very military!

Then there were the Russians, apparently parachute troops occupying all the Teheran barracks. Their field grey was emblazoned with red stars and medals. We had our usual share of communists on the unit, but when they discovered that lesser ranks were supposed to step into the gutter when encountering a Russian officer on the pavement their socialist enthusiasm tended to wane.

A Scottish bandsman strode by in kilted glory. The reaction of the locals was strong: stupefaction, disbelief and then grins. Bony knees swung along under the kilt and the Scot ignored them all.

Beyond the city in the Elburz mountains bordering the Caspian Sea to the north, towered the Demavend mountain. Its shapely white cone cut into the clouds. At sunset, it glowed pink and was almost phosphorescent. It was actually a volcano in suspended animation but smoke sometimes rose from its fissures. From the summit crater, filled with snow and ice, 50,000 square miles spread out below in clear weather. Otherwise it was a lifeless place. When we moved south later we were to find out that we did not lose sight of the Demavend for 150 miles.

We returned to Hamadan in record time. On the way we encountered locals relieving a donkey or horse of its skin. This was apparently a custom and we saw many such remains by the roadside. What remained was left to the birds.

We returned to find an HQ under snow. An entry in the Operations Record Book was "Snowfall today, 6 inches. Unit under canvas without sufficient heating." We countered this absence of warmth with charcoal fires until a Medical Officer arrived, had a near fit and banned them, due to carbon monoxide. So we were chilled again.

A signal came in from one of our posts in the mountains, from a driver known to his familiars as 'Loopy Lewis'. He wasn't all that bright; two planks short of a shed. Anyway, Lewis asked for advice. He had been on a fast run somewhere and his engine had started to overheat. So he climbed down to a mountain stream and collected a bucket of water. It failed to dawn on him that this water would be near freezing. He even broke some ice to obtain it.

The inevitable happened. His signal said that water was emerging from his exhaust pipe. What could he do about it? The face of the Sergeant MT was a study:

"The damned fool has cracked the engine block. What he's 'going to do' is collect a stoppage on his pay for a long time," he gritted.

❖ ❖ ❖

Mick had a heavy dose of flu and on CO's inspection was discovered buried in blankets with three day's growth of beard. The CO, who happened to be Greek, offered his "grandmother's cure". We were not sure what this implied, neither was Mick, but Zachy, the CO, meant what he said and rolled into the tent that night carrying all kinds of gear. A candle was lit and six aluminium cups produced. A little cotton wool was dipped into methylated spirits and twisted inside each cup in turn. The resulting blue flame was blown out, the cup inverted, and banged down on Mick's bare back.

"Ouch!" said the invalid.

"That's the first lot," said Zachy.

Mick looked like some weird kind of porcupine as the cups were held in place by suction. While this was going on the CO regaled us with some more stories of his estimable grandmother's cures.

The invalid wriggled and the bed creaked.

After three or four repeats, the last cups were removed with another lot of satisfying "plops" and the treatment concluded with a hearty massage. What all this was supposed to do no-one was quite sure. Perhaps relieve the congestion on the lungs? Anyway, Mick was left, apparently for dead and the CO departed, bearing his instruments of torture. The interesting result of all this was that Mick was soon out and about. Perhaps from sheer terror of a repeat!

We continued to place guards at night but they rarely saw any villains; probably too cold. When Guard Commander I had some odds and ends to perform – reveille, wake the camp, check the defaulters, and keep an eye on any men in detention – of whom we didn't have many. The nights on guard had become extremely cold; at 6,000 feet above sea level snow lay everywhere. I had adapted my uniform with a Russian-type fur hat of astrakhan bought in Hamadan. It was soft, warm and lined, with the usual ear flaps. I only found out later that the fur was from the skins of very young lambs, often beaten out of the pregnant ewe. To misquote Shakespeare, Henry IV pt. 2:

> *Is not this a lamentable thing,*
> *that of the skin of an innocent lamb*
> *should be made a hat?*[3]

❖ ❖ ❖

Another visit to hospital for me. That made the fifth! Four of us had been down to Hamadan, where we had heard of the local baths. After the usual anteroom and concierge we descended into the lower regions and the heat intensified. A whitewashed passage led off, with a number of doorways. A custodian opened the last door and we entered another anteroom hung with blankets, with a low divan and benches, and thickly carpeted. More tables, chairs, trays and coat hangers. Evidently no convenience spared! Beyond were two more doorways leading into the main bath and showers. The water was extremely hot and we sweltered in the steam arising from water flung over a brazier. It was hotter than Iraq in the summer – so much so that when I tried to dry down the perspiration still streamed over me and I was as wet as ever.

---

[3] In this, "hat" substitutes for "parchment".

~ Under the Red Eagle ~

When we returned into the cold of the afternoon outside, snow was deep around us and the air cutting and frigid. We pulled our greatcoats tight around us. We hailed a droshky – an open four-wheeled passenger carriage of Russian origin – drawn by two weary horses and piloted by a Persian local. We waved a hand in the general direction of camp and said "*Polski Oboz*" which was our rendering of "Polish Camp", near which our own camp lay. This turned out to be wrong and we ended up at what we later found out was the Field Post Office. Perhaps "Polish" and "Post" sounded much the same.

With some help in translation from another local, we regained the right road. The horses trotted on feebly until we got to a slight rise, when we suffered a horse-strike. The driver descended and spoke angrily to his not-so-fiery steeds. They took not the slightest notice. Grabbing the assortment of leather goods passing as a harness he hauled on his two-horse-power contraption, omitting the precaution of looking where he was going. The inevitable happened. The wheels on my side tipped into the ditch and we gracefully tilted over accompanied by remarks like: "Here we go", "Abandon ship" and the like.

We ended in the ditch, after a nose-dive from seat to soil, then silence, apart from the tinkle of broken glass. Then… "Sahib, sahib," from the driver, "Anyone hurt?" from Bowler and "Neigh!" from the horses, struggling to regain their hooves.

We brushed ourselves down, checked our limbs, shoved the droshky back onto the road, righted the horses and harness and slung in all the pieces. There was no further comment until the horses baulked again, when we piled out rather sharply to avoid a repetition and announced to the driver that we would walk the rest of the way, which we did. The droshky-man did not get tipped.

It was not until I got back to camp that I found my boot full of blood. A day or two later I could not walk and had acquired septicaemia. I was transferred to the hospital and was treated by an Anglo-Indian doctor.

Back at camp a few days late, I found a promotion awaiting me. That meant a posting in due course. But where, I wondered…?

~ Under the Red Eagle ~

❖ ❖ ❖

About this time we heard something of two Hitler Directives. The first was number 41, dated for April 1942. This chose to strike south for the Caucasian oilfields and east towards Stalingrad. The first move would extend the German flank past the main body of the Red Army and drive from Rostov to Maikop. The eastern drive was to be the responsibility of Army Group "A", created for the purpose. Hitler had obviously recognised the psychological as well as the military significance of Stalingrad and intended to use its occupation as a lever to hold firm while the main attack would wheel south.

Later in the year came Directive 45. This extended the intention to push both west and east of the Caucasus – the first towards Tiflis and the second towards Baku on the Caspian Sea. Intelligence had some suspicion that gas might be used.

24 Wireless Unit now lay astride this planned attack line, to the south of Tiflis. The enemy success in taking Tiflis would also cut one of the main British supply routes to Russia.

The implications of these Directives were formidable. An assessment at this time was that German forces from northern Africa and Russia could meet in Iraq and Iran, secure all the oil they needed, and link up with a Japanese invasion of India. Intelligence planning on the Allied side contemplated that German forces would attack northern Iran before the end of 1942. Winter conditions would then close down operations until the Spring of 1943. Russia, on the other hand, intended to make a fighting withdrawal into southern Caucasus, and on to Iran if necessary. The outcome hinged on the struggle for Stalingrad.

About dogs. This being a British unit, they seemed to attach themselves to us. One airman had a gazelle hound – a tall, rakish animal rather like a greyhound, white in colour. He had a fair turn of speed, which he would need if he were to outpace a gazelle. He felt the cold and sported an overcoat made out of an old blanket. He wandered round the camp all day to show off his attire and cadge some food. At one time we had a great many dogs and they attracted more. These were "pi" or "pye" dogs, which is a name for the half-wild animals that run free, probably something to do with "pariah". In the end they had to be shot; so many simply could not travel with us.

❖ ❖ ❖

A message came in from one of the posts that they had shot a boar. Would we like it for an HQ dinner? Certainly! I left with a three tonner to collect the carcass. These animals were quite common in parts of the mountains, as were wolves. The wild boar was, of course, the "*sus scrofa*" of antiquity, the emblem of Richard III, famed for its bravery in the chase and an excellent meat. They are large, dark and hairy animals. The sow is a very dark brown with six-inch hair along the ridge of its back, like an Alsatian. It will kill to protect its young, and can weigh 300 lb or more. It was extinct in Britain three hundred years ago. Shakespeare had it right about the boar:

> "*Being moved he strikes whate'er is in his way;*
> *And when he strikes his crokked tushes slay.*"
> **Venus and Adonis**

The one shot was a big beast with a huge shaggy head and wicked tusks. When we hauled him into the back of the truck we lashed his back feet over the bars, his body hung down, and his head lay along the floor. That made him nine feet in length! If properly roasted, the flesh has a sweet flavour with a resemblance to pork but less pronounced. Back at camp, I passed over the remains to the cooks and left it to them. This was going to be a great delicacy. A roast like this was a rare event and when brought to table in huge joints, it looked good. The eating began, but not for long…

"Pah! What the hell's wrong with this meat?"

It was uric acid. The cooks had failed to drain the blood.

9. The Spirit of Christmas

"Now there are diversities of gifts, but the same spirit."
1 Corinthians ch.12 v. 4

The Persian moon rose high in a clear black sky, with the glittering and deep snow encrusted by a savage frost. The tent canvas crackled if touched. From behind came a different crackle, this time from the fire which glowed red and its dancing blue flames flickered over the coals. Outside the moon radiated silver light and around us, both near and far, rose the jagged white masses of the mountains. Lights glittered from Hamadan below, matched by the million stars coruscating like tiny electric bulbs. Two airmen tunelessly sang, "Keep the home fires burning…" as they scrambled round searching for their tent – or anyone's tent.

That night it snowed again in a frost twenty or more degrees below. It took two hours in the morning to get our staff car and the lorry moving; brakes, gears and radiators, were all frozen solid. Finally, however, two oil burners under the gearbox shifted the freeze and we were away at last, heading north to carry mail and extra Christmas rations to fifteen RAF signal posts guarding the road to Russia and the skies above, through the mountains. The Germans were driving south through the Caucasus towards us so any merry Christmas might herald a less happy new year.

As we swung along the narrow track through a long pass a UKCC truck ahead had halted by the side of a wanderer and, to our surprise, the driver was offering alms. This was at least unusual since these drivers, speeding supplies to Russia rarely stopped and strained to cover maximum mileage in minimum time. Closing on them we saw that this traveller wore a green turban and was evidently on a deep winter trek to Mecca – the *"hajj"*. The pilgrim's refusal of a lift was courteous; he salaamed and plodded on with a small stick and bundle on his shoulder.

We called at post after post as we rolled north, exchanging Christmas toasts and collecting mail for homes far away. Evening closed in and we finally halted for the day outside a local staging post at Turkestan. It possessed nothing more than a single room hung with dirty hurricane lamps and pictures of snow-bound Caucasian scenes relieved by a large picture of a striking Persian actress with hand tucked thoughtfully under her chin. An amalgam of races and uniforms thronged the tables – two red-capped military police, a turbanned and heavily bearded Sikh, men from an Indian Regiment, a few Persian army officers … and a score of locals. We added the RAF to one or two British squaddies. The uniform colours ranged through grey, khaki, blue, to the mustard-coloured swinging cloaks and spurs of the Persians. At least four languages were being spoken but much convivial approval was beamed on us as we called for the best house wine and passed the bottles around. Glasses clinked.

The time wore on to midnight. There was no room at the inn for us since all the beds had been pre-empted; shades of Christmas long ago. So we turned in at the side of the road, back and front of our vehicles to frustrate any prospective thieves, and piled on the blankets. The Plough, as we knew it, stood on its tail below the Pole Star.

I awoke to a grey morning, flashing orange in the east. Four days to Christmas. There was 4 ½ inches of snow over my blankets.

The last post to be visited was number 15, near Kasvin and the Caspian Sea. They had found a good flat spot, pitched their tent and aerial and were busily engaged with the evening meal. The extras we had brought were received with acclaim and the welcome was warm. We could bed down here for the night before the run back.

An hour later the tent flap suddenly pushed back and the formidable nose of a PPD-34 appeared, followed by a young officer sporting a red star on his cap. This time the uniform was strange. Later we discovered that this was an infantryman from one of the Russian guards regiments; not elite troops but men who had distinguished themselves on the field of battle. Two more of these uniforms appeared behind him, also with red stars and assorted flashes.

The officer's expression was that of a towering passion. A cogent order was spat out so we did the obvious – put down our tea and raised our hands. None of us spoke Russian, so schoolboy French was attempted. This, with much repetition and broken exchange, seemed adequate. But the Russians' French was more elegant, especially that of the officer, who turned out to be a Moscow University graduate. Slowly it became evident that, unknowingly, our post had pitched its tent inside the southernmost Russian lines. They had breached a signal received at HQ a month before, "Russian occupied zone not to be entered until further order." Our visitors, having spotted the aerial, had found what was, to them, a nest of spies. More guns were waved around. More bad Gallic explanation. A signal to Base was permitted, although the operator had the snout of a gun poked into his ribs while he tapped the keys. A reply came in, and the officer studied it. It now transpired that one of the visitors could read English and accepted that the signal came from a British Commanding Officer, being suitably terse, that the uniforms were RAF and that the post was legitimate, if misplaced. The Russians lowered their guns with some regret; no decorations from Stalin on this occasion.

Now the atmosphere became less frigid and, after a meal and vodka, positively warm. The visitors helped drop the tent and we all rode, singing, behind the Russian staff car to a spot some miles south. By this time it was full night and the tent had to be repitched with the aid of headlights flashing over the cleared snow. Tea was brewed again. As midnight approached, the Russians disappeared into the darkness of Christmas.

The following morning we moved off south with the staff car leading the lorry. The mountains and passes loomed before us, black and threatening. Sheer slopes closed all around. Suddenly there was a burst of firing from the right and the snow spurted as bullets struck.

Owen   "Out and under the vehicles lads! Where the hell are the rifles and ammo?

Kelly "In the tail of the car and the cab of the lorry. I'll get them."

Owen "What a bloody place to have them. We'll know better next time. Watch your step Kelly."

The intensity of the firing increased. There was a machine gun around.

Owen "Who the hell is doing the firing. Locals? Where's it coming from?"

Harris "I've spotted them. Behind those rocks. Three fingers at three o'clock from that scrub tree. I can see part of a half-track and the helmets are German.

Owen "German? What on earth are they doing here? They're supposed to be the other side of the Caucasus."

Harris "Maybe a long range patrol, to reconnoitre the area. But they're a long way south…"

Kelly crawls back with the rifles and a Bren. Owen takes over the Bren and rapid fires up the hill. The bullets chip pieces out of the rock and the helmets duck. The others use the rifles, one being a grenade-throwing Lee Enfield which manages to lob its grenade onto the stone barricade. It explodes and unsettles the rock, which slides forward some feet and exposes the enemy behind.

Owen "There they are! Fire at will."

The Germans retire to their half-track, firing as they go, and disappear round the edge of the mountain.

Owen "That seems to have cleared them. What were you saying about a patrol, Harris?"

Harris "A pure guess… If they've got down as far as this they had to by-pass the Russians, but they could have done that through the mountains."

Owen	"Maybe so. We had best get down quickly to the nearest post and signal Base and Command."

We retired and examined the vehicles, finding an assortment of holes but no serious damage – except for the small goat presented to them by 15 post when they left.

Harris	"Do you believe it, they shot the goat. Lucky it was already dead."
Owen	"So he's been shot by the enemy? 'Wounded in action'. We should put him up for a posthumous decoration."
Kelly	"If he had been a Yankee goat it would have been the Purple Heart, if that can be awarded after death."

We laughed, climbed into the vehicles and headed south again, leaving splintered rock and holes in the snow.

❖ ❖ ❖

There was a profound quiet at HQ when we reached it. Most were down in the town, so a colleague and I, Jew and Gentile as it happened, also headed for Hamadan. As we already knew, this had always been a sacred spot for Jews because of the alleged tombs of Esther and Mordecai. We traced a battered copy of the Old Testament and found that the Jew Mordecai took for his own daughter Esther, the "fair and beautiful." She was later to become queen and to save her people. Finding the shrine proved to be difficult. "Nay maloom" – no understand – was the usual answer. We found a shop which bore a notice in the window: "French and English spoken. American understood." Ha! A wit in Persia; a bit unexpected. The following ensued:

"Where is the tomb – grave – of Mordecai?" (digging motion)
"Motor car. You want spares?"
"No – tomb – grave" (more excavating motions)
"We no sell motor cars."
"No, no. Esther and Mordecai."
A lad in the rear of the shop came forward.

~ Under the Red Eagle ~

"May I help?"

"Good heavens, English."

"I speak a little, from school."

"Sounds as though you speak it well. We are looking for the tomb of Mordecai."

"Mordecar? I don't quite…"

"No – Mordecai. Esther and Mordecai."

"Ah Mordecai" (pronounced differently as "*Morh deakai*")

He spoke over his shoulder in rapid Persian and there was a general dawn of intelligence. An even smaller boy was summoned.

"This is Omar. He will take you."

The noise of the main roads faded behind us and our small guide indicated a building tucked away behind others. It was topped by what seemed to be a modern cupola but was otherwise old in time, surrounded by high walls and iron railings and buried in snow. The doorway was low – so low that we entered on our knees and crawled into a candlelit room. There was a tap on my shoulder and an old woman, brown and wrinkled, proffered a tray of sweet cakes and amber tea in exquisitely chased silver holders.

Then we passed through another low inner door into the central domed area. To the side was an alcove where women and girls murmured in prayer. Apart from us and the caretaker, there were no men. Before us were two wooden sarcophagi inscribed with Hebrew characters and hung with gay cottons, velvets, silks and embroidered meshes of every kind. Even under candlelight the colours glowed.

To the left was the tomb of Queen Esther, to the right that of Mordecai. Esther's was original and its wooden carvings had stood up well to more than two thousand years. Mordecai's tomb had been rifled "fairly recently". (That, we later found out, meant about 1,500 years ago!) Below the sarcophagi lay the tombs themselves. The caretaker lowered a candle through a hole and its feeble light flickered over old stone and candle grease.

We were invited to join the prayer circle and readings. We stood, with the women cross-legged on a brilliantly carpeted floor, spread with Persian rugs and with another tray of candles in the centre. The precious Scroll of the Law lay above them in a small walled alcove, also hung with gay cloths. Its skin was white with age, and the lettering superb. Unusually, not one of the women or girls had made any attempt to veil themselves.

Deep snow, pilgrims, no room at the inn, three Russians to stand in for three kings and the soothing hum of prayer for long-dead ancestors. This was the true spirit of Christmas, if alien and far from home. We hailed a droshky and clattered back to camp. Our watches ticked quietly towards Christmas Day.

10. The Shade of Omar Khayyam

> *"Awake! for Morning in the Bowl of Night*
> *Has flung the stone that puts the stars to Flight;*
> *And Lo! the Hunter of the East has caught*
> *The Sultan's Turret in a Noose of Light."*
> **Rubaiyat**

It was the early New Year of 1943 and we had moved to a new position, placing our posts along the Kasvin road, close to the Russians and, for that matter, the Germans. Setting out from Hamadan we picked up post after post in the mountains and laagered overnight in Turkestan. While eating the local version of supper, eggs and *chapatti* – a flat coarse unleavened bread resembling a pancake – we were joined by several Russian officers. They occupied the northern provinces of Persia on an east-west line drawn through Kasvin and south of Lake Urmieh. They had no English, we had no Russian and even our French failed us on this occasion, but we made ourselves understood and called for the best house wine, which was well received. It occurred to me to draw a rough map of Europe and show how we were likely to advance on Germany. This generated immediate enthusiasm and one of the Russians pencilled in their own intentions. We exchanged badges and some rank items and shook hands all round.

Again, as last time, it was a camp bed under the stars and a repeat of snow on my blankets in the morning. We rose early and drove to Kasvin and through the Russian barriers. No problems on this occasion and we were waved along with great friendliness. By this time the situation to the north had changed. The Russian counter-offensive before Stalingrad had isolated the German army and removed the immediate threat to northern Persia, while the battle of El Alamein had lessened the pressure on Egypt. So the presence of 24

~ Under the Red Eagle ~

Wireless Unit so far north was not necessary and by the end of January 1943 we received orders to move south to the Mediterranean.

In my camp bed, under canvas outside Teheran, I awoke to the cooks' tom-tom beating of a petrol tin; breakfast imminent. No bugles or flag-raising here, we were in the field, not at a drill centre. My timing was just right to hear a slither from the opposite corner as it collapsed, letting in a blast of cold air. Despite our regular attempts to clear the roof of snow during the night, the dawn fall had been too heavy, the ropes had tightened up, out came the pegs, and my companion was buried under loving canvas, sopping wet. We assumed that the half-collapsed tent would hold for a short time longer and sought our meagre breakfast. On the way back we were in time to see our tent haul out the remaining pegs and subside entirely. We spent the morning rescuing our kit and bundling up the tent prior to moving into the next one. The unit was due to move, anyway.

The convoy started away through Teheran, escorted by police riders, which attracted much attention. Once out of the city we turned south and the metalled road soon disintegrated into the usual stones and grit under the snow. The scenery was desolate – no vegetation, no life and a long shallow valley so grim that it rejoiced in the sobriquet "Valley of the Angel of Death." It looked like it.

We entered Qum – or Qom or Kum – as the sun sank, flashing and firing over turrets and minarets and a towering dome plated with solid gold. We had seen the distant glare of the aureate light from many miles away and it had acted like a beacon, drawing us towards it. It was the mosque of "Fatima the Good". We laagered overnight and in the morning saw the words of Omar Khayyam translated into a living scene as the "turrets caught in a noose of light."

This mosque was one of the most famous in the East and Qum is one of the most holy towns – second only, I believe, to Mecca. Everything here seemed to be "out of bounds" and all the Services had been advised not even to look at the mosque when within the town. I noticed, however, that there was a local army hospital not far from the mosque and obtained permission to climb onto the flat roof. Qum was now spread out before me and the golden dome rose like a huge lustrous breast from the huddle of houses. Making sure I was unobserved, I took my photograph.

As the convoy left the following day we could look back from the hills and see the dome smouldering through the morning mist. Would we ever see its like again?

We completed a huge semi-circle from south to west through Sultanabad. Again it had snowed overnight and the cold was intense as we passed through valleys and over ranges under heavy lowering clouds. We were whipped by white flurries streaming over the ground in threads of icy flakes. Entering another of the long, shallow, valleys we reached Hamadan.

The following day we clocked only 65 miles, being faced by the Asabad Pass for the second time. We crawled up slowly, accompanied by many UKCC and military vehicles. Gears threshed through narrow passages and tortuous curves carved out of the heavy drifts. A blast of bleak and frigid wind tore over the summit, then we dropped at increasing speed, chasing one another into Kermanshah.

We encountered a potential suicide, just above the Paitek Pass – or that was what he looked like to Soapy Simpson, the unfortunate driver. The native ran from his blind side and straight into the radiator. The convoy halted behind a frustrated Soapy, not realising that anything was amiss until keening women rushed past and a small group congregated from nowhere. The body lay on the road, groaning. We dug out a stretcher from the medical lorry and with a dozen over-enthusiastic helpers conveyed the injured man to a doctor about a mile away. It turned out that the man was not badly injured despite the blood – mainly shocked and lacking some front teeth.

The wife was the star turn in all this. She did not know how badly her husband had been hurt – any more than we did – and assumed the worst. She wailed and rubbed mud into her hair, presumably a version of sackcloth and ashes. She hung on to Soapy's lorry. She wailed and upbraided him incessantly and refused to let any following vehicle pass over the spot on which her husband had been lying, so the convoy all steered round elaborately. The local mullah had to mutter words over the spot until it had been "cleared", it appeared.

11. The Road to Cairo

> *"Think of it, soldiers; from the summit of these pyramids, forty centuries look down upon you"*
> **Napoleon**

Following our road accident, we found that all could be put right, except for the teeth and a still demonstrating wife, by the application of a few rials. So we all remounted and passed on our way down the Paitek Pass, and over the border back into Iraq. We drove south through a slowly heating atmosphere, despite the fact that it was winter, and through desert and dust re-entered Baghdad.

There was a marked difference in the city. Iraq had recently entered the war. "Allies" restaurants appeared on all sides and our taxi driver gritted through broken teeth, in English, that his new enemy was "sonofabitch."

We travelled on to Habbaniya and found ourselves in the presence of 32 and 38 Wireless Units, who had followed us down from Teheran. The mess rang with song. It was the anniversary of our embarkation from the UK, being 13th February.

The three units left together in the early morning as the sun yellowed the Damascus road. It was an enormous convoy of some 50 or 60 vehicles, so a long line of wagons chased one another along the thin thread of road slicing towards an ever-retreating horizon. It was flat from skyline to skyline. The light dusty surface of the desert slowly reddened our skin and turned it from tanned to bronzed. We left the road and the desert was now so smooth that we could move into line abreast. The drivers were not loath to take advantage of this, closed on one another from time to time and shook hands between vehicles.

~ Under the Red Eagle ~

We still tracked the pipeline, although it was now buried and identified only by aluminium telegraph poles. The hearts-blood of oil continuously streamed west unless there had been sabotage and plumes of fire rose into the sky. These were the first leaks and fires that we had ever seen, in all the distances travelled along the northern section of the pipeline.

We bowled over the frontier into the true desert of Transjordan – merely a few empty barrels of oil lining the track and a small notice. Our first white, racing camel, appeared.

Mafrak with its fort was a large dirty village with a central road deeply rutted and flanked by grey hovels, "out of bounds" again but no hostility, certainly not from the many raggedly-dressed and tawny children yelling "*baksheesh*". Although Mafrak was so grubby a real flare of colour touched it that evening when four Arab Legionnaires trotted in from the desert on strong-boned camels. The men wore long scarlet robes with ornamental gold trappings slapping the animals' sides. They were armed to the teeth. Against the sparse green grass and under the setting sun, it could have been a film set. They rode in a flare of western orange light and darkness then fell rapidly. The riders simply vanished into the coming night. Shades of Lawrence of Arabia!

At dawn, we entered a barren, boulder-strewn, region which halted any more hand-shaking tactics. The scene was now one of mountain grandeur as we followed the tortuous Trans-Jordan Valley Road: the night's heavy mists lifted quite suddenly as the sun got a grip.

The plateau dropped slanting towards the River Jordan. Recalling the negro spiritual we certainly "looked over Jordan." but not, I was relieved to appreciate, to see any "band of angels comin' after me." What we did see was a road dropping lower and lower round many hairpin bends until we passed a faded notice saying "sea level", and then dropped again to the river itself. Strange that one could now make the claim of having been below sea level in a staff car!

I don't know quite what I expected of Jordan, but here it was not wide, probably because we passed over it fairly high up towards its source, below the Sea of Galilee.

Oranges! A profusion of groves all around us. Huge golden globes, real Jaffas, some of the fruit as big as a baby's head, not for export presumably, since we never saw oranges so large in the UK, even in peacetime. The vehicles of the convoy seemed to 'break down' repeatedly and large baskets of fruit were later to be seen nestling securely in dark corners of the lorries. The locals didn't seem to mind – they even tossed the fruit over the tailboards.

We laagered only a few miles from the Mediterranean, in another orange grove, with faint strains of the Warsaw Concerto floating over the hiss of the Primus. Who had the record, I had no idea.

The country near Gaza verged towards the English Midlands in character – blossom on the apple trees – except for the first blue of the Mediterranean seen over white dunes and with surf pounding the shore. This was something new.

We left 32 and 38 Wireless Units here, passing their long line at the roadside with waves and the usual drollery. On to El Arish, the 'capital' of the Sinai Desert, where we found ourselves in barracks, or, more strictly, in what had formerly been a convalescent camp. We were only a short distance from some excellent bathing – and under the welcome shade of eucalyptus trees. Crush a leaf, and the smell was as powerful as any liquid. Along the edge of the surf lay brightly hued shells, as far as the eye could see.

We got some idea of why we were in this location. Apparently El Arish was one of the few spots along the coast that had trees, and German aircraft pinpointed it for raiding inland. We also watched the sea for enemy ships.

We took the staff car to inspect the posts down the Ismailiya road. Constant wind whipped the sand from the loose surface and it "duned" ahead of the blow. The wind was strong; one post had had its aerial blown down twice in the day. It was desolate country with little sign of life until we reached the top of a rise and to our astonishment saw half a ship moving across the desert with only funnels and masts above a line of green palms. Half a ship? Of course – the Suez Canal. Here it was a channel of blue-green water perhaps fifty feet below the level of the desert. We crossed by the ferry, a contraption hauled across by chains, and checked ourselves through a military post unhindered – principally because the natives were being thoroughly searched by Egyptian Police. For what? Drugs? Arms? To our left we were flanked by a strip of water bearing the picturesque name of "Canal d'Eau Douce" or "Sweetwater Canal". The irony of this euphemism was that the services were convinced that if one fell into this canal one was due for a series of inoculations – the belief was 32 – to protect against assorted fevers and diseases.

On to Cairo – *El Qahira*. As we looked forward, we noticed two oddly pointed structures which appeared about ten or fifteen miles away. It was some moments before I realised that I was looking at the pyramids.

Then into Cairo itself – increasing traffic, narrow streets, clustering buildings, brought us into the centre, where we checked in at Air Headquarters and then into "Lions Rest House."

Cairo was loud, very loud. It was a bustling city where West and East met with a clash. It had a hundred hotels, more restaurants, and shops packed with goods and people. The buildings towered above us and every service uniform thronged the streets.

We did little that night except dine and attend a film at the well-known "Metro". At the conclusion of the performance the British and Egyptian anthems were played and all stood, to the evident delight of those Egyptians lacking English, when the troops sang "salaam malik".

They would have been less pleased if they had known what the words were that were actually being sung, as was revealed earlier. If there were Egyptians in the cinema who understood English, this refrain could result in brawls.

There was a story going the rounds that some airmen were offered a lift to their base and sang this and similar melodies all the way, only to discover that the stout driver was King Farouk himself. Doubtless apocryphal, but believed.

~ Under the Red Eagle ~

In the city a long loping figure sidled up. Would we like to see the bazaar, pyramids, Citadel or Blue Mosque? This was Abdul, the dragoman, a professional guide having official sanction and fees.

We opted for the Blue Mosque. Farouk had just attended and cleaners were sweeping away sand, dropping flags, and dismantling barriers. We entered through a heavily-studded bronze door. Profound silence – apart from our shoes which echoed solidly on the granite floors. Abdul waved at the intricate and abstract mosaics and also pointed without comment to spots where the mosaic had been damaged and pieces torn away as souvenirs by vandals.

"Who did that?" said we.

"Soldiers," said Abdul.

"English?"

"No. They know sacred. Others."

We did not pursue the matter further. But who would be such depraved desecrators?

We passed to a small shop in the depths of the bazaar with bracelets and filigree work of silver, much as we had seen in Iraq and Persia but finer and more intricate. The designers were at work in the back of the shop, using long silver thread – all youngsters between six ands sixteen years of age. Apparently their eyes did not last on such close work and they could only cope with these delicate, almost lace-like, designs until they were about twenty. Then they moved to machines and the handwork was taken over by small boys. Next door was a perfumery; Abdul pushed aside a beaded curtain and we were in a tiny room rioting with colour and having shelves full of small bottles. These were the essences from which blends were made, originating from flowers. We spent an hour under persistent sales patter. Perfume was only one offering. Others were drugged cigarettes, ambergris used in the manufacture of perfumes, and fiery spirits. We were not misled: doubtless Abdul got a cut from our purchases.

The street vendors were prolific. Hordes of unpleasant people tried to sell one fly whisks, Arab chewing gum, sunglasses, shaving brushes, hand-tinted pornography and much other trash. They ran backwards in front, grinning through broken and blackened teeth

~ Under the Red Eagle ~

and shoving and kicking each other away. They included small boys trying to sell a shoe-cleaning service. These were vicious. I said "no" and was threatened with a brush loaded with black boot polish to be thrown over my immaculate khaki drill. I avoided the threat and chased him down the main street with alacrity. He vanished into an "out of bounds" area.

The Pyramids followed. Not quite in deep desert as most selected viewpoints suggested, but at the end of a tram route!

Dragomen reappeared, with camels this time, touting for business on the short ride to the stones. I walked, with excited dragomen objecting to one of their number, with camel, not attending!

The hot stones were unexpectedly big – so much so that it required a massive scrambling effort to climb to the apex of the Great Pyramid. What can one say of these massive structures that has not been said a thousand times before? Impressive, significant, momentous, stirring and overpowering.

The Sphinx stared over a village, again not apparent from most pictures and photographs. Someone, I believe Napoleon's troops, had shot off its nose. What was it, anyway. A cat?

On the Sunday I saw our old 24 Wireless Unit CO, "Zachy" the Greek, at Groppi's and we took many coffees. What he was doing in Cairo we did not find out. Probably acquiring his half ring.

Back to El Arish. News from the Military Police that floods were expected down the wadi at El Arish at about 22.00 hours. So we slept until morning at the wadi-side, when the water had ebbed.

At the camp, I found a signal, posting me to "Air Headquarters, Western Desert."

So ended the first part of the long trek from the snows of White Waltham to those of Persia, from Cosford to Cairo.

Now into the full battlefront and what has been termed "a hideous wasteland."

12. The Murderous Mediterranean

"Tomorrow we shall sail again on the vast ocean."
Horace

I made a personal farewell to the unit and caught the night train. A few came down to the station to see me off and at 22.00 hours precisely the train pulled away and the shadows waving goodbye slid back into the darkness, and into time.

The dawn was grey and the green fields of the Delta and their waving palms glided by. A fox wandered through the trees and a brown-skinned native washed in the muddy ditch irrigating his fields.

The objective for me was 29 Personnel Transit Centre, and a few days later on to 24 P.T.C by the Alexandria train. Kit was hurled to porters who carried huge amounts and looked like camels when fully burdened. I wondered at their enthusiasm at first – Egyptians usually avoid heavy work – but my particular porter shouldered four kitbags, bedding and some side packs, total weight at least 180lb and probably more. Then I found out that there was a standard rate of one piastre per item, so they maximised what wind and strength allowed, and then dashed back for more.

The carriage was completely full. One airman had no seat. He disappeared. Then a stentorian voice bellowed, "All Army personnel move up the train; this carriage RAF only." Two disgruntled squaddies rose and departed. The airman nipped round the other door and briskly took one of the vacant seats, announcing cheerfully "O.K. Room for one more of the lads now!"

We reached Aboukir and the P.T.C. in mid-afternoon to find that we had missed this week's passage up the Mediterranean and had to shake down here for seven days. There were few parades or commitments, so we were released into the city. It was a base port for the Navy, but not one warship, nor anything else, was in sight along the waterfront, which swept round in a great semicircle. We were looking in the wrong place; later on we discovered both dock and harbour, and a welter of merchantman and warships, lolling at anchor.

The streets of Alexandria seemed even narrower, busier, louder than those of Cairo. We adopted the 'Fleet Club' as a base, where RAF were welcome but not the Army – a result of a rough-house between Army and Navy, it appeared. There was a more rigid blackout as well, and one fell over one's feet at night in the approved UK fashion.

Alexandria lay in flat country; in fact, the nearest high ground was 2,000 miles away in the 'Mountains of the Moon.' It was a "city of secrets", rather like Baghdad. It was also cosmopolitan, and shared by a number of races, not to mention sexes. Hookahs could be seen in the streets, in the cafes, and were kept alight by attendants.

There were heaps of garbage. The stalls were of watermelon, fish, and almonds. Water was thrown over hot pavements and an unmistakable sweet smell arose. The city was like an old prostitute, once beautiful and even now not wholly fallen. It was an ancient place, founded by Alexander the Great and had been occupied by many in its time. Now it was occupied again, by us.

History repeated itself. Once more we were aboard a trooper, at a table lit from the side with kit overhead and hammocks stowed. This was the *Rohna* of 8,600 tons.

The gossip of the Fleet Club made us uneasy; that there were many German and Italian operations against Allied supply traffic, by air and submarine. We realised what a tempting target we would offer and how enticing the through-Mediterranean traffic would be; its volume actually exceeded the number of vessels crossing the Atlantic.

We pulled out of the harbour at 06.00 and moved into the dusky orange of sunrise, edging slowly past the grey vessels at anchor, with their many different flags, and with the dark city outline behind us. There were some 21 ships in the convoy and an escort of five or six destroyers. We swung into the usual lines and turned west for Tripoli, through dangerous waters (at this time, Air Intelligence had estimated that the Luftwaffe strength in the area was 820 aircraft). The sea was smooth, with little but a ruffle on its surface. We passed another convoy five miles to port with a comment from the rail.

"What a bloody insult to Jerry – convoys passing in the Med!"

This disparagement was to be taken up, more than once.

We had our first indication of incipient trouble with "Crr-umph, Crr-umph" from a swiftly moving destroyer and a long bellow from the ship's siren. Eyes shifted to the deck notices:

One long blast: air raid.

There was a noticeable tightening of lifebelts and atmosphere. But an air raid alarm followed by depth charges? Divers wits suggested submarine aircraft or winged U-Boats. But there was no gainsaying the depth charges, so we retired below in the approved manner. Nothing else transpired, so back on deck to resume quoits and relight pipes and cigarettes.

Two more alarms followed during the day and more depth charging from the escort. We recognised the procedure. Air raids we were long used to but not with many fathoms of sea below. Little we could do would assist the crew, and one could hardly move out of range! In the event, it was much as I had already seen in the Atlantic. First a blast from the siren, then switch in course. The destroyers picked up speed, their bow waves lifted, and they did their "helter-skelter" bit around the ocean.

One destroyer pointed its bows to the spot where something lurked below and its sister hared past at a good lick. Over went some black specks and things happened. If the charge were deep the whole surface of the sea creamed and was lifted a few feet, accompanied by a rumble and a heavy clang as the concussion struck our steel plates. If the charge were more shallowly set a plume of water rose high, again with the rumble and clang. We had a good idea of what this meant below from the shiver of our own plates, and we were not the target.

We passed near a desolate coast. The Eighth Army and Desert Air Force were long past this point and near the Mareth Line.

~ Under the Red Eagle ~

There was an impromptu concert that night, with an even more impromptu ending. The Captain and his morning rounds came up for satire but he grinned hugely. There were also some very strange females in Egyptian belly-dancing dress, who aroused enthusiasm and cheers. Only the crows nest spotted the first attack and above the chortles and wisecracks came the sharp chatter of machine guns, the quick thud of cannon, and the deeper five-shell "whoof.whoof." of the Bofors. The audience dispersed rapidly and some went on deck unmindful of standing orders.

"There's the kite. Down it!"

The first bogey – enemy aircraft – came in low over the sea, heading for the outside ships with guns blazing. The reception was hot and he flew through streams of shells marked by the red glare of tracers. Cordite fumed pungently around us. More aircraft appeared and the action intensified.

Glowing arcs of tracers swept over the convoy. Uproar came from the screeches of black-crossed planes, guns bellowed, and the "Rohna" alarms were sounded. The middle of the convoy, with everyone blazing away at low-flying 'planes must have been hell. An aircraft loosed a bomb, which fell close to us but missed, resonated on our steel plating and flung up a huge spout of water which fell back over the decks. Then a second bomb, and metal fragments from the trooper behind flew upwards in black bows of destruction.

This was about as much as the few on deck saw and the messdecks began to fill. I was late enough to see two Hurricanes circle in from the coast, quickly banking and weaving as they sought the wave-hopping planes. Then they made a long dive away to the north. We were not misled by the departure: this was probably a reconnaissance with more to come. It did, and a second phase opened with staccato bursts from the flanking destroyers and long stripes of orange from their gun muzzles placing black puffs close round the diving aircraft. Nearly all were below when I climbed down through the hatch. We could only sit and register the thuds and explosions above our heads. Then the "Rohna" guns opened up as well and since we were directly under stern armament of heavy calibre it shook both ship and us.

Then came the first dull clangs from bombs. It was time to don steel helmets. It was noticeable that the Palestinian troops on the deck above promptly stopped singing and a distinct and apprehensive silence fell. We hoped they didn't move on to panic as they were between us and the deck. Night was nodding to a fall now and after about half-an-hour the "all clear" sounded. On deck, I could see only 19 of 21 ships. Both troopers in front of us and behind were absent and had been hit. The destroyers accounted for some of the 'planes, which had blown up in the air and cartwheeled into the sea. We heard that the very first attacking aircraft had been accounted for by the Hurricanes twenty miles away.

Things had been fairly warm.

There was an early stand-to the following morning, with expectations of a repeat attack, but nothing happened. Normal routine. The coast was no longer visible as we had moved out to sea.

Into Tripoli. The Desert Air Force had pretty well wrecked the harbour and it was chock-full of sunken shipping. In fact, the actual number of wrecks found after the war was 87. Attempts had also been made by the Germans to block the harbour mouth and the *Rohna* only managed to scrape in, literally, and discharge us to shore by lighters, packed herring fashion. As we boarded them, the destroyer which had led the escort swept past and a stentorian megaphone on the bridge bellowed: "Goodbye, Commodore, and good luck."

This was our first intimation that the Commodore had transferred to the *Rohna* after the loss of his own ship in the raid.

We saw little of Tripoli; too busy heading towards the battlefield. It was of continental style and well laid out. The white houses and buildings bore battle scars but the town itself seemed to have escaped heavier damage.

Then a short drive along the coast to 39 Personnel Transit Centre, an old Italian fort surrounded by the usual lines of square tents set amongst trees and palms.

At least we had got through – most of us, anyway.

❖ ❖ ❖

Later that year the *Rohna* was sunk off Algiers when in convoy KMF-26. The story was grim. The convoy was escorted by ten warships and the aircraft carrier *Colombo*. They were attacked from the air three-quarters of an hour before sunset, much as we were. Some sixty glider bombs were released, one of which hit the *Rohna* on her port side near one of the troop decks. The ship lost control – no steering gear or engine power, no means of fire-fighting, a ten degree list, and communication only by word of mouth or messengers. She became a vast fireball. Rescue work went on all night. There were over 1,000 dead amongst the American and other troops on board and 120 of the 195 crew were lost. Eight He177s were shot down, but that was poor consolation.

On reflection, this attack was very similar to that made on us and we might well have sustained similar losses.

Fortunes of war...

13. Into Battle with the Desert Air Force

*"He paweth in the valley, and rejoiceth in his strength:
he goeth on to meet the armed men."*
Job ch.39 v.21

We were left to our own devices to travel on from the PTC and after a little investigation I found an RAF padre who had come down from the front to pick up a beer ration for his Wing. Forward with the beer, cock-a-hoop! We joined an Army road convoy and headed west.

For some miles we were in living country of olive groves and cultivated fields over which were dotted the homesteads of former Italian settlers. Then this habitation faded and we entered the desert area around the Tripolitania-Tunisia border. Perhaps 'desert' was not quite right; Tunisia, bare and sandy though it was in parts had evidence further on of rural if not urban civilisation. Farmsteads appeared again with grape vines, olive groves, and fruit, and the inevitable prickly pear studded the coast along which we were passing. It was sundown and as we approached the border we found its buildings badly damaged, walls riddled with shot and shrapnel, the water tower blown up and collapsed across a crater in a welter of broken concrete and wrenched steel. Italian grenades were strewn about the floor and the passing British had left their mark in "Kilroy was here" painted on walls still standing. A large hole below the words reminded me of the Bairnsfather cartoon of the Great War as between a new recruit and an "old soak" sitting on a pile of stones:

Rookie: "What made that hole?"
Old Soak: "Mice"

~ Under the Red Eagle ~

We kicked away the debris and bedded down on the floor for the night. Since the roof was absent this meant that we had an open view of the stars, sparkling frostily.

The next morning we moved into Tunisia proper. This country was about two-thirds the size of the UK with 7m or so inhabitants.

We moved through scrub and rough roads under repair. Scores of blackened vehicles were strewn along the roadside, rusting. Black crosses were well in evidence, as was the palm and swastika of the Afrika Korps. The Desert Air Force had passed this way.

The Mareth Line was ahead of us, with roped and wired areas marked either "Mines" or "Minen". German and British crosses surmounted small mounds marking the human detritus of battle, Amongst these was a small batch of graves of Scots Guards who had died attempting to take the rise in front of them. A far place of little consequence now, but it had been the scene of desperate hours. The village of Mareth itself was a torn place. The full weight of the 8th Army heavy artillery had been thrown into action here and the battle had raged without pause for five days. Rommel had been forced to employ virtually all his armour, whereas Montgomery had retained most of his in reserve and depended on guns. The decisive stage was reached directly the 8th Army breached the Mareth Line, and their subsequent advance linked them up with the 1st Army and the Americans, coming east. This sealed the fate of the Axis in Tunisia. The Italians had fared badly: nearby was a wadi where an Italian Division had been captured entire.

There had been problems for Montgomery in assaulting the Mareth Line and he ran into trouble. Vigorous action by the Desert Air Force prevented a crisis and they became Monty's favourite airmen. The Army tended in the past to think that wars could only be won on foot with guns in the hand. That might have been true of the Great War, but it was not of this one and here was a case where the Air Force settled the day.

We again pulled in for the night and the convoy dispersed into the trees of an orchard – a necessary camouflage because we were in the company of high octane, explosives, and ammunition. We spoke to some of the locals here and I noticed a change to a Moorish cast of feature and a transformation to red headgear and colourful robes.

The Goums were in the hills, and were a tough bunch. A story came back that they attacked a German camp and a Goum crawled into a tent where three Germans were sleeping, and cut the throats of the two on the outside. When asked why he did not kill all three he said, "When the one in the middle wakes up he will be useless and will scare his friends as well. Long live the Goums."

Finally I arrived at Air Headquarters, where I had been posted. Here I found that my final destination, near Sousse, was to 239 Wing, one of the most famous – if not the most – of the Desert Air Force. This was a posting beyond any expectations.

Machine gun fire, the blaze of Very Lights arcing through the sky, and flares and bonfires illuminating the valley. But this was exultation, not battle, and harmless except for the stray bullets hissing through the air and driving into the grass. There was also a group of loons in the nearby American camp levelling their gun to the horizontal and firing through the spaces between the tents. Megalomaniacs in an over-excited celebration. The war here was over and Alexander was able to say in a signal to London:

> "Sir. It is my duty to report that the Tunisian campaign is over. All enemy resistance has ceased. We are masters of the North African shore."

A peculiar camp, this 239 Wing Headquarters. How might one imagine it? Surely a bustle, a sense of urgency, a great coming and going between squadrons. Not at all. It was quiet during the day with few airmen about and all the work going on behind the scenes in the Squadron Operations Room and Flying Control. The landing ground lay in a long, shallow valley some miles inland from Kairouan, another holy city, and to the north and east blue hills surrounded us, from which came occasional gunfire where the last remnants of the Axis were being rounded up.

The Wing had six squadrons: 112, 250 and 260 (RAF), 3 & 450 (RAAF) and 5 (SAAF). 112 was clearly identified by the "shark" motif on the noses of the machines – savage lines of pointed teeth around the air intake and a staring eye behind the propeller. 250 was the 'Sudan' squadron. 260 was formed in the Middle East in November 1940. 450 Australian were the "Desert Harassers", so named by Lord Haw-Haw. 3 was also Australian, originally formed for Army Co-operation but now developing that role. 5 was created, of course, in South Africa. All the ground crews were RAF. This made the Wing as a whole of joint and experienced British/Commonwealth stock, existing together as a good-natured, well-knit, and easy-going mob. The dress was informal to say the least and the archetype uniform was khaki battledress top, drill shorts or longs, "brothel creepers" (alias suede sandshoes),and, for pilots, silk or nylon scarves to deal with perspiration and friction, often carrying printed maps of the desert for forced landings.

The main contribution of 239 Wing in the desert had been to back up the 8th Army with ground attack and defence against bombers. Severe conditions were imposed by the desert – landing grounds on sand, rough and stony, sandstorms, dust devils, wind always wind, heat and more heat, and the thieving Arab. Aircraft engines naturally suffered from sand until special filters were produced but they had the disadvantage of cutting down speed.

As for tactics, the Germans used four planes in two pairs which was superior to the old "Vic" (three aircraft in V-formation) of the British. Later on the Desert Air Force created an alternative – three pairs who went "weaving", which meant that the ones on the outside dived under the leader and the ones on the inside would also transfer. Alternatively, especially later on in Italy, where they were less likely to encounter opposition, a group of planes on a mission would be in line ahead, each plane removed downwards from the leader. This was more casual, but effective.

A word about the Australians. The airmen of 3 squadron had a pronounced ability to scrounge and acquire regulation or non-regulation items, either for their own use or to keep the aircraft flying. This they knew as "cliftying" and 3 squadron was the "Clifty Squadron." Amongst other items acquired were many strange vehicles, enemy ones as well. So when there was to be a vehicle inspection dust tracks marked disappearances in all directions in the desert and only the official vehicles were ready for inspection.

All the Australians were a wild bunch It was usual at a Mess party for them to pile up paper, wood, and cardboard and have a bonza barbecue in the centre of the Mess tent. Their own Mess tent was put out of bounds to them from time to time. If they felt more active they might whoop around the tents and fire off live ammo. Several tents had unexplained holes in them. I recalled that something like this was going on when I joined the Wing at Kairouan. Then there was always the event of boarding a gharry and doing a little pig-sticking around the local farms. I think the farmer got paid – I think. The other side of the picture was their superb flying and impressive decorations. By the time that I joined the Wing their score was:

DSO	1
DFC and Bar	2
DFC	15
DFM	6

One thing the pilots were quite clear about was their debt to their ground crews. Much of the Desert Air Force efficiency was attributable to them. They suffered from shortage of supplies and difficult working conditions but, like their colleagues in 3 squadron, were also adept at "cliftying" to add to hard work and ingenuity. They solved most Kittyhawk problems themselves: they did not need to be instructed by "Flight" or anyone else. Even the "admin." relieved pilots and other staff from considerable potential strain which would have inhibited their flying. It was, in all, a considerable teamwork.

The temporary respite here in Tunisia had a touch of nostalgia in it. There were still some "founder members" of the Wing who had spent up to three years in the desert. They had endured a harsh climate where sandstorms could blind and choke, the sun seared, and chilly nights set the teeth chattering. They had always been exposed to a vicious enemy whether they flew or not and had the same touch of flamboyance and swagger. They were true desert veterans looking with friendly prevalence on their white-kneed comrades of the 1st

Army and its air units. Some, it must be admitted, appeared slightly "puggle" – not completely off their heads, since the desert demanded restraint, but dippy enough to take sun, Sahara, sand and the Afrika Korps, in their stride.

The surrender in Tunisia found the Desert Air Force in complete control of the skies. It stood as a strong force of fighter and fighter-bomber squadrons. The Americans provided heavier bomber and transport squadrons. Its flying decorations were formidable – about 70 or so in total, ranging from D.S.O. to D.F.M (some arguments about these distinctions because all pilots did the same job), and there were about 35 pilots claiming 5 or more victories. This apart from their main job of tackling enemy troops, guns, tanks, dumps, other fighters and a whole array of ground targets.

During the last days of the Tunisian campaign, Montgomery issued this message for the 8th Army:

> "On your behalf I have sent a special message to the Allied Air Forces that have co-operated with us. I don't suppose that any army has ever been supported by such a magnificent air striking force. I have always maintained that the 8th Army and the R.A.F. in the Western Desert together constitute one fighting machine, and therein lies our great strength."

The aircraft 239 Wing were using when I joined were mainly Curtis Kittyhawk fighter-bombers having a maximum speed of 350 mph and cruising at 280 mph – in theory with a ceiling rather over 20,000 feet and a range of 600 miles. They attacked with 250 and 500 lb bombs. The latter was a big bomb for its time, capable of destroying a block of buildings. In practice, the Kittyhawk was a much better flier at 8-10 thousand feet. It was heavy – over three tons in weight – and dived faster than the ME 109, which proved to be an advantage when one got them down to a lower level.

Flying operations with these Kittys required skills similar to those of the Hurricane and Spitfire. Keep a sharp lookout, turn into any attack, and act at once on any instruction from the leader. He, or others, might well see what you could not and "Behind you" was capable of saving your life. Waltz around the sky if there were enemies about and don't fly straight and level for more than 20 seconds. This was very different to the required perfection of peacetime flying, which could kill in the desert. "And, by the way, don't try to dive at more than 60 degrees simply because, unlike the Stuka, the Kitty hasn't got air brakes."

Pilots were talking in the Mess. The experienced one said that the Kittyhawk to them was the P-40 to Americans. The "P" was for pursuit, and it was made to bomb and strafe. Could it, asked the recruit, dive it like a Stuka? The experienced one grinned; one didn't need to persuade the Kitty to dive … it dropped like three tons of lead. The real problem was pulling out afterwards. A third pilot visiting from 260 squadron chipped in that was correct; he got his Kitty up to 500 mph in a dive to the sand and it took him ten thousand feet to pull out. "And I lost a chunk of my cowling."

One required a strong right arm to control the aircraft. When dive-bombing it could pick up speed fast, but rolled to the starboard. This could be trimmed out with the left hand but on emerging from the dive there was a counter-roll to port if one were careless. This needed to be offset by trimming out halfway down the dive and holding the stick central by bracing the right arm against the right leg and the cockpit side. If not flown smoothly, the kite would also "fishtail" and "skid", which did not improve the pilot's aim. Someone had given a definition of this as "Russian roulette at 300 m.p.h. and zero feet. Quite bucked one up if one were a little barmy."

The Kittyhawk had been adapted to carry bombs but that didn't make it a bomber, since the target could often not be seen – the nose and wings got in the way. Conversely, if one came in too low the target might be seen ahead but the bomb skipped and bounced past. So the dive needed to be steep and the aircraft aimed bodily at the target. What had been said about sixty degrees was about right. Any more and you wouldn't get away with it.

It was a good operational aircraft even if some pilots had doubts about the Allison engine. There had been too many crashes with aircraft bursting into flames. For pilots, it was wise not to take up a 'plane with which they were not happy. The Kitty was certainly idiosyncratic and the higher the fewer – of good performances anyway. One pilot claimed that he had been out-climbed by a Liberator, a four-engined bomber. Admittedly, it was not bombed up and had released its load. But as a ground strafer and fighter-bomber, the 'Kitty' was a success.

Into Tunis at last; 'in at the death', as it were. The first noticeable change was the women, mostly French; chic and well-groomed they made the best of the poor circumstances and themselves. The city was not much damaged but had a war-weary appearance. No entertainment facilities, but then it had only been hours since the 8th and 1st Armies and the Air Forces had entered. Now there were also Americans in steel hats to contrast with English side-caps and the occasional Scottish Tam-o-Shanter. A French unit contributed flaring red. Flags had appeared from nowhere, hoarded pending "the day" – mainly French but with some Union flags. Civilians were gay in red, white, and blue ribbons in lapels or pinned to colourful frocks. Food was short and if one needed to eat, it was the ration. Grey dust powdered everything from the hurriedly-dug trenches at the roadside. The London Irish, smart in their green cockades, marched along piping and got a roar of welcome.

Back to camp as dusk fell, past German and Italian P.O.Ws in cages – tattered remnants of once formidable troops. The 90th was the last to surrender, which explained the gunfire in the hills a few days ago. Where was Rommel? The rumour was that he had handed over to Von Arnim and left for Berlin. If so, it was kept quiet, probably not to jeopardise German morale any further. The Desert Air Force had never stopped fighting in the weary wastes: now it had to invade Europe proper. Churchill said of the 8th Army and Desert Air Force:

> "Ever since your victory at Alamein, you have nightly pitched your moving tents a day's march nearer home. In days to come when people ask what you did in the Second World War, it will be enough to say: 'I marched with the 8th Army.'

Or flew over it, which was just as tricky.

14. Poised for Europe

"In the nightmare of the dark, All the dogs of Europe bark,
And the living nations wait, Each sequestered in its hate."
W H Auden

We retired from Tunis back to Zuara, on the shore. It was obvious, we thought, that the Sicilian invasion would be next; this was the calm before the storm. We exchanged old for new equipment, put our weapons to rights, went in for rifle practice, cleaned the weapons again, exercised our driving through the sea, drilled and endured 'gen' parades. The Adjutant – 'Bushy' Hine – took advantage of the last and stood in front of us with his large moustache bristling and remarked: "Get ready for some action, boys. We shall be wading through blood and surf!" Blood and surf, eh? It sounded like the Salvation Army's "Blood and Fire".

We were watched from the skies; the high drone of reconnaissance planes passed over and anti-aircraft guns belched fire and shell. We were also the subject of frenzied activity by the "fifth column" the Germans had left behind.

One evening the AOC – Air Officer Commanding – dropped in with his familiar "Fieseler Storch" and Lord Trenchard also appeared. This was characteristic of some big operation.

It was a Sunday and the declining sun threw long shafts of golden light across tents and palms. A thin crescent of moon rose, with a bright unblinking stare from Venus. Candles and a cross stood on the improvised altar and as we rose to "Abide With Me". I glanced down and realised that the supports to the benches were Italian bomb fins!

Information came in the following day that an aircraft carrying Wing Commander Burton and Squadron Leader Hanbury, plus the actor Leslie Howard, was missing. We could ill afford to lose experienced men like that. Burton was due to command the Wing and Hanbury to be promoted Wing Commander.

❖ ❖ ❖

On less sombre matters, I was in 450 squadron mess one evening and discovered that they were great ones for song, which were relayed all over the Wing. Here was one, based on their nickname "Desert Harassers".

THE HARASSERS *(To the tune of "Lili Marlene")*

Get the right deflection, check reflector sight,
Give your skid correction, and see the range is right,
Then you can press the tit old man,
The Hun, to kingdom come,
    And poor Marlene's boyfriend,
    Will ne-e-e-ever see Marlene.

Belching ammunition, petrol tank ahead,
Glorious condition, to fill them full of lead,
A flamer for you is a grave for Fritz,
He's all in bitz, right where he sitz,
    And poor Marlene's boyfriend... etc

Half-a-thousand rounds of anti-personnel,
Eighty dozen rounds of the stuff that gives them hell,
And after the bomb-dive zoom away,
And live to fight another day,
    And poor Marlene's boyfriend... etc

Back to Harasser House you'll steer,
To drink a beer, with ne'er a tear,
    For poor Marlene's boy friend,
    Who'll ne-e-e-ever see Marlene.

And again, still 450 squadron:

HARASSER THEME SONG (Tune of "White Horse Inn")

"Raise up your glasses and drink, Harassers,
We're taking the air at first light,
To fly in Rommel's direction,
To bomb and lay off deflection,
And when the war is a memory,
The Desert Harassers will be,
A name they'll always remember,
So – drink to 450 with me.

From Canada and from Kiwiland,
From Perth and the Outer Barcoo,
From near and far they will straggle,
To join once again in the gaggle,
The years roll on and you're clapped at last,
In the desert, at home, or at sea,
You'll always be an Harasser,
So, drink to 450 with me.
Sgt Pilot Minchin

Haw Haw named the squadron "Desert Harassers", as mentioned, and "regretted the loss they had suffered". 450 squadron did not see it that way… hence the song.

450 was not the only squadron with a song. Here was one penned by Flight Lieutenant D.H. Clarke of 250 Squadron. The tune to which it was sung is unknown:

THE END

"After weeks of damn-all liquor,
Comes the beer; then, in a flicker,
Mighty milling crowds on the Mess descend
And you say "Let's have another,"
But you're told "You've had it brother"
It's the end, I tell you fellows, it's the end.

When you've drunk all you're able,
And you stagger from the table,
And in an alcoholic stupor seek your bed
Man appears, at dawn's first gleam,
Yells, "Get up, you're on the team,"
Its the end, I tell you, fellows, it's the end.

When you're jumped by twenty snappers,
And you're dicing like the clappers,
And your cover's disappearing round the bend
A voice pipes as you're weaving,
Bullfrog blue, are you receiving?"
It's the end, I tell you fellows, it's the end.

When you're shot to rags and tatters,
And your clapped-out engine clatters,
And you're heading, willy nilly, for the deck,
And the Spits, your plight discerning,
Cry, "We're coming boy, keep turning,"
It's the end, I tell you, fellows, it's the end."

I was Guard Commander. A signal came in of a landing near us, from an enemy submarine. I doubled the guard but we neither saw nor heard anything more, but those off duty kept their weapons close to hand. There was to be a consequence, however.

It produced some light relief. After a roaring evening in the Mess, Winco retired – or, more properly, was put to bed. In the small hours the insistent demands of nature woke him and he wandered out of his tent, naked, looking for a desert rose. After a suitable period, he returned and crawled into his tent.

But it wasn't his tent.

The scene shifts. First to awaken was the Orderly Room Corporal, who vaguely saw a white figure and jumped to the conclusion that it had something to do with the submarine. So he grabbed the first thing to hand, which happened to be an overloaded waste paper basket, and hurled it complete with contents, feeling around at the same time for his rifle. The others in the tent woke abruptly to find paper, paper, everywhere, loud grunts and an incoherent uproar. The white figure was submerged under four bodies. He emerged with head bloody but unbowed and was recognised with some horror. Heaven protects the "tight". At this juncture my doubled guard arrived requiring to know "What the hell…?" A much more sober Wing Commander was escorted back to his tent.

Laugh? The Wing nearly had hysterics.

July 2nd 1943. My birthday. The heat suddenly intensified and built up into a tearing blast of dry, shrivelling, incandescence, straight out of the Sahara. This reversed the former cool breeze from the sea. It was as though a furnace door had opened with flames leaping towards us. This was the "khamseen" – Arabic for fifty days – the fierce southerly wind that blew from March onwards. The seasalt dried on our skins and "crept" with the heat.

A word about Mediterranean winds in general. The *khamseen* – or *khamsin* or *kamsin* – was described somewhere as, "like a brown night taking over the day." It looked like a vast rolling cloud stretching from distance to distance and maybe up to eight or more thousand feet. It was a strong wind, perhaps up to 9 on the Beaufort scale. It interfered badly with aircraft in the air or trying to land on the strip. They could be bowled wing over wing. It blew out of the Sahara pretty well all along the North African coast from Egypt to Tunis. These were the other winds:

Vendaval	A steady westerly blowing through the Straits of Gibraltar.
Tramontane	A dry cold wind blowing south or south-west from the Italian mountains to the western Mediterranean.
Bora	Violent dry and cold wind from Alps to Trieste and down the east coast of the Adriatic, usually in winter.
Mistral	Strong cold dry wind blowing through the Rhone valley and southern France to the Mediterranean.

Sirocco	Similar to the *khamseen*: hot, oppressive, dusty: blowing in Spring from North Africa to southern Europe.
Levanter	Easterly wind in west Mediterranean in late summer.

One could go on with this listing since there were about six more, but often the same wind with a different name. The Mediterranean was a sea of humours rather than tides and its colour could range from blue through purple to wine. The Greeks called it the White Sea, which it still was to the Turks, and the Arabs had it as the White Central Sea.

My birthday also heralded new information from the "Tripoli Times", which reported from a foreign radio that tomorrow was the invasion day. It was true that our "A" party had vanished in the general direction of Sicily and "B" and "C" parties were occupying themselves in the sea. This usually meant donning dark glasses, sitting waist-deep, and reading a paperback.

I rolled over about 07.00 to see a long layer of black cloud above the landing strip. There was only one cause for that – burning aircraft. They seemed to throw up a peculiar oily blackness in the thick smoke. A Kittyhawk tyre had blown as it took off in squadron. Its wing tipped, touched, and the aircraft swung into the one racing parallel to it. The one following crashed into both. Luckily, the three pilots got away with it, but the aircraft were write-offs. Expensive.

The 8th Army landed on the tip of Sicily in the south-east and the Wing busied itself with its usual cover duties. It was in full action for the first time since Tunisia. A signal came in from the Army:

"Much gratitude. Fields in front of our troops alight. Thanks very much. Twice a great success."

The basic intentions for Sicily had been created at Casablanca with the so-called "Mediterranean Strategy" finalised in January 1943. The main effort was to be made in Sicily and not across the Channel.

❖ ❖ ❖

If the North African campaign were to be followed up, Italy knocked out of the war, the Russians relieved, and German forces drawn away from Normandy, then we had to land on some terrain north of the African coast.

There was some unease from General Marshall that this option might presage a deep action involving a long trek up the mountain spine of Italy. In the event, he was proved correct. It did. But there was also the British calculation that the Allies were not strong enough to undertake the Channel crossing in 1943. This was almost certainly true if one now considers the narrow margin by which the Normandy landings succeeded.

In the event the landings in Sicily began on 10th July 1943 and we were on our way into Europe.

❖ ❖ ❖

Prior to this time, known only to a few and to us not at all, not even to the top brass of the Command, was the deception initiated in London as "Plan Mincemeat" or alternatively "Plan Trojan Horse".

This has been written about and filmed elsewhere, but it should be mentioned here since it was an integral part of the Sicilian operation, was ingenious and saved many of our lives.

The idea was to mislead the enemy about the Allies' invasion intentions – into Sardinia, Corsica, Greece and so on. A question was put to Sir Bernard Spilsbury, the pathologist, on what the condition would be of a body that had been floating in the sea for some days after a plane crash. He advised.

A suitable body was located – that of a young man in his thirties who could pass as a Staff Officer. "Major Martin" of the Royal Marines was created. The body was to carry personal papers, including letters from an infatuated fiancée. Also in the briefcase was a letter from General Alexander implying landings in Greece and Sardinia, and another from Mountbatten stating that "Martin" was an expert in seaborne landings, with a jokey reference to his bringing back home some rationed "Sardines" which the Germans might interpret as "Sardinien."

The corpse was encased and loaded into a British submarine in a Scottish loch, great secrecy being involved, and, after a luckily unsuccessful attack by three British aircraft, the submarine surfaced off the

Under the Red Eagle

Spanish coast. Naval tradition came to the fore and a bizarre burial at sea was carried out with due ceremony.

"Major Martin" floated away on his last action, and the submarine dived deeply. Just after dawn the body and briefcase were picked up by a Spanish fisherman and turned over to the Spanish Navy, supposedly neutral. They were not that neutral, however, and the local German agent was soon copying the documents to Berlin.

Whether or not the German general staff fell for this was uncertain. But Hitler did, and that was good enough. German troops were shifted into Sardinia and the Sicilian cupboard left rather bare.

So we landed under the shadow of "Major Martin". What would the man himself have thought of this use of his corpse? Perhaps, with Shakespeare:

"Expect Saint Martin's summer, halcyon days." (Henry VI Pt. 1 sc.2)

❖ ❖ ❖

The call was sudden and "B" Party was on the move into Tripoli harbour with its many battered and sunken wrecks. Huge doors opened up in the prows of the LCT (Landing Craft, Tanks) and we were the first vehicle on board, up the purring lift and carefully reversed into our allotted position, ready to drive off at speed.

All quiet. No, it wasn't. Aircraft with black crosses swept down. Quick – under the lorries. Two airmen near me did so from either side of their vehicle with a brunt of heads and some forthright language. Gunfire poured down on us: we did not lose equipment or men, but later we did find a few holes in the lorries.

We up-anchored at dawn and the LCTs followed nose to tail out to sea. Quite uneventful until two or three miles out when signal flags whizzed up and down. A corvette had developed engine trouble. We returned to dock and swinging at anchor again. I counted up the number of hospital ships – three inside the dock and five outside. Hmm. Someone anticipated a bloody landing.

Time pressed now, so we moved out again without benefit of Navy, into growing darkness with the lights of Tripoli dimming and lowering. Africa lay behind us.

~ Under the Red Eagle ~

Long afterwards we were to realise that July 1943 was when the tide ran to flood after its turn at El Alamein.

On 21.7.43 we were renamed from "Western Desert Air Force" to "Desert Air Force." This was less localised and distinguished that we were the first RAF into Europe.

15. Interpolation

Retrospect
*We crossed the Iraqi wastes of sand
Beneath a flaming eye,
Where Euphrates swirled and Moslem prayed
And some remained, to die.*

*We struck east towards the mountains,
Through pass and hills grey-grim,
Where snow and the frigid breath of height,
In Persia, touched the skin.*

*Then south past rock and valley,
Domed mosque of sullen gold,
Back to the winter desert sand,
And Jordan's song of old.*

*South and west into the setting sun,
And the shade of the old Pharoah,
In Egypt, where Nile and weathered stone
Recorded time in its transient flow*

*Onward west through dangerous sea,
Where torn steel and shrapnel flew,
In diabolic plumes of white,
Rent from the rolling blue.*

*So to Tripoli's battered shore,
And past the ravaged farm,*

~ Under the Red Eagle ~

Over the Tunisian border track,
To Gabes, Sfax, Kairouan.

The roar of war resounded then,
As the final act was played,
Until the grey-clad hordes were pinned,
Behind wired barricade.

Now we look out across the blue,
Edged by its creaming foam,
Towards Europe, and await the call,
To invade, avenge, then – home.
At Zuara, June 1943

16. 'Husky' and the Sicilian Slaughter

> *"But thy most dreaded instrument,*
> *In working out a pure intent,*
> *Is man – arrayed for mutual slaughter,*
> *Yes, Carnage is thy daughter!"*
> **Wordsworth**

The full invasion of Sicily began on 10th July 1943. It was to prove a brilliant success: the whole island was captured in five weeks. But there was also a dark side.

It was the night of 9th July that about 2,500 landing craft and ships carrying 180,000 men approached the Cape Passero point of south-eastern Sicily. They were to land on the coast running from Syracuse in the east to Licata in the west. The former were the British landings, the latter the American. Airborne troops preceded them and many were to be lost at sea or in faulty landings. This was the "Sicilian Slaughter": more of that later.[4] But the main invasion went more or less to plan and was the biggest amphibious operation ever attempted. It was to provide invaluable lessons for the later D-Day in Normandy. Facing the landing troops, however, were 300,000 of the enemy.

Sicily was not, in fact, a small territory, being roughly one third of the size of the UK and with a population of about three million. It was a hard land, mountainous in the centre and arid. The volcano Etna pumped out smoke and lava.

We were introduced, on the way over, to a fearsome beast under the sea. One of the LCT cooks emerged from below carrying a pail –

---

[4] For an insider's account of this airborne fiasco, read *Operation Ladbroke: From Dream to Disaster*, by Alec Waldron, who was privy to the planning of this operation and also took part as a glider pilot. Published by Woodfield at £9.95.

the "gash" or food remnants from the galley. He hurled it over the side. There was a sudden flurry of water above a long, surfacing, grey shape and the garbage disappeared.

"Hey, look at that!" Harris yelled, leaning over the side. "It's like a 112 squadron kite!"

One or two within earshot gathered around Harris.

"What have you seen?" asked McLeod.

"Look for yourself," said Harris, pointing.

"Strewth!" said McLeod, observing a large triangular fin. "It's a shark!"

"Shark?" said Harris, "it's more like a whale. I thought there weren't any in the Med?"

A member of the crew came up behind.

"Yes there are," he said, "the sea off Sicily is a breeding ground, and what's more that could be a Great White."

The grey shape rolled over, displayed its white underparts and exhibited rows of large teeth again. More gash disappeared.

"Well…" said Harris, stepping back a pace, "I see what 'Bushy' meant about wading through blood and surf. I don't mind the Germans, but having that around is not my cup of char!"

A sharp nose broke the surface again, disposed of the remaining gash and the selachian dived away into the depths.

Ahead of us, on land, we and other Wings increased the air power available. Our own destination was Pachino, in the far south of the island, where we were to replace 244 Wing, the Spitfires. They were sisters, mainly engaged in covering 239 Wing missions.

Some quarter of a million British and Commonwealth troops finally went ashore from landing craft, under Montgomery. The moon was light enough to help the assault by paratroops and gliderborne infantry and after it had set it became dark enough to allow the seaborne forces to land. To the west of the island, American troops landed, under Patton.

Mussolini had already admitted that the Italians had neither the bombing force or fighters to cover them and that they would be on the defensive. He asked for the Luftwaffe to counter-attack any landing or drive onto any forces coming in from the sea. Kesselring brought in some paratroops and a Panzergrenadier division, which the 8th Army was soon to encounter.

The faint outline of the Sicilian shore could now be seen over the misty sea, and later an inexplicable spray of flares arced over us as we entered Syracuse harbour. The Luftwaffe met Mussolini's request; fighters appeared out of the sun, swept over us in numbers, and gunned the docks and landing craft in a repeat performance. Under the trucks again, without ceremony, was the order of the day – not only to avoid enemy fire but to escape our own shrapnel from the anti-aircraft guns. The L.C.T. cannon and guns added to a deafening roar. The sky became flecked with hundreds of puffs of smoke. Things were hotting up.

We emerged again in due course and recommenced the unloading. The harbour was crammed with craft, with a submerged hospital ship off the shore. This was the British "Talomba" which, we gathered had been brilliantly obvious with bands of light and electrically-illuminated red crosses on its sides and deck. The nursing sisters, wounded, and crew, had appealed for help in a black night of despair,

The ship sank by the stern and her lights were extinguished deck by deck. Other hospital ships saw what had occurred and circumspectly doused their own lights. Doubtless some Nazi squadron received Iron Crosses for this terrible breach of the Geneva Convention.

We moved smartly away from the docks and headed south to Pachino, which 244 Wing had now left. Somehow we found ourselves aimed in the wrong direction – a signpost indicated that we were heading for Catania, which meant the German lines – so we backtracked hurriedly and found a rough track to Pachino. 'A' party was already in residence and gave us a breezy greeting.

It was a surprise to find that this landing ground was in the midst of vineyards; we pitched our tents between the rows. We could stretch out a hand for grapes, and did so. No one was aware that the picking season was some weeks away, and that the grape type was not an eating one. Vengeance followed: the next morning many were "relieved" in the evacuation sense!

The clamour of planes resounded continuously and the sky was rarely empty. The Wing was extremely busy supporting the 8th Army as it moved up the east coast into central Sicily. The Yanks were not far away, on another airfield, showing a very different landing approach to ours. They came diving in, climbed fiercely, circled, usually with a coughing engine. The Kittyhawks reserved their style for the battlefield itself, arrived sedately under a steady engine, touched down, and taxied off gracefully to dispersal. Enemy aircraft were conspicuous by their absence during the day and arrived only at night, when the Army around us made its feelings known by spewing up shot and shell – quite often, successfully. Black-crossed metal lay around in the vineyards.

The Sicilians were a revelation in their reaction to us – cheers, fruit and flowers, and wine. On second thoughts, perhaps, we were less surprised. After all, over the centuries, these islanders had had plenty of "liberators" and could easily adopt a deceiving goodwill. So we took the gifts and benevolence with pinches of salt. We then received regular demands for food and materials, which the locals evidently felt was their due. They claimed to have despised the "Tedeschi" who had disposed of their fowl, pigs, sheep, and anything else available, and once the Allies arrived the Sicilians thought their troubles would cease. This was probably an illusion; troops are troops everywhere but we could hardly "half inch" what was not there. The urban Sicilians were offhand and not particularly helpful. These included the lads with sharp Italian suits and pointed shoes, the smug Catanians with overcoats draped over the shoulders, sinister toughs who wore perpetual sunglasses, and every other variety of town Italian. When we got into it we found Catania choked with crime and the whole city controlled by the "men of respect" as the Mafiosi described themselves.

A curious sight were Italian soldiers, still in uniform, carrying rifles and policing the beaches. Further, during the advance up the east coast we and the 8th Army were accompanied by civilians who pointed out the sites of booby traps, and mines. This must have saved many lives. All in all, the Sicilians were a curious bunch!

The inhabitants of the farm, on which we were later to move, at Agnone, were four – father, mother, daughter Marie of some fifteen years of age, and Antoinette, a child of six. The last was a prime favourite with the airmen. Watching the way the Wing made itself at home with them, sitting outside the farm door every evening,, was an insight into how "Tommy" and "Erk" could settle in with all locals. The family, and their farm labourers, even joined with us in Sunday services.

"Strange," said the Padre," to think of the Commando graves out there, and to remember that the people they came to attack are with us here tonight."

Attacking civilians? Surely Arthur had not got that quite right? We took it as metaphorical.

Around us, the villages were small but full of life and we viewed and were viewed by, healthy looking youngsters as brown as nuts and giving us the "V" sign.

There was a dark side to Sicily; the Mafiosi. They were hoodlums of the worst type who terrorised and intimidated the locals with blackmail, extortion, mutilation and killings. They also "took a 'cut' of all trade carried on. The Sicilians themselves were to blame for this imposition since their authorities lacked both will and ability to act against the Mafia, who also had the rule of 'omerta' – the code by which they did not inform against one another and exacted any necessary revenge themselves. Mussolini, it appeared, had tried to repress them with some savagery but they were still here.

In the early days of the war it was alleged that the Americans had made the Mafia a secret ally through the use of expatriate Mafiosi. "Lucky Luciano" was one of these and he agreed to help the Americans in Sicily. Otherwise, there were Mafiosi imprisoned on the islands around Sicily and after the landings these were released to become a "resurrected Mafia." They attained positions as town mayors, were political allies of the Americans, and acquired a bastard civil power. The island was later largely abandoned to them and they remained long after we had passed on into southern Italy. An American spokesman later admitted that they had failed to contain the Mafia. We, on the east of the island, saw little of them except in Catania. Perhaps the 8th Army and the Desert Air Force were a little too much!

We were not long at Pachino and moved up close behind the Army to a strip at Agnone, south of Catania. The Hermann Goering Division, other Panzer Korps, and an Italian Littorio Division had defences through Catania and along the slopes of Mount Etna, where they employed commanding fire over the Catania Plain.

We convoyed up over a ridge to look down on this open country. It was a spectacle. Thirty miles north was the huge conical mass of Etna with its smoke drifting away from the crater. On the plain itself the Simento River curled windingly down to the sea. Beyond the river, Catania shimmered under the heat. It would have been a striking scene in peace, and still was, but for the vicious shell explosions a mile or two away, at the river, tossing up reeking clouds of cordite. Two armies faced one another in deadly conflict.

The valley plain below was like a huge amplifier. Sounds rolled away in great ponderous waves. A gunshot started as a sharp bark then developed into a sullen resonance as the hills reflected the sound.

At Agnone, we were in a field under a low hill. The landing strip had been a rapid effort of construction, in twelve days, and we were the first to occupy it. This put us far enough forward to receive attention from German gunners, who tossed over shells with enthusiasm.

There was a third enemy here – the mosquito. We learned later that although 8th Army battle casualties were 9,000 the losses from malaria were well over 11,000. The insects were counterattacked by elderly Lysanders spraying the marshy areas with the new DDT, but this had not yet cut the incidence of the disease. The mosquitoes swarmed when the sun went down and continued to plague us all night. It was impossible to keep them out of the tents. We were issued with small yellow pills of atabrine, a proprietary name for mepacrine, but this did little to ward off the symptoms and nothing to halt the pestilence. It was a palliative rather than a preventive. The malaria came later on. This gave rise to a song that always featured in Wing concerts. On came the chorus, usually dressed in *tu-tu* garb and delivered this, sung to the tune of the "Ovalteenies"

> "We are the Mep-a-crinies,
> Darwen's happy boys,
> We have no fear of "bull" or charges,
> 'Cos we came in L.S. barges,
> You can hear our song and story,
> You can share the joys,
> And though we may so scruffy seem,
> You know we came from Alamein,
> And 'cos we take our Mep-a-crine,
> We're happy ma'aleesh[5] boys.'

Finally we had to move as many of the Wing as we could take onto the hill above and leave only skeleton crews in the valley. Our small two-man tents – "bivvys"– crouched under the olive trees. Before we moved onto the hill, however, there was a nauseating job to be done. Severe fighting had taken place over the ridge, centred on a stone house. Half-a-dozen of the enemy had been caught by hand-grenades lobbed into the back of the building, and by the look of it the whole lot had been strafed by our squadrons. Very bloody and very effective. In the house, they were annihilated.

The bodies had been there for a fortnight in Sicilian summer heat, and the result can be imagined. It was now impossible to bury them in the usual way, since we would have needed special equipment. So the only thing possible was done – the house and putrefying corpses were drenched in petrol and a match applied. The flames roared and a pyre of black smoke towered into the sky and drifted out to sea. The more practical were then for blowing down the building onto the remains, but the Wing Padre would have none of this and volunteers

---

[5] "Ma'aleesh" was Arabic and roughly translated as "don't care".

were called for to bury the charred remains; an ugly job. The RAF was not usually so close to the havoc it wreaked.

About this time the Wing came under heavy attack. As mentioned, the German guns were near and regularly bombarded the strip. Then, one night, the Luftwaffe paid even closer attention. At 22.30 a brilliant Sicilian moon was flooding the dispersals and the characteristic wavering notes of unsynchronised engines approached from seaward. Enemy aircraft. Flares blazed. Long streams of silver rain cascaded down like waterfalls of light from dimly seen parachutes. Red rage swelled from the 8th Army anti-aircraft around us, punctuated by the dull concussions of bombs and the myriad small explosions from "jumping jacks."

This was the first serious attack on the Wing since John Darwen had taken command six weeks earlier. He and his jeep clattered through the smoke and roar as he marshalled the fire parties to critical points. The raid developed in flame, reeking smells, explosions, the stink of cordite, and the touch of incandescent cinders. Every sense was excited.

Beating out flames, I was close enough to see and hear Darwen. "I've had enough of this," he yelled and ran towards his personal Kittyhawk. The flames were dangerously near but he clambered into the cockpit and belted up with the aid of the mechanics. He roared off dustily followed by two or three more of the Wing. They climbed swiftly and two or three Spitfires from 244 Wing joined the gaggle. Diving onto the bombers they shot down five.

Touching down again, Darwen spoke with feeling when he saw the row of shrouded bodies outside the hospital tent. They were all ground staff.

"Flight," he said, "We'll take a service at 9 am tomorrow, on General Parade. Best kit, medals, decorations, and a fired salute."

He strode away.

The following day he came into his element again, and the Wing attacked enemy vehicles on the Catania front and around Etna. A long string of lorries and cars were fired and ditched. Enemy entrenchments were also bombed and strafed and a characteristic 8th Army signal came into the Wing:

> "Troops report excellent results. Enemy C4601 effectively attacked. Thank you."

A lighter side of our sojourn in Agnone. I was accommodated with the Senior Medical Officer at the time and had the opportunity of seeing his report on "Controlled Prostitution in Agnone."

Here are some extracts:

> "Without in any way disparaging the work of MPs, no amount of "out of bounds" notices or threats of arrest, prevented the airmen finding willing women in Lentini. The final blow was struck when three itinerant prostitutes set up a lucrative brothel in the Squadron Dispersal Area. The challenge to virility was there and the alacrity with which it was accepted dispelled any doubt about homosexuality becoming a real factor in the Wing.
>
> A farmhouse adjacent to the L.G. was commandeered as a 'convalescent depot'. The S.M.O. then visited the local controlled Italian brothel, the institution being managed by two sisters of formidable mien who had graduated from active participation in the business some eight years previously. We decided to employ them.
>
> A jeep set out for the Wing, from Lentini, with an unmilitary complement. In front, the rather more attractive of the two sisters, her most striking features concealed behind correspondent sun glasses. The back seats were occupied by an interpreter – the cashier of the local bank and rather disapproving, and the elder sister who favoured black sequins, tight lacing, and a pompadour coiffure. The journey to Agnone was made without mishap except for meeting the C. of E. padre on the road. On the return we were stopped only once on the way, by an inquisitive M.P.
>
> The next day a three-tonner and a 15 cwt pulled up outside the local brothel. It was unfortunate that it was the main street,

that all the might of Empire was being dragged up it, and that the British soldier is so glib with his repartee. A cherished memory will be that of a British cavalry officer skipping nimbly between Bren carriers with a portable bidet clasped to his bosom, madame shrilling admonitions about this essential adjunct to her calling. Off we rattled in the 15 cwt with the two sisters, a cook, and one small but active young woman. It seemed a large ground staff to have only one operational type. As Mount Etna was lit by the rusty glow of the setting sun our charges were installed and a guard placed over them by courtesy of the R.A.F. Regiment."

(Then follows some medical matters, and the admin)

No alcohol, and drunks turned away by the guards. It was considered redundant to advertise the project. How right we were. The water bowser called and both driver and assistant were pressed into action. Madame sat on the porch shelling peas. The scene, bathed in the morning Sicilian sunshine, reminded one of a musical comedy staged by a provincial touring company. The airmen co-operated. Madame coped with any suggestion of indecorous behaviour. The prostitute was treated with respect and became one of the family. By the end of the day we had two operational types and Madame was left to hold the fort alone. The two were Rosetta and Marie. We never knew the surnames. Rosetta was small and agile and averaged four-and-a-half minutes. She wore two garments, both of which buttoned down the front. Marie was blonde and better upholstered, of a placid disposition, with an average time of eight minutes, No single case of V.D. was ever traced and the rate on the Wing dropped to zero.

The end of the story makes dreary reading: the powers heard of it and heavy-footed redcaps invaded our Nirvana. The entire circus vanished like the mists of dawn.

The documents in the case are confidential, but they only go to show that discipline and training in the R.A.F. are not easily discarded.

A parthian shot to this was that back in 1939 Alanbrooke had threatened to sack Montgomery, then one of his divisional commanders in France, because the latter had suggested opening brothels to stop his soldiers contracting VD. Presumably the "powers" in this report did not consult Montgomery!

Completely contrasting incidents from the American side are worth a mention as well. These were the "slapping incidents". The rumour as it reached us was that Patton had encountered a private in hospital who had said "I just can't take it." So Patton both kicked and slapped him and had him removed from hospital "I don't want yellow-bellies like him hiding their lousy cowardice around here, stinking up this place of honour." There was a further incident in another hospital, with Patton's reaction to a second private who had claimed "It's my nerves." Patton hauled out a gun, saying "I ought to shoot you now goddam you…" to the shock of doctors and nurses. It became a topic in the 7th Army and was relayed to us.

Apparently the medicals reported on the incidents and the papers finally got to Eisenhower's desk, who ordered an extensive apology. It was a savage punishment for so "proud and cocky" a general. Patton later said "I wish I'd kissed the sonofabitch" and even later "I've learned my lesson. If I get another chance I'm going to keep my mouth shut."

Patton had an unusual attitude for a two-star general. More of his remarks that went the rounds were:

"No bastard ever won a war by dying for his country… You do it by making the other bastard die for his."

"All my life I've wanted to lead men in a desperate battle. I'm going to do it…"

To Rommel: "You magnificent bastard… I read your book."

On an old Carthaginian battlefield, reflecting his belief in reincarnation: "I was here. I fought in many guises, many names."

Of Hitler: "I'm going to Berlin to personally shoot that paper-hanging sonofabitch."

To a medical officer: "Wear your helmet! If you need to use a stethoscope, then cut holes in it."

Patton is alleged to have been described by the Germans as "a magnificent anachronism." He finally returned to the U.S.A. without plaudits. Montgomery, on the other hand, was received by the King and became Chief of the Imperial General Staff.

Very different outcomes.

Reports emerged about this time that all had not gone well in the initial attack on Sicily. The assault had been spearheaded by the British First Airborne Division and the American Eighth Airborne, as the biggest aerial attack ever launched. All four drops ended in disaster. Some pilots in the towing aircraft freed their gliders too soon and the craft plunged into the sea. Apprehensive gunners in the invasion fleet shot down paratroop 'planes by the score. Fearful American aircrews dropped their paratroops all over Sicily and even further afield in Sardinia and Southern Italy.

When the planes carrying dead and dying got back to bases in North Africa the paratroops who had not been employed had to be confined to camp to avoid a bad blood confrontation.

It was both disaster and scandal, hushed up at home for decades, and only in time to become known as the "Sicilian Slaughter." The rest of the operation, according to General Alexander "went according to plan." Economical with the truth. The Sicilian landings made a difference to the German onslaught in the East, from where Hitler was forced to withdraw troops to reinforce this new southern front. This helped relieve pressure on the Russians.

Towards the end of the Sicilian day forty Allied squadrons were flying from twenty-one airfields. The enemy were still holding out, however, in the steep narrow valleys and mountains which were ideal to cover withdrawal. So far as 239 Wing was concerned, with its fighter-bombers, strafing and bombing on spotted German positions was more difficult than it had been in the Western Desert. The flak was intense and the enemy valley ambushes had telling effect. But the

Kittyhawk got through. At the Casablanca Conference it had been decided that the Sicilian invasion should take place in June 1943 and that the campaign in Italy would be pushed as far as Pisa. In the event, Sicily became a rehearsal for the more serious operation in 1944, across the Channel.

Before we left Sicily the "Africa Star" was awarded to veterans of the desert. We drew a ribbon from Stores to sew on our battledress tunic. The "Star" itself would be issued at a later date. The ribbon also bore a silver rose to denote the Desert Air Force, or an Arabic "8" for the Eighth Army. The ribbon was pale buff (for desert) with a wide central red stripe (Army) flanked by narrower light and dark blue stripes for R.A.F. and Navy. The Wing tended to interpret the expanse of buff as the extent to which we were "browned off."

On August 17th 1943 the last German soldier was flung out of Sicily and it fell wholly into Allied hands. The enemy had fought hard, the difficulties of the terrain had been formidable, and malaria had run riot. However, once the Desert Air Force had landed and become operational the issue was never in doubt.

On the last day of fighting 239 Wing were intercepted by six Macchi 202s which attempted to down twelve of 3 RAAF squadron. They were fought off with one shot down, and three badly damaged.

No loss to the Kittyhawks.

17. Avanti

> *"A man who has not been in Italy is always conscious of an inferiority, for his not having seen what it is expected a man should see"* **Boswell: "Life"**

Plans had been set for the 8th Army to cross the Straits of Messina – "Operation Baytown" – and for the US 5th Army to go in at Salerno – "Operation Avalanche."

The trek forward would be at least a thousand miles until we reached the German borders, over a country a quarter bigger than the U.K. but with about the same size of population.

There were firm objectives for the campaign. Montgomery's message to the 8th Army and Desert Air Force was:

1. Having captured Sicily as our first slice of the Italian home country, the time has now come to carry the battle to the mainland of Italy.
2. To the Eighth Army has been given the great honour of being the first troops of the Allied Armies to land on the mainland of the Continent of Europe. We will prove ourselves worthy of this honour.
3. I want to tell you, soldiers of the Eighth Army, that I have complete confidence in the successful outcome of the operations we are now going to carry out. We have a good plan and air support on a greater scale than we have ever had before. There can only be one end to this next battle, and that is: ANOTHER SUCCESS.
4. Forward to victory! Let us knock Italy out of the war
5. Good Luck, and God Bless you all."

~ Under the Red Eagle ~

All this was ultimately fulfilled, but only after major battles.

Still in Sicily, we had our first intimation of the rainy season to come. Etna was lost behind grey clouds. The northern sky was sombre and menacing. Clouds piled up inland, with air heavy with anticipation. Large, warm, raindrops spattered onto thin khaki drill. The olive trees around us rustled and dust rose for the last time for some months. The main body of the storm drove north and a watery sun gleamed again, developing into a fiery sunset.

The visibility became clearer and we saw the faint but definite outline of the hills on the Italian "toe" at Calabria. The enemy became more active and swept down in sorties. On our side, the sky became full of aircraft heading towards Italy – Spitfires, Bostons, heavy bombers and Kittys. White stars and old roundels identified them as Allies. Fighters swept round and above, revolving round the bombers like satellites. The whole sky shivered under the bellow of engines.

Another campaign had opened.

On 3rd September 1943, four years to the day after the war began, the 8th Army landed on the beaches before Reggio and began their drive into Italy proper at 04.30. The first pebble in the rumour pool was cast by an airman rushing past with his tousled hair half-combed: "Italy's thrown in her hand … she's capitulated!"

This was confirmed by the first "gen" talk at 20.00 hours. Up came Darwen in his jeep, well oiled from a squadron tour. He swung the jeep round to throw its headlights onto the mess wall carrying a full-scale map of Italy. 239 Wing was to be the first fighter-bomber Wing to go in with the 8th Army.

I reflected on the war being four years old. As a teenager I always thought that the four years of the Great War of 1914-1918 must have seemed an impossibly long period to live through – now here we were in the fifth year ourselves and there was more to come. The conversation regularly returned to demobilisation but few wished to go back while the war was still raging and a Channel invasion still a matter for the future.

As to the state here, it appeared that German troops were coming over the Brenner Pass in droves, without any agreement from the

Italians. Northern Italy was being treated as an occupied country and German military currency was being issued.

The first parties moved off at 04.00 the following morning, 11th September and we headed for Catania. The Salerno landings were coupled with ours with the Germans "looking down US throats from the mountains and passes." We were likely to have our throats examined, too. I volunteered to drive, since I was now fully authorised on any RAF vehicle – an accolade – but I did not bargain on being asked to deal with the mobile cooker. Still, we always had the rations.

The vehicle seemed to be pulling hard up a rise and finally flagged out. A hooting convoy pulled up behind and I dismounted to wave them past and grab a blazing oily rag from a feedpipe. Who was that fool? Up came the fitters:

"How do you expect us to tow you with your handbrake on?"

"As a matter of fact, it's not on."

They discovered that all servo brakes were binding on red-hot drums. Someone had not serviced the damned thing and it had been standing around immobile for too long. We released the oil from the brakes and were towed ignominiously onto the docks at 23.00 hours.

At this juncture, George's mepacrine failed him, and he was carted away, delirious, at midnight. He was out of the running for this invasion.

We took an entirely different route to the 8th Army and circled round the Golfo di Squillace into Taranto, which we found full of Italian sailors. Pronto, Marinaro. The opposing services eyed one another tentatively: the order to salute higher Italian officer ranks failed to be observed.

We heard that Kesselring was deploying sixteen German divisions across Central Italy, had disarmed the Italian Army and was preparing defences across what he called the "Gustav Line", based on Monte Cassino. One hardly needed to be a military strategist to foresee that attacks on a relatively narrow front up Italy, mountains striding up the middle and all rivers west to east, was not going to be a sinecure. The country was ideally suited to defensive operations.

~ Under the Red Eagle ~

We were not long in Taranto and moved forward again to an Italian aerodrome near Bari. On the way we encountered no hostility from the civilians of what was, after all, a defeated nation. They seemed to accept us as "liberators", which the British serviceman – essentially pragmatic – did not expect. It seemed that the Germans had left a bad taste behind them. Children chased up to us, grasped hands, and were entirely satisfied with affirmation to their query "Inglese?"… and with the chocolate.

Arriving at Bari we ensconced ourselves in the main block, which was similar to a Station HQ at home. We scouted round the buildings to see what was about and entered a deserted officers' mess. We stood astounded. The far wall was completely covered in mirrors, which served to reflect hundreds of bottles of wine and spirits on the shelves. No one had ever seen so much alcohol. Well, after all, these could be taken as spoils of war. We removed a few bottles and introduced ourselves for the first time to the sweet Italian Vermouth Cinzano Bianco. We retired and celebrated our surprise that the Italians had declared war on Germany; so they were now Allies.

Again, we were not long at Bari and moved forward to 'Foggia Main' on 3.10.43, which opened new possibilities since this also was an aerodrome and not an LG. Formerly, fighter cover had been coming from Sicily and could remain over our Kittyhawks for only fifteen minutes. Now they covered the Wing completely, while the heavy bomber could range far and wide throughout Italy and strike at Austria and transport centres in the Balkans.

Foggia had been torn apart. We had been told in our "gen" talks before the invasion that bombers would go for railway junctions south of Rome to discourage the supplies coming down the Italian "ankle" and that is what has happened to Foggia – railway, aerodrome and town. The last had also been looted. The Germans had ordered the townspeople to move out as they were going to hold Foggia, and the civilians went, leaving houses and flats locked and household goods packed away. Now chests, cupboards and drawers lay open with contents strewn across the floor. Doors were smashed in, beautiful furniture attacked with crowbars, and locks shot away. The

Germans had concentrated on small valuables and taken them as booty, smashing the rest. They had destroyed the civilian life of Foggia even more than our bombing.

Only remnants of a town had been left behind. The streets which old postcards revealed as handsome were now squalid. A few children begged while grubby women hung onto rags from which peeked the faces of hungry babies. Other adults drifted about the streets with hopeless looks – the men old and worn, the women dispirited and all dressed in black. There was devastation everywhere, not least in the marshalling yards formerly a railway centre; the station was virtually flat with sheds and warehouses in ruins.

Looting was a crime for the British, so when I arrived with a guard into a wasted town, I was astonished to find a small R.A.F. group, with lorry below, struggling to extract a grand piano through a first floor window.

"What the hell do you think you are doing?"

"It's a piano for the mess: we have an O.K."

"Do you now… Where is it?"

A "chit" is produced, worded as a "requisition"

"Can't you find something a bit smaller than a grand. What about an upright?"

"No, that's all we can find."

"You're aware that you can be shot?"

"Shot? By whom? Why?"

"By my guard, you loons. Don't you read your DROs? But since your C.O. has been unwise enough to give you a 'chit' then get on with it and clear off."

Trust the R.A.F. to "requisition" rather than loot!

A twenty-six-year-old Italian lieutenant of the Regia Aeronautica became attached to the Wing as a Liaison Officer. After the armistice he flew a bomber from central Italy to an airfield in Allied hands. He was chased by an Me109 but evaded it and reported for duty with the RAF. Since he turned out to be one of the pilots who had attacked the Wing at Agnone, when we lost over forty killed and injured, we were not too welcoming to the new recruit. He simply said: "I want to rejoin my wife and child and live in peace again."

A typical sortie at this time might be outlined. It was much of a routine except when the pilot ran into trouble. That might be enemy fighters, flak, engine trouble, loss of control and forty other possibilities.

Kittyhawks looked handsome with their well-proportioned lines and large air intake. They had a rather snooty nose-in-the-air angle The big radiator was not always an advantage, especially in a hard crash landing, since it dug into the soil, and could toss the machine onto its back.

The driver would reach for the recessed grab handle, haul himself on to the steeply sloping wing, slide back the canopy, and sling his chute onto the seat. When seated, the flap and undercarriage selectors were at his left hand. On the right were the manual hydraulic hand pump and the curved lever for the radiator shutters.

In front, the nose canted up steeply and blocked the view ahead; hence the need for someone on the wing to direct one around dispersal. There was a primitive gunsight consisting of a set of concentric rings and a separate blade foresight.

One started things up with two hands and a foot, and the engine settled down into an idle. Taxi away and gun the motor a little. Then let it go and the ground slid away below with increasing speed. Bump, bump, then a smooth rise under power. Up to 5,000 feet or so, which would take five minutes. Now to the target, which was often a long line of transport in the enemy's back area; it could be seen down to the right and then it swung in front as the Kitty turned over into a dive. At 350 mph the rudder pedals became stiff to move but the elevator could be shifted with an effort, as could the ailerons. The aircraft now had a strong yawing motion to starboard and the right wing was heavy. Trim tabs countered these expected forces. Bomb released. The 'plane felt lighter and rose as the bomb fell away. It exploded on the road below and a truck overturned and fired. The pilot turned away and drove down the line of trucks, strafing, climbed and rejoined the formation. The LG was only twenty or so miles behind so it was less than five minutes before the familiar strip appeared, with the village lying behind. Sixteen seconds to drop the gear, four seconds for the flaps, open the radiator shutters and check boost pump.

The power was chopped as the strip disappeared under the nose, and the aircraft's weight was eased onto the steel plates. A member of the ground crew was picked up on the wing to assist in taxiing into dispersal. Halt. Final adjustments to flap and mix and the canopy was shoved back. The ground crew grinned.

"OK, sir?"

"No problems. Thanks boys."

Out of the cockpit and into a jeep; just enough time for a snorter in the bar tent before the evening meal.

Another day and two or three 'flamers'.

❖ ❖ ❖

I was nearly 'killed on active service' one day at Foggia. We were in an open three-tonner running back across the airfield with about eight men aboard, heading for HQ. We bowled up the dispersal road and turned across the end of the main runway. As we curved round I glanced back and saw a Hurricane banking towards the runway, about fifty feet above the strip; its undercarriage was not lowered. The plane was obviously in trouble and not under control. I suddenly realised that the lorry was heading straight into the line of flight and that the driver could not have seen the aircraft. I hammered on the cab and bawled for him to stop. Since I was able to drill squads at long distances, the driver heard me all right.

He reacted fast and locked all four wheels in a skidding halt. The plane was now almost touching the strip and coming in under power a few feet ahead of us. The propeller hit the deck and shivered into fragments. The fuselage ploughed into the surface, its long range petrol tank tore away, and petrol gushed over plane and ground. A blade of the splintered propeller arced up and drove into the tarmac three feet from our lorry, sticking in like a knife. I had a momentary glimpse of the pilot flicking up his switches and bracing himself against the cockpit side. The margin of escape couldn't have been slimmer, with the Hurricane skating past us a few feet away and drenched in petrol. We leapt over the side to rescue the pilot before the whole lot caught fire. It didn't, by luck, and he had braced himself so well that he climbed out only dazed after turning off his klaxon, still racketing an alarm.

The "blood wagon" appeared at speed, racing the crash tender. The airfield controller hared up in his jeep, followed by the R.S.U. crane.

There was nothing else for us to do, so we left them to it, still perspiring, and drove round the trail of wreckage. Why the pilot was in trouble we never found out but it was a near enough miss.

We were lucky to be alive.

18. Death of a C.O.

> *"Group Captain John Darwen DFC arrived to take over 239 Wing command."*
> **RAF Operations Record Book, 30 June 1943**

This chapter goes back a month or so to Sicily, when John Darwen arrived, and follows his short period as CO until his death in central Italy. His work during the enemy attack on the Wing in Sicily, has already been mentioned.

John Darwen entered the mess tent, its large canvas roof shading trestle tables and benches. Of medium height, he was dressed in spruce khaki drill and the silk scarf of the desert pilot. The diagonal flash of a DSO, a faded DFC and the Africa Star lay under his pilot's wings. His brown hair waved freely over a high brow and he had a strong, slightly cleft chin with thick eyebrows and piercing eyes long accustomed to far desert horizons. The four rings of an RAF Group Captain were blue on his shoulders. He was 27 years of age.

"Gentlemen," he said. His senior and junior officers rose. For most of these men, the Desert Air Force had been a unique period in their lives. Young and athletic, they lived in relatively primitive conditions with only the bare necessities to sustain life. It was as far removed as it could be from the life of a home station or the pleasures of Cairo. Creature comforts were few. In the desert they had been in daily combat in a land naturally hostile to their existence and as implacable a foe as the Afrika Korps and the Luftwaffe. It had been a harsh climate where sandstorms gritted the eyes and choked the throat, where the scorching sun could stun and chilly nights set the teeth a-chattering.

~ Under the Red Eagle ~

Although Darwen was in his everyday uniform, casual but neat, among these men he appeared dressed as for parade. Commonwealth and British were well represented and their uniforms were a motley collection. A few pilots wore battledress of army type but there were also cardigans and sleeveless pullovers in various shades of khaki and, like Darwen, the inevitable silk scarf doing double duty of absorbing perspiration and acting as a map for forced landings – now a useless addition since the desert was behind them. Many elected for calf-length mosquito boots or suede, while others made do with sandals or scuffed shoes. The headgear tossed onto the table included RAF peaked and forage caps but added variety with two Luftwaffe caps, some Australian slouches, woollen scarf caps, and one Arab fez. At least half the assembly were sporting full naval beards or the long fierce moustache, usually extending beyond the ears, of the desert airman. They had panache and a slight swagger. Decorations were everywhere.

Darwen was an unknown quantity but it would not be long before his unusual loathing of the Germans became apparent. To the older hands the Germans were simply public enemies whom their duty called them to oppose by military action, but to Darwen, Hitler and his Nazis were vermin to be utterly destroyed. A savage experience lay behind this psychology – his wife and small daughter had been killed on the grim night of the Café de Paris bombing. The café had been a glittering urban nightspot advertised as London's safest venue, lying as it did beneath the Rialto cinema. That night it had been packed with fashionable society types and officers home on leave, all bent on forgetting the war for an hour or two. At the height of the dancing two bombs plunged right through the Rialto and onto the dance floor below. One exploded and the other burst and threw yellow filth in all directions. Thirty-four people were killed on and around the dance floor and sixty badly injured. Marjorie Darwen was amongst them. She died in her husband's arms. It was a macabre scene and a night of deep personal tragedy which left a scarred mind. Darwen became a man with a mission – to avenge and annihilate without compunction. His Wing colleagues understood and were not surprised.

Some time after Darwen's assumption of command, the Wing was in Sicily – the aircraft flying in and the ground staff going in by landing ships. But they were not south very long. The 8th Army pushed up the east coast far and fast enough for the Wing to move into the Catania Plain at Agnone, where mosquitoes existed in their millions: "The insects could not be counted in any cubic foot of air space," read a medical report.

Apart from the "bumph" which Darwen abhorred, his days were packed with sorties and missions on enemy motor and rail transport, gun positions and any opportunist target that offered itself. By this time the enemy had had enough, was trying to withdraw, and 239 Wing had operated with great distinction against their shipping in the Messina Straits. Now, troops and airmen faced the "toe and heel" of Italy. Then we needed to push towards the Foggia and Rome areas and create the conditions required for 'Overlord' – the D-Day Channel crossing – and the other prong of Allied forces entering southern France.

Cross-country communication was poor, since both armies, 5th American on the west, and 8th British on the east, had to force their way along the flanks of the central mountains. Only the air was a free highway and the Wing made the most of it, battling over both coasts, the central 'spine' and the warm seas on either side.

This was the background for the *coup de grâce* for John Darwen on the fatal day of 7th October 1943. There was no operational flying until late in the afternoon when Darwen led the first recce. Approaching a valley near Guglionesi, he looked down and spotted a German convoy threading its way along a narrow road in the valley and gave the order to attack. The other pilots glanced down as Darwen dived, followed by his Number Two. Intense and accurate light ack-ack poured upwards from what now looked like an ambush and both aircraft rammed into the focal point of the fire. The wings of Darwen's aircraft disintegrated in a seeming explosion and its shattered fuselage ploughed hard into the ground alongside the convoy. The plane of his Number Two, also hit, was last seen limping away with white smoke pouring from the engine, never to be seen again,

~ *Under the Red Eagle* ~

nor ever found. The surviving flight leader took over command and gave the order to continue the attack. Harry was "Tail End Charlie" of the gaggle and checked the skies above him. They were clear. Whilst flying level the convoy below was obscured by his wings, so he circled in the vortex of aircraft and then followed the others forward and down, into the dive. He eased the stick and exerted a strong arm-thrust, knowing that his Kitty would now accelerate fast and tend to roll to starboard. They always did. Halfway through the dive he trimmed out, with the left hand removed for a moment from the throttle. The aircraft then revealed another idiosyncrasy and attempted to roll to port. Bracing right arm against right leg and the sides of the cockpit Harry held the stick central with a hard thrust to fight the rolling, fishtailing, or skidding, calculated to spoil his aim.

Dive-bombing like this was always a near-vertical business – but not too much so. It was a tricky technique. Although the Kittyhawk had been adapted to carry bombs, that did not make it a bomber, and its missiles did not go into free fall and curve down onto the target. Aiming the aircraft itself aimed the bombs, like strafing.

The altimeter unwound and Harry's straps gripped his shoulders.

The valley bottom came at him, thick with trucks, but an aircraft was already below, so he broke hard right and then left in a turn that reversed his course. 'Back to line astern,' he thought, 'and I'll get another chance to clobber this convoy.' As he came in again the air in front of him had now cleared of smoke and as he dived he saw trucks blown off the road with their undersides exposed. All seemed to be in a peculiar slow-motion – trucks in the ditches, trucks burning furiously, truck colliding with other trucks. He aimed his three tons of Kittyhawk into the middle of the chaos and released both 250lb bombs at 1,000 feet. The kite lightened, now free of its burden, and he pulled out of the dive, reversing the trim tabs with his left hand to combat the roll. The G-force drove blood into his legs and bright flashes crossed his vision. He "browned out" for a moment.

The Kitty juddered slightly on release. Harry heaved on the stick and the nose came up, slowly and unwillingly, as he toggled the electric trim-tabs and fought the port rotation. She straightened and came back to level flight, then began to soar into the climb. The ack-ack spat tracer past his wings and holes appeared, but his aircraft was still flying under control.

Below, after seconds, Harry's bombs struck on the centre vehicles of the convoy. The black-crossed lorries erupted in a cloud of debris and smoke. At the same time, other aircraft bombed both the tail and head of the convoy. It was now completely blocked, Small figures dived into ditches and flames roared along the convoy from end to end. The streams of ack-ack stopped dead.

All the aircraft swung round into staggered line astern and turned south. The Wing Leader dived in salute over the shattered and scattered remnants of the CO's aircraft, from which rose a plume of black smoke. They reached the strip, touched down one by one, and taxied into dispersal in a very sober frame of mind. Wing operations laconically wrote in the Record Book:

> "It is recorded with profound regret that G/Capt John Darwen failed to return from an operation he was leading over an enemy target at MR Napoli 1:500,000 HR.7167 at 17.00 hours today."

Darwen had commanded the Wing for just over three months. Some weeks later the Chaplain asked me to join him to find the spot where Darwen had been killed – a necessary official procedure of identification before "missing, believed killed" could be translated into "killed in action." Wing Operations provided a map and a pinpoint near Termoli. It was 100 feet north of the Guglionesi-Montecilfone road on the side of a hill. We arrived in a long low valley of black earth and rich grass. Two labourers were ploughing in a field and guided us to where a propeller blade thrust skywards from the soil, a silent witness to the crash. Beyond, down the hillside, was a three-hundred-foot scar and a scatter of torn metal – the largest parts being the cylinder block, the guns and a section of fuselage and rudder. The grave was marked by a white cross, probably by courtesy of the 8th Army when it penetrated this far. It was incorrectly lettered, "Wing Commander, D.F.C., R.A.F." but the Army had done its best, almost certainly from torn rank bars and a decoration they would recognise. We had brought another version which read "Group Captain J. Darwen, D.S.O., D.F.C. and Bar C.O. 239 Wing, Desert Air Force." We looked hard at the grave. The corpse had been interred only lightly and from the look on Chaplain's face I realised that he was having thoughts about recovering his commanding officer and reburying him more suitably. However, after five weeks it was impracticable, since we did not have the kit, and in any case the War Graves Commission would transfer the body soon, to a military cemetery.[6] But there was a torn and stained battledress blouse with its tarnished decorations only lightly embedded in the soil, so we recovered it and put it aside to take back.

It was apparent that the aircraft had indeed been hit in a steep dive and had exploded in the air. John Darwen was probably dead before he hit the deck. Around the wreckage on the hillside was the havoc of destroyed lorries and a staff car, with some German graves. The C.O. lay among the debris of his own Wing's attack.

It rained hard as we tidied up the grave, and then the sun broke through. I found it hard to believe what then happened. A magnificent double rainbow arched over us. We saluted the grave and turned away. Darwen had rejoined his wife Marjorie.

As I looked back from the road the white cross stood stark against the dark hillside, with the end of the rainbow dipping towards it – a striking spectacle.

There was a Parthian shaft to this. Back in camp I had the usual unpleasant duty of collecting together Darwen's effects. A copy of Richard Aldington's *The Crystal World* lay on the side. A female hand had endorsed the first page "John Darwen, 22 August 1942, in the Western Desert, from Pat." Who, I wondered was "Pat"?

On the back page of the book there was a rough draft in John Darwen's own hand.

---

[6] Darwen was reburied in May 1944 in the War Cemetery above the station of Torino di Sangro on the Sangro River. Plot X, Row E, Grave 27.

~ Under the Red Eagle ~

The bright new silver shaft of love,
Is new and clear, Yet still behind,
The ancient love is warm,
And all-suffusing all our hearts,
But bright and silver shines the new love
And still brightening and now shining
Than a star's first birth into conceiving space
On, on, and outward.
Upward climbing – a bright spark,
Out and still more far and climbing,
Far out into the chill and cold of space,
Far, far beyond the ancient golden warmths,
Then caught in other gravities, How cold and lone,
How far beyond the help and heat of deep remembering,
Is it for this we strive, and striving,
Forget the cold infinity of loneliness,
Only to be alone and in all space
In nothingness find nothing,
Endless, remembering the far warm gold.

Well, it seems that we may now have a good idea of who 'Pat' was, as the 'new love', although 'the ancient love' was still warm. Then, as I turned the pages of the book, these lines sprang to the eye:

Your sun of life goes flaming to its doom
Be thankful for it; think, you might have died,
Like common men who deal in pounds and stocks,
Poor sensual men who never come alive.

It was a good epitaph, on the death of a good CO.

19. The Italian Dambusters

> *"Great things are done when Men and Mountains meet."*
> **William Blake**

Montgomery wrote of this time:

> "The Allies in Italy held the initiative with well-established air forces. They would constitute a very serious threat to Germany in several directions: east into Austria, north into south Germany, and westwards into southern France. They could play on this and thus help OVERLORD."

One might have added to this: were the invasion across the Channel to fail – not a far-fetched scenario – then resuming the push up Italy and over the Alps would have been an alternative. But it would have been bloody, since Hitler would have shifted his divisions into the Italian north.

As mentioned already, Italy did not favour an attack from the south. The area in which the 8th Army was operating was poor and undeveloped with marshes on the coast and mountains up the centre. Rocky valleys flooded in winter, and the rivers ran across country and were major obstacles to the advance. The Germans did not fall back as expected; they fought in the heights below Rome and destroyed all communications to the south.

When the 8th Army reached the defensive line across the Biferno, Montgomery put his few landing craft to good use in hopping round by sea and turning the flank, while his main force attacked frontally. The rains took a hand; the Biferno rose to a height which prevented fording and the approach roads became a sea of glutinous mud in which tanks and vehicles stuck hard. The Italian "General Mud" had started to play a part.

450 Squadron were out and about and broke up an enemy attempt to counter-attack the 8th Army south of Termoli. They bombed from 500 feet and strafed everything that moved in a spectacular half-hour air-ground battle. The Army was more than pleased and congratulatory signals arrived. The "Harassers" were at it again. The Wing had also been asked to attack in Yugoslavia, and an increasing number of missions were directed there. Calls for aid came direct from the partisans and on one occasion the Wing sallied into German troops trying to land on the Peljasan peninsula – so successfully that the enemy gave up the attempt to land by sea.

The constant strafing on the Termoli 'hinge' (as it was designated) broke the German defences and they pulled out. Operational sorties rose over the hundred mark and the Wing was almost continually airborne and having to 'queue up' over targets. One of these was a petrol dump, from which flames rose very satisfactorily hundreds of feet into the air. "Whizzo prang, that…" remarked one of the newer pilots, but the desert veterans did not use such homeland RAF-ese – *quaieskateah* (very good) was more likely. The Kittys also acted as 'flying artillery' and were liable to descend with a whistle onto any recalcitrant strongpoint.

The armies moved steadily along and up over the mountains and the Wing operated over them as the weather permitted. We now had the Kittyhawk IV, which was lighter and could carry a heavier bomb-load – one 1000lb and two 500lb.

Of these Wing operations a Sangro River observer said:

> *"I watched the most fantastic and daring operations I have ever seen the R.A.F. perform. For scarcely a single minute was the sky clear of our planes. Waves of fighter-bombers swept in at zero feet, bombing and machine-gunning.*
>
> *Later I saw German prisoners coming down the long road through the valley. They were so weary, shell-sick and bomb*

dizzy that their faces were grey, their eyes bloodshot and their actions uncontrolled."

We were still operating from Foggia, but it had become congested with heavy bombers, which were uncomfortable bed-fellows for lighter aircraft, so we moved a few miles further forward to Milene, onto a farm. Back into tents for most of us, except those who took over a stable, which was spacious and had a large fireplace in which log fires blazed. They had many guests.

Others found a pigsty with its occupants present. The pigs were turfed out into other quarters by the farmer and their mess cleared away. The walls were scrubbed and some distemper found. Apart from the low headroom the new animals had a warm and dry snug. They had fewer guests than the stable but their main problem was the wits who passed, who tended to grunt and snort.

Not all operations from Milene went well. The pilots flew out on one occasion with two 1,000lb bombs on board – one under each wing. In normal circumstances the aircraft would probably use about 45 gallons of fuel an hour, which offered a range of about 800 miles and 4-4½ hours flying, but with this heavier bomb-load this time was probably reduced by an hour.

On one of the livelier occasions a squadron bombed a railway bridge, which was demolished, and did a little strafing on the way back. Fred's brakes jammed on landing and over the Kittyhawk went, tail over nose. In these circumstances, it was wise not to panic and release the safety belt – otherwise Fred could have dropped on his head and broken his neck. So Fred hung there on his straps and awaited deliverance. The fitter Flight Sergeant was able to grip Fred's shoulders, take the strain, and lower him to the ground. A case for a little restorative in the mess – for Flight, too! The aircraft was bent, but not a write-off and the redoubtable Frederick flew again.

In a report, 'Relation of the Mediterranean to Overlord' it was assessed that the Germans would attempt to hold both Allied Armies for as long, and as far south, as possible. If they had to retire they would fall back and defend strongly a line running east from Pisa, to

Rimini. Churchhill observed that the Allied offensive, "should be nourished and maintained until we had secured this line." We failed to see why we should not push on beyond it into the Alps and south Germany.

A word on the Italian peasant, the *gente di campagna*. The American 5th and British 8th had rather different attitudes to these "gentlemen of the country." The former shoved them out of the way and they stood by the road in forlorn and dispirited groups before returning to their wrecked homes to salvage anything that was left. The 8th Army treated them rather better and could be found fraternising with the families and children in the evening. They even assisted in reconstruction. The war meant little to the Italian peasants, who had been rolled over for centuries by one army or another. The one thing they were sure about was that whoever won, it wouldn't be them!

The Wing now put more organisation into its work for the two armies. This was "Rover David." In the desert the targeting had been in completely open and flat space. Here, it was more confined and mountainous. The Wing therefore adopted a forward mobile unit at Brigade HQ to be in direct radio contact with the aircraft. Both unit and pilots had photographs of the terrain bearing a fine reference grid by which targets could be identified. The squadrons then patrolled over the battlefield in line astern or "cab rank" as it came to be called. This developed procedure was a roaring success and later came to be adopted in Normandy and Burma.

Having complete control of the air, we now had sufficient elbow-room, to be given a respite – 'rest' (not leave) as it was called – on the 'Divine Coast' at Amalfi and Pozzuoli on the western shore. We registered ourselves for a few days away and departed in a Jeep. This was an occasion when we needed to cross the central mountains, and we twisted and turned on tortuous roads. There was more grass and trees here and usually a village perched on each hill. The Italians seemed to adopt hilltops for villages, churches, shrines – or at least, something. It was as if they wanted to diminish the scale of the landscape. Reaching the western coast, the sea lay below us and we started to descend at speed. This was the area where the Germans had "looked down the throats" of the Americans landing at Salerno. The views were magnificent as we plunged towards the sea, through small steep valleys and chasms showing outcrops of rock and many trees.

The sea below us was a deep azure and glinted as the sun reflected from many ripples in otherwise millpond water. We reached the coast road to Amalfi, with one corner after another, mile after mile, and walls protecting the Jeep from diving into the sea. Each corner presented a new scene and a constant succession of views. Many times we were too near the walls as the road corkscrewed its way towards and then through Majori, Minori and many other tiny villages of white cottages and houses, each bearing window boxes and small plots of flowers. There were orange and lemon groves – the latter being much bigger than we were accustomed to buying at home – throwing black shade across the road and gardens. The poplars did the same with foliage almost as dark as the shadows, putting a suggestion of death into the landscape. This was a scenic symphony of colour, sun and shade. It was startling to recall the butchery that had taken place just around the corner, at Salerno.

Amalfi itself was a glorious spot with hills dropping sheer to the sea and the town huddled in the bay, rising back into the fold of the hills behind. One of the hotels taken over was the "Luna Conventa", a conversion where we found ourselves in old monks' cells. The central cloisters of the hotel were dated about 1200 AD and it was a graded Italian building where nothing could be changed and little added. Large palms shaded the cloisters and the central well, with its goldfish, and the winter sun did not penetrate here. It was, after all, December. Bougainvillea hung over the walls and a lemon tree crouched in the corner. The hills around were topped with a sprinkle of snow but the weather near the sea was like an English summer and there were roses everywhere. Over dinner at night we listened to songs sung by a small Italian girl, maybe in her early teens, accompanied by her father, who simply boomed quietly across the mouth of a pot or gourd carried on his chest. As she sang, the lights dimmed lower into a complete blackout. Candles were brought in and the dinner became highly romantic – or would have been with female company.

I walked above Amalfi into the high village of Ravello, which was even more beautiful. It also had a striking record. I was taken aback to see two plaques in a church, one below the other. The top one was to a captain of the 1914-1918 war, killed in the vicinity. Below it was one of the same surname to a Flight Lieutenant 'son of the above' who had been killed here in 1943 – a strange coincidence.

Then there was Naples, which one supposedly saw and then died. The old tag was true except that airmen had only to smell Naples to pass out! The city stank with putrescence, simply because the sewers had been destroyed. Apart from this, it had also been well knocked about. The Germans had even taken the trouble to blow up the central post office, now one huge heap of stone, concrete and rubble; 140 people were killed there, we heard. Many children were in torn and dirty tents, wandering about aimlessly and enduring filth, pollution and sickness. Black-eyed ragazzi often accosted us with:

"You like my sister, Johnnie? Ver-r-ry clean…"

"*Cosa dice mai!* (You don't say) – but I think not, *grazie*."

The side streets – well postered 'Out of bounds: VD' – were the real heart of Naples. High buildings crushed together towered over narrow streets; the shadows were thick and dark and the solid stone underfoot was deep in rubbish and stank of urine.

In the distance the formidable cone of Vesuvius loomed darkly and heaved steam, gas and lava into the sky. We were not to know that on its own timescale, an eruption was imminent and that the mountain would 'blow its top' within a few weeks.

We got round to the female company lacking at Amalfi when we transferred for the second week to the *Terme Puteolone* at Pozzuoli. Here the hotel actually arranged evening dances which the local girls, with chaperones, attended in numbers. Around the girls, two cultures clashed. We would have danced with any girl, and preferably all of them, but the chaperones grimly regarded such freedom as licence. There was a serious possibility that too many dances with one young lady and one was on the way to being affianced. I managed to find

~ Under the Red Eagle ~

Giuseppina and a more willing chaperon. Giuseppina was vivacious, had striking dark eyes, even more notable dark eyebrows and a mane of jet-black hair. She must have been in her late teens, was extremely light on her feet and had a seraphic smile. We swung around the floor in high style and I made what conversation I could in fractured Italian and schoolboy French. The band pounded away with Italian rhythms and the lights were low. Thronged with pulsating couples, chaperones eyeing us from the walls, the temperature of the room rose. I perspired and she glowed. We abandoned the dance floor for a balcony overlooking the bay. There was a brilliant moon, quite full, pendulous in a sky of scintillating stars. A long highway of moon silver stretched away to the horizon. Suddenly I heard an Italian squawk and Giuseppina's mother descended on us with a crash. Her daughter was hauled away protesting, "No, no madre!" As she disappeared, she flung back over her shoulder "*E stato un godimento continuo*" which I grasped as something like "enjoyed every minute" ... Ah, well!

Vesuvius was a strenuous trip. About twenty of us chartered an old Italian bus, which got us about half way up the volcano before petering out and refusing to budge any further. We had some fitters with us, however, and they got her going again on most cylinders. The lower slopes of the volcano were farmed, but this gave way higher up to sparse grass and lava. The highest we managed was about five hundred feet below the crater with, perhaps, a mile of climbing to follow. It was stiff work over great folds of solidified lava, accompanied by smoke, rumbling, flame and red-hot lava. We arrived at the edge of the main crater and saw within it separate cones, erupting regularly about every two or three minutes, blasting glowing recrement into the air. There was a steep slope up to one of the small ejecting peaks – one minute up, a quick glance, and down again before the next eruption. At its edge I could look down into the sulphurous smoke. The colours ran through red, orange, yellow and white-hot, and the lava pool below bubbled evilly. A minute here to absorb what would be a lifetime memory, then back down quickly as Vesuvius vomited its next burst. We beat a retreat to the tiny vehicle far below. The bus started down well enough, even if we tore pieces off two farm carts that got in the way and neared, uncomfortably, a wall on a hairpin bend, seeming to loom over the very heart of Naples.

The full-scale eruption of Vesuvius three months later – in mid-March 1944 – would certainly give us pause for thought… Observers of what happened reported a distant roaring as if a massive beast were roaming the sky, which turned blood-red.

> "What looked like great clumps of fire were hurled into the air with giant orange sparks as Vesuvius spat fury and venom into the night sky. Bright streams of lava emerged from the slopes, bleeding down the volcano's flanks like giant stab wounds. A massive belly of cloud gathered over the top with the eruption as a low, growling, roar beneath it. There were louder sounds, like a great hoarse voice and a pillar of fire shot up from inside the cone, hurling itself towards the cloud and the terrible sky."

The war news in Italy was quite overshadowed by this natural disaster and a second eruption in the week spewed rivers of lava 150 feet wide and 40 feet deep over the villages on its flanks. In an Italian newspaper a boy of twelve years said: "Vesuvio made noise and smoke. Ashes were flying – not little ones but heavy like this" and he hefted his hand to show how heavy they were. "The wind blows ashes onto the roof and it burns. It was dark for two days. No sun. Just ashes."

❖ ❖ ❖

Next day we were back to our mud bath of a camp.
Montgomery reported to Mountbatten:

> "I shall be interested in the years to come to read the judgement of history on the campaign in Italy."

It was obvious that he thought the campaign had not received its due measure of honour at home. He said further that it had been vital to get to Rome before the weather broke, which could have been done easily. Now the armies and air force were faced with low cloud, rain, and mud. None could operate properly; the whole tempo of offensive operations had been cut down. The mud was quite frightful and no vehicle, wheeled or tracked, could move off the roads.

The severity of the Italian winter also came as rather a surprise to us, accustomed to home talk of "sunny Italy". But the locals had no illusions and emerged with fur caps and black woollen cloaks. Our desert gear, and even the blues, had to be replaced with flying or rubber boots, Syrian sheepskin or heavy coats, mufflers and leather waistcoats – for those who could persuade Stores to issue them.

The weather had broken up at the end of October 1943 and heavy rain became common. In an hour 2½ inches of rain could fall and water also came down from the mountain slopes into the small valley where our tents were pitched. Everything became completely waterlogged and mud was inches deep. The Wing vehicles had to stick to the road, otherwise they were into feet of "chocolate sauce".

The living conditions themselves became rougher. The tents were of 'bivouac' type and slept four. If the ground allowed we dug a hole below the tent and laid down rubber groundsheets. This 18 inch, or deeper, hole had been known to save lives when shrapnel or anti-personnel fragments whistled over the LG. Most had some kind of bed, usually a filched canvas one, or slept hard on the ground. A little trenching round the perimeter of the tent was also wise, so that rain cascading off the canvas would be carried away. If flooded, it was a case of hanging out everything to dry when the rain passed over, which it usually did in an hour or so. At night, if we were able to light the tent, it would be with a blackout in mind – shaded candles, hurricane lamps, or home-made lights of one kind and another.

Many felt trapped in the ugliness of the camp in winter. Trees without leaf, everything dun in colour, canvas marked and soiled and mud, mud, mud... The only escape was to leave camp on some business, which I was able to do from time to time, or climb into a Kittyhawk and rise away like a bird on the next operation. Even then, there were clouds, clouds, clouds.

~ Under the Red Eagle ~

We moved again, this time to a landing strip two hundred yards from the sea at Cutella below Pescara. We pitched a tent in a cobbled yard behind a house, with mallet and pickaxe, although what persistence and prescience caused us to choose and work that precise spot turned out to be curious.

It was the New Year of 1944. The sun went down behind gathering clouds and a bitterly cold wind rose from the north-east. I awoke suddenly about 03.30. The wind was now whining ferociously round the tent, which was shuddering violently with one collapsed side. It swayed and strained under an increasing crescendo of wind, even in this sheltered spot. I put down a hand and touched water. Where? Now fully awake, I lit the hurricane lamp and peered out to see the Scots Firs by the house bent in arcs against the wall. No question of further sleep, so I sat by the "Valor" and brewed up some hot liquids.

We had been fortunate, we realised, when we saw what had happened to the beach camp. Nearly all the tents were flat on the ground and even those partly standing were soaking wet and rent. Poles had snapped like matchsticks and personal possessions lost. All were haggard and drawn and the strip was deeply under seawater. Aircraft had broken their restrainers and had been overturned like toy models despite scores of airmen trying to hold down the mainplanes. Vehicles were down to their axles. The Wing was completely out of action. Chaos reigned.

It had been a freak Adriatic storm, one of the worst ever known in the district and certainly the hardest weather conditions that the Wing had ever experienced. Even the discomforts of the desert had been less arduous; at least it had been dry! Nevertheless, by midday all the vehicles had been dug out, the aircraft righted for repair, tents mended and repitched as far as possible, indents issued for more repair materials. It had been a Merry Christmas, perhaps, but not a Happy New Year. We even found that our capricious weather conditions had hit the press headlines at home.

At Cutella the order of battle changed when we took delivery of new Mustangs. The official figures were that these planes could achieve something like 430-440 mph at 25,000 feet and reach an operational ceiling of 42,000 feet. We thought these figures optimistic, but they were certainly an advance on what could be done with the Kittyhawk. The P-51 – as the Americans called it – turned out to be the best piston-engined fighter of the war, despite two faults. The first was the gunsight. It had protuding edges, on which it was not wise to bash one's face. The Kittyhawk had some protection against this. The second fault was that the brakes tended to overheat and could clench the wheel. The first fault was remedied by the inventive CO of 53 RSU, an ex-Flight Sergeant fitter of the desert, who removed the gunsights from the old Kittys and added a large rubber pad. This was fine. The second fault had finally to be eliminated by the manufacturer. But in spite of these oddities the Mustang was a lady to fly and the lucky pilots thought it "whizzo".

There were four Cutella incidents worth mentioning. The first was the epileptic. I happened to be standing on the dais in the Nissen Hut that served as the Mess, smoking a pipe and not thinking of very much. In front of me was a man I did not know well and he was swaying a little. Suddenly – thud! He had flung back both hands and neatly connected with the end of my pipe. I spat out the bits. My assailant promptly fell off the dais onto the floor, convulsing and shaking violently. The paroxysms intensified. The Orderly Officer for the day happened to be present and jumped forward with presence of mind, jamming a cloth into the man's open mouth.

"Lend a hand, lads – he's in an epileptic fit!" Exuberant helpers leapt forward. "Sit on him". They did so, and were flung off like flies. More volunteer sitters came forward. It finally took no less than fourteen men to hold him down. Then he collapsed into a coma and was borne away, foaming, to Sick Quarters. Later we were to learn that we should not have held him down as we did, but simply done something about his tongue, cover his head and let him work it out on the floor. Hindsight! Next day he seemed fine again and was a very apologetic – which his friends waved away – but an epileptic on active service?! Now all I needed was a new pipe…

The second episode involved two lads from the Orderly Room, who customarily walked along the railway line for exercise in the evening. They were returning under the moon when they saw someone lying across the track.

"Hello… he's a bit tight," said one to the other, "let's move him before a train comes down."

Unfortunately, the train had already come and gone.

When they got to the soldier there was no head to the body; it lay in the grass twelve feet away. The shoulders were a pool of blood. They contacted Sick Quarters and the body was removed. It turned out to be a member of the Pioneer Corps who, strangely enough, were going back to the UK. Perhaps that, in some way, was the reason for the suicide. The worst part of this for the two airmen was that they had actually greeted and spoken to the soldier, then sitting on the line, when they were setting out for their constitutional.

The sequel to this was pure black humour. The following morning's Duty Driver had a call to pick up some Italians for work on the railway. He duly jumped into the cab of the first three-tonner he saw, drove to Montenero, where he was to collect the Italians, and told them to jump aboard. One came to the driver and said there was someone asleep in the lorry. The driver squinted through the tailboard to see a figure lying on a stretcher covered with blankets. One of the Italians pulled back the covers to reveal a severed head and much blood, whereupon all the Italians "baled out" of the truck rather smartly, yelling *cadavere!* (corpse) and fled back to town. The shaken driver returned to camp. The Pioneers buried their comrade the following day.

The third incident was another accident. I found Sick Quarters, next to our billet, a hive of activity when I returned. A train coming through our station, where the medicals were based, had already picked up its "docket" and had travelled on without stopping. An Italian from the local village had panicked, since he wanted this station, and had jumped for it. He hit the platform, lost his balance, and fell between platform and train. The wheels passed over one arm and the axle boxes hit him one after the other. But he had some luck, since this happened only feet from Sick Quarters with the Senior Medical Officer attending. The arm had to be amputated but as his skull had been fractured no anaesthetic was used and it had to be morphine. His cries and screams were sickening. All his wounds were dressed and he was removed to Vasto in an ambulance, a white-sheeted and now silent figure. He survived and, long afterwards, came back to thank the medics.

The fourth incident was a coincidence or worse. There was a superstition among the pilots that if they were photographed with their aircraft they were bound to be killed. Darwen was so photographed at one time. Most of 5 SAAF squadron, for example, believed this absolutely, except for the CO, Major Bob Morrison, who posed in front of his bombed up machine, hand on propeller, and with a large grin. On 13.9.44 he was leading an attack in his Kitty, diving over Vergato. Ack-ack was seen to burst near his aircraft and he never pulled out of the dive. This, of course, did nothing to abate the superstition.

One night when I was on duty as Guard Commander, a wandering stranger turned up in the small hours. His odd uniform bore strange flashes (an astrolabe cap badge in white and silver) and he spoke a language unknown to me. I tried French, which he did not speak, fractured German, which he refused to speak, and some anglicised Italian, to which he did respond. He turned out to belong to 'Popski's Private Army.' This unit I had heard of, but never encountered, in the desert. Formally, they were No.1 Long-Range Demolition Squadron, which had created its own style of reconnaissance in North Africa. "Popski", properly Vladimir Peniakoff, was born in Belgium of Russian origin and had developed a taste and ability for desert navigation. He admired the British way of life and was in his late forties. His unit was over 100 strong and highly mobile, using Jeeps which carried heavy machine guns. British troops gave up the "Peniakoff" and as a joke made it "Popski." But the name "Popski's Private Army" was accepted by Middle East command – not all the Army wits were privates – and the unit had retained this personification ever since. Further south in Italy, Popski's major coup, dressed in khaki and passing himself off as an Italian, was to acquire the ration list of a complete and premier German Division!

~ Under the Red Eagle ~

I gathered from the visitor that they now co-operated with the Italian partisans, harried small German garrisons, and reconnoitred routes for the Allied armies. I found the incomer a bed and a meal. He wandered off north the following day. Why he was on the loose I never found out.

Montgomery departed from Italy in January 1944. His last message included this:

> "I am also very sad at parting from the Desert Air Force. This magnificent air striking force has fought with the 8th Army throughout the whole of the victorious progress; every soldier in this army is proud to acknowledge that the support of this strong and powerful air force has been a battle-winning factor of the first importance. We owe the Allied Air Forces in general, and the Desert Air Force in particular, a very great debt of gratitude."

Montgomery was succeeded by Lt-Gen Oliver Leese, who almost immediately received an addition to his 8th Army of the Polish Second Corps under Lt-Gen Anders. They were soon to play a vital part at Monte Cassino.

Leese's troops in the vicinity of Campobasso were being nightly "inconvenienced" by a large long-range gun mounted on a railway flat carriage. It fired at night and retreated during the day into a railway tunnel near Bolano. How to deal with this pest? In a tunnel?

Four 260 Squadron aircraft were detailed to liquidate the scourge by coming in at low level and "skipping" 500lb bombs with delayed fuses into the tunnel mouth. A complication was that the hill over the tunnel was 150 feet high, so a fast climb out was rather necessary. All four aircraft bombed from about 100 feet. The bombs were seen to bob into the tunnel mouth and others to bury themselves into the embankment. There was intense but luckily inaccurate flak and no aircraft was badly damaged, although they acquired a few holes.

The Army sent a congratulatory message reporting that they were no longer having sleepless nights. Later, on overrunning the spot, they found the tunnel entrance plugged and a huge hole in the hill. The gun was still there, impotent, together with a small tank engine locomotive which had bounced off its rails. A large section of the tunnel roof had caved in. The leader of this attack acquired a D.F.C.

At more or less the same time, both 260 and 3 Squadron Kittyhawks encountered six enemy aircraft and brought down two. Within the Wing, Mustangs were now fully replacing Kittyhawks and being greeted by the pilots with considerable enthusiasm. They practised on a target just off the beach with shaking concussions and shattering explosions, to the accompaniment of comments such as:

"Evens he doesn't make it."

"Yes, he did. Pay up."

A sudden reversion to desert days this morning; a black scorpion in my shoe. Evidently they are found as far north as the River Po. Ugh!

A strange story was relayed to us from a sister Wing on the west coast. Some Spitfires in the Anzio beachead were grounded for lack of spares. Three attempts were made to fly in a stock but in each case the aircraft crashed due to foul flying conditions and an uncertain surface. The Engineering specialist – a Flying Officer in rank who had never, in fact, flown – took off in a Spitfire, landed safely and serviced the aircraft on the spot. Alarm ensued at his Wing and he was hauled back pronto.

Having thus flouted all the Regulations he gathered together his engineering band and announced, "Flying a Spit is a doddle."

Opinion on 239 Wing was that he should get an immediate award.

Not so. A Court Martial now loomed. Later, in Administrative Routine Orders, we followed the further trail of the intrepid Engineering Officer:[7]

> "*Flying Officer --- of --- Squadron was on 15.3.44 found guilty by General Court Martial of:*

---

[7] The Engineer Officer in question was Greggs Farish of No.72 Squadron, whose amazing story is told in full in his book *Algiers to Anzio with 72 & 111 Squadrons* also published by Woodfield at £9.95.

(a) An act likely to cause damage to one of His Majesty's aircraft in that not being a qualified pilot he improperly and without authority took off and flew a Spitfire.

(b) Conduct to the prejudice of good order and Air Force Discipline he flew the same aircraft without authority contrary to K.R. and A.C.I. para. 693.

It seemed hardly necessary to split the charge between "taking off" and actually "flying"! In the event, he was sentenced to be severely reprimanded and to forfeit 12 months seniority as a Flying Officer. The finding and sentence were confirmed. We on 239 Wing still thought he should have got a decoration and wondered whether we could get him posted to us? We would promote him.

On 22 January 1944 the landing at Anzio, behind German lines, took place. This was "Operation Shingle." It was a near disaster. At first, the beaches had been found deserted since the Italians had been evacuated and the Germans had pulled out. The US commander, Lucas, ordained that the redoubt be strengthened before pushing on, as the British wanted to do, and in consequence gave the Germans time to hold down the bridgehead with reserves and artillery. Had Lucas pushed on, Kesselring might not have been able to stabilise the Anzio front and the chance was lost to slip into Rome and cut the German supply line.

In company with other Wings, 239 helped save the day by relieving the pressure on the troops and so enabled them finally to break out of the bridgehead.

A little mention of "friendly fire"… Everything was quiet at Cutella when there was a roar of aircraft coming down through a break in the clouds and the dry rattle of guns over the landing strip. Six Thunderbolts climbed away over the sea. We had been thoroughly strafed by an American squadron. Both ground staff and aircrew pelting for the slit trenches were blasted off the ground, riddled with bullets, and aircraft were set ablaze. This was a performance by 3425th Fighter Group (306th Wing) US Army Air Force.

~ Under the Red Eagle ~

It was alleged that the lead Captain's navigation was shaky and he thought he was fifty miles further forward than he actually was. There below him were the clipped wings of the Mustangs, which he mistook for Focke-Wulfs. It was a serious mistake because there was no other LG up the Adriatic coast that even resembled the two strips at Cutella. These were either side of the River Biferno and we had adopted the lower of the two. The LG was the usual metallic link strip with dispersals and tents next to the railway line. There were also Nissen huts, one being the mess. This should have shrieked RAF, but not to the Americans, apparently. Amongst others, they managed to kill the Warrant Officer of air/sea rescue, who had hauled many Americans out of the Adriatic. They also put bullets through the Operations Officer, killed a number of ground staff, fired the Operations Trailer, and shot up three aircraft.

The Australians on the Wing waxed particularly furious, saying, "Let's bomb up and pay 'em a return visit!"

We heard semi-officially that the American Air Force had been ordered in consequence not to bomb or strafe south of Pisa. Since that was well over 200 miles away, it was something of an implied criticism. Subsequently the colonel commanding the American Group heroically turned up at 239 Wing to apologise to Lt Col Wilmot, a tough South African, now commanding the Wing. While he was thus engaged some Wing comedians got busy with paint brushes. When the colonel emerged from Wilmot's tent he found several RAF roundels added to the row of swastikas on his machine!

Subsequently, in May 1944, there was an American Court Martial at Foggia where the Captain of the Thunderbolt squadron was standing trial. It was a very formal affair; he collected twenty years' imprisonment but was also told that he would be released at the end of the war.

The Wing anniversary was on 24th April 1944, so we thought up a concert, which I arranged, and decided to have a programme printed. This meant a trip back to Bari. Two of us made a fast trip to Foggia with lunch amongst some trees. Airmen usually avoid woods; crashing into one is about the last thing a pilot wants to do because the trees become like knives, cut the fuselage to ribbons, and probably the pilot as well. But here we were on our own, near the banks of a small river and with spring budding the trees. At the side of the water there had once been a small power station, now blown to pieces. The war had passed on. Then on to the south. The sea to our left was glassy, with small craft and occasional "Landing Ships Tank" making a passage along the coast.[8]

In Bari, I had a slight altercation with the Military Police. I had parked the 15-cwt in the centre of the town and on returning saw MPs climbing all over the truck, which had its engine racing. I stood back for a while, let them get on with it, and then approached.

"This truck," said they, "has not been immobilised."

I stood round some more. They failed to move it. The engine continued to race. Then I thought enough was enough and pulled the connecting rod for the accelerator from my stocking.

"I don't think you will move the vehicle without this chunk of metal." I said.

They had the grace to be good-humoured about it.

"All right Sir, you win."

We collected the anniversary programme, Wing crest in gold with underneath a list of "Foundation Members" still serving. A buffet menu was laid out – a good one – and then there was a cyclostyled insert "The First Book of the Twothreenyne" or "The Line from the Blue". Chapter One started with: *And the High Priests at the Ay Em said: "Let there be a Wing at Gambut in the midst of the sands and it was so.* This doggerel continued to the end, which was: *And the Erks of the Aitchkew the Twothreenyne and they that did bind them took counsel together and charged each other, saying: "We have dwelt together for two years and so what?" And a feast was arranged and there was much rejoicing.*

---

[8] For a fascinating account of the activities of these vessels in the Mediterranean and elsewhere read *This is My Story, This is My Song* by Raymond Oram, a RN coxswain who went on to command a LCT to Omaha Beach on D-Day. Woodfield £9.95.

I particularly liked the 'photograph' on the back page – again cyclostyled of course – which was a void expanse broken only with a horizontal line saying "sky" above it and "sand" below. The caption was: "The above photograph of Gambut, secured at enormous expense, is believed to be the only one 'taken from round a bend'.

The programme met with general approbation when we got back: copies would disappear all over the world.

In one of the most impressive feats of this campaign, on 5th May 1944, the Wing scored direct hits on the great Torre Dam, west of Pescara, well behind the German lines. This dam provided hydroelectric power for the railways and towns of Central Italy.

The object was to help along the attack on Rome which, although an "Open City", was a prime objective. It would disrupt the power system, and flood the Pescara valley down to the coast. This latter was particularly important since it would prevent the Germans making any substantial attack down the east coast to counter the drive on the capital, along the west coast. This Wing effort in fact released a number of Allied divisions to reinforce the drive on Rome, under the security of an Adriatic coast free from attack.

Three squadrons from 239 Wing were used, led by 260 Squadron and the Wing CO, Colonel Wilmot. They came in fairly high over the country to the south of the dam and released drops of 500lb and 1,000lb bombs. This was one of the biggest loads that Kittyhawks had attempted. The bombs arced down one after another as the aircraft completed their 60 degree dive, and smashed into the dam, raising huge spouts of water from the relatively small target. 260 Squadron then climbed fast to provide cover for the other two squadrons as they dived in. The briefing beforehand had insisted that only heavy underwater explosions had any chance of bursting the sluice gates so the need was to get the bombs as close to the dam wall as possible.

The two squadrons followed in line astern and most of the Kittyhawks managed to hit as designated to reinforce the strikes of the earlier bombers. Streams of ack-ack poured upwards. The gates tore away, opening a huge hole in the top of the dam, and a wall of water swept down the valley carrying houses, animals, trees and much other debris before it. By noon the following day the river west of the dam was virtually empty with no more than a thin stream of water trickling through the shattered sluice gates.

All pilots returned safely and there were high jinks in the Mess that night. They celebrated their "grandstand view" of a great bore of water flinging debris high in the air below them.

This mission of course recalled the 617 Squadron (RAF Lancaster) attack on the Moehne and Eder dams in the Reich twelve months before (Operation "Chastise"). The difference was that the bombs used here were straightforward 500 and 1,000 lb and not the "bouncing" 9,000 lb Barnes Wallis invention. Further, the Wing attack was with fewer and much lighter aircraft, although admittedly on one dam only. It was not a matter of level flight and bombing with special equipment.

It was probably natural that our professionals claimed theirs to be an at least equal undertaking, especially as it was carried out as a routine and not anticipated by special and specific training. Further, while there had been some doubt about the war-shortening effect of the Scampton dam-busting, there was none about the Pescara raid. It prevented a German counter-attack, freed the 8th Army to support the drive on Rome, and advanced the end of the war. Finally, no pilots were lost in Italy against eight out of nineteen aircraft missing and fifty-three aircrew killed in the German raid.

None of this diminished the sheer bravery of the Scampton mission but it came hard that the papers at home said virtually nothing about this second classic success.

It was truly a "wizard prang."

20. The Agony of Cassino

"The blood-dimmed tide is loosed."
W. B. Yeats
"Beyond is agony."
Greville

The Wing still played a vital part in dealing with enemy guns and had started carrying 1,000lb bombs, sometimes two of them. The Germans had heavy artillery on the hills beyond Monte Cassino and commanded the area through which the Allies were forced to bring supplies. Their guns were difficult to engage for the Allies because they had a range of 35,000 yards, whereas the Allies' range was 5,000 yards shorter, hence the crucial contribution of 239 Wing and other fighter-bombers in acting as "flying artillery" and "keeping the Germans' heads down."

On 11th May 1944 the 8th Army Spring Offensive opened with a tremendous barrage of 1,000 guns. The 5th Army also went into action on the west side of the mountains. On their right flank were the Polish and British XIII Corps. The former circled to the left to attack Cassino while the Corps crossed the Rapido River. A French and Canadian Corps drove towards the Liri River. 239 Wing was in the middle of this attack and was assisted by the Spitfires of 285 Wing, which not only undertook reconnoitring but also led the 239 squadrons into the attack and distinguished some targets for them. The push forward was successful and the 'Gustav' Line was hamstrung, as was the 'Dora' Line close behind.

The Germans backed off towards Rome along Highway 6, the Frosinone and Terracina road and came under further Wing attack, both from 239 and 285. Over one hundred vehicles were destroyed and columns of fire and black smoke rose from Highway 6 for miles.

On 18th May the Poles finally climbed to Monte Cassino and raised their red and white flag above a landscape littered with corpses and across which, as in Flanders many years previously, blew the red poppy petals of spring. They extricated a handful of wounded Germans from the piles of stone and rubble. The monastery as such had ceased to exist.

The convoys now in full flight were bombed and bombed again. It was a famous, if bloody, victory. Two weeks later the Anzio beachhead troops broke out and linked up with the Cassino victors.

As we approached what had been the Italian country town of Cassino signs of the fierce fighting multiplied – defoliated trees looking like a madman's view of hell, thousands of bomb craters overlapping one another, shattered and burnt-out German transport and tanks, and awe-inspiring ruins with something of an obscene quality about them. In front rose Monastery Hill, which looked as though it had never known grass or trees and was smothered in piles of rubble. There were no town street scenes here, simply because there was no town. So intense had been the bombardment that if this bastion of the Gustav Line were to be reconstructed, deeply buried mines could explode fifty or so years hence.

To our right lay the smaller but precipitous Castle Hill, also a shambles. We looked over the desolate scene, which replicated the mud and slime of trench scenes in the Great War, with some understanding of the holocaust that had howled over it. All that was left were a few bricks loosely piled and earth that had been churned into a morass. Over the whole hung the unmistakable, sickly-sweet, odour of putrefying flesh from the unburied bodies in the refuse, debris, and trash, where it was as yet too dangerous to dig them out for decent burial. There was also the pungent smell of human urine and faeces, and the acrid perfume of smoke-shells and cordite. These had rained down without compassion on ruins and hidden soldiers and civilians alike; the civilians had fled long ago, had been expelled, or were dead. The area had been so heavily mined, and was in such a state, that I was moved to comment at the time: 'I would not be surprised if the Italian Government, when it again gets a grip, decides to leave this area as it is. It will need somehow to be defused, or straggling and curious strangers and seekers after souvenirs will probably be blown into gory shreds'.

The fighting here had certainly been severe – but a stronger word than severe was required; nauseating, perhaps? Only our fighter-bombers had been able to get through under the frequent overcast until the heavy bombers found a break in the clouds and effectively pounded Monte Cassino to bits.

We recalled that two months before, in the March of the year, the Ghurkhas and New Zealanders had encountered an already chaotic battlefield. It had been so bad as to face them with a major obstacle – even tanks could not penetrate Cassino at all, had to halt on the outskirts and leave the infantry to its own devices. Those men had to fight for yards of ground, as in the Great War. That tanks failed to support infantry was a highly unusual state of affairs.

When we as a Wing were engaged at Cassino, in May, the battle line came off the west coast at Argento, about 50 miles north of Naples, then zig-zagged across the country to Cassino, then went roughly north to Castel di Sangro and Villa San Maria, and finally curved round to Civitella and on to the east coast at Ortona. 239 Wing, then at Cutella, would have been about 25 miles south of that eastern flank. Very near the battlefront, in fact.

Now here we were in the centre of Cassino, or what might have been the centre. We looked across a stinking quagmire, dirty yellowish-green under the slime of stagnant water. It would be plagued with mosquitoes. The ruins of the Benedictine Abbey stood above us on the top of the hill but were nothing more than a few shattered walls. This had in fact been an advantage to the Germans, who could shelter under and behind all this near scoriae and debris.

Written to describe the sheer hell of the trenches in the Great War, Siegfried Sassoon's description fitted Cassino just as well

"The place was rotten with dead; green clumsy legs

> *High-booted, sprawled and grovelled along the saps;*
> *And trunks, face downward, in the sucking mud,*
> *Wallowed like trodden sandbags, loosely filled;*
> *And naked sodden buttocks, mats of hair,*
> *Bulged, clothed heads slept in the plastering slime."*

An older Army officer, who had seen something of the Great War, concurred that it was "Passchendale all over again."

Apparently, before the Allied invasion of Italy a joint staff exercise of the German and Italian High Commands had concluded that Cassino was impregnable. It did not prove to be so, but it had been a Herculean task to liberate it. All that was left was now a stricken place, no longer on the map. As one official Administrative Officer bitterly observed, "There's nothing here left to administer."

21. The Holy City

> *"Hurry, we burn for Rome so near us,*
> *for the phoenix moment."*
> **Cecil Day-Lewis**

We attacked towards Rome and the 'Gustav' and 'Hitler' Lines. The Wing was called together and the plan outlined. An opening barrage was to commence from 1,100 guns laying down 65,000 shells. The Spring Offensive had begun. There was to be a three-pronged drive: the Russians had lunged forward two days ago, we were headed for Rome and the Channel invasion could not be far off.

At 23.00 hrs exactly the first glow in the sky came from the west and north but the guns were too far away to be audible. The initial glow strengthened into a flickering halo. The Poles swung to the left to attack Cassino from the north-west while the British XIII Corps pushed across the Rapido River, and the French and Canadian Corps shoved northwards from a bridgehead over the River Garigliano. 239 Wing were on "Cab Rank" duties above the battlefield, covered by Spitfires of 285 Wing. The enemy guns were either damaged and put out of action or simply blown to bits by direct hits. Four congratulatory signals from Army Command.

The Gustav Line was breached, and so was the Hitler Line, hastily renamed 'Dora'. The Germans fell back along Highway 6 to Rome, again under constant Wing attack.

From San Angelo a squadron departed on an armed recce. How the information came in is not clear, probably Italian, but the evidence for the mission was that a convoy near Frosinone included a high-ranking German Officer en route to Cassino to take over its defence.

~ Under the Red Eagle ~

Our lead pilot put the flight into close line abreast and one by one they dropped down to 2,000 feet and let go their bombs. Then they strafed the convoy low on the deck and turned into the sun. No. 2 aircraft called up the leader and said they had missed the general's car, so all curved round into another strafing run with guns chattering and flaming. This wasn't the cleverest thing to do. Training says, "Don't go round again in case the guns are waiting for your next run." They ignored this and even went round for a third run. The worth of the training caution then became apparent as the leader was shot to pieces, although he had by that time reduced the general's staff car to a flaming pile of metal.

The lead pilot failed to get back to the LG and crashed, severely wounded, behind the British lines. It was England, home and glory, for him, but he had survived. The general, we think, did not.

Up and down Highway 6 the Wing went, tossing down bombs and shells. We had casualties. Planes returned damaged and crashed across the landing ground. A Mustang did so carrying a bomb, which burst and tore into shreds much of the thin metal runway strips. The pilot got away with it but with badly burned hands and fingers blown away. I happened to be in Sick Quarters when he was brought in, bandaged with field dressings and black with burns. He had an immediate blood transfusion and was sent back to Termoli with two Medical Officers. While all this was going on, three Ju88s dived on the Wing from the air, so we dug ourselves in even deeper, anticipating trouble around the strip.

We needed to get closer to the forward troops and therefore moved west. The signal was sudden and so was the move. I drove as leader of a convoy of some hundred vehicles. We climbed steadily into the Appenines through green fields and waving corn humming with insects and looked back to an Adriatic blue with haze. Heavy bomber formations bellowed over us and then the insect hum was resumed.

We set camp about 15.00 hrs, having found "A" party in residence on a hillside amongst the vines. This was San Angelo, in a shallow valley glorious in the sun. Squadrons and strip were down in the valley by the river. An Italian town crouched high on the hilltop above.

On this move, as on others, we passed through towns where the locals thronged the streets and waved us through with cheers. You would have thought us liberators, which we were in a way, I suppose. Children waved flags – where on earth did they get the Union Jacks? – and girls rushed forward to kiss us, which was very well received by us. The older people tended to shout *"Guardi il RAF!"*

On another note, we even 'thumbed' trains if we had any distance to travel and the rail was convenient. They carried everything – in one that I was on, the first carriage was full of corpses being transferred to war cemeteries. Most towns were at last recovering now the battlefront had passed and they looked less desolate than they did when we first passed through. I often wondered where all the civilians disappeared to when we entered these towns and it now appeared that they "went to earth" ahead of the fighting. Then they returned to find the hated field-grey replaced by khaki and – in celebration – shoved up all the prices! Inflation appeared: the lira was 95/£ before the war, now it was 400/£.

The sun was getting higher now and we began to see where "Sunny Italy" came from. There were continuous missions from this LG and the German front appeared to have collapsed. We had connected with the Anzio bridgehead and the Allied armies were pushing along the west coast with a bomb line on the Tiber. There was a race for Rome: we were driving north and we heard that a Panzer Division was coming south to hold Rome. All pilots reported flamer after flamer on the roads and were exuberant with the chase. Prisoners so far numbered 9,000.

There was a heroic exploit when Flight Sergeant Casson of 250 Squadron, already crippled in all four limbs, was hit again with cannon fire by a shell penetrating the cockpit. He radioed: "My leg has been pretty well shot off." This statement was so calm that Operations thought he was referring to his undercarriage and warned the crash crews on the strip. He brought back his aircraft, could not crash-land due to lack of rudder control, circled three times because Kittyhawks were lining the runway for take-off, and finally touched down perfectly. The plane then slewed violently across the strip and he was unconscious when the ground crew got to him. Despite blood transfusions from three of his squadron, he died at about 16.00 hours. The Medical Officer called the flight "a miracle of courage". The "leg" nearly amputated was his own, not the Kitty's. Immediate award of the Conspicuous Gallantry Medal. A brave man.

The Germans were still pulling back. One morning No.3 RAAF Squadron found a big convoy of 200 lorries, pranged its head, middle and tail and then flew back to give the position. 239 flights then attacked all morning and by noon there were sixty blazing vehicles with a pall of smoke rising to 9,000 feet. The day ended with some 170 lorries destroyed and littering the enemy back areas.

Yesterday, Trinity Sunday, the forward troops crossed the Tiber at sunset. Mobile columns drove straight through Rome and on north after a retreating enemy.

Two days later, 6th June 1944, we picked up a major report from the German news that the Channel invasion had commenced, with airborne troops having landed along the Seine. There was some hesitation at accepting this news from such a source, because we had waited so long for it. But they should have known!

So we crossed the Rubicon and entered Rome – the first Continental capital to fall – and did so before the Channel invasion! In years to come that may well be forgotten. Rome had been declared an 'open city' and Jerry evacuated in such a hurry that he left eleven bridges across the Tiber intact and 25,000 of his wounded lying in the hospitals. As Rome was entered by the Allies, church bells rang. People emerged from cellars, nervous at first, but then, realising that the Germans had gone, became bolder and pressed on the troops kisses, roses and wine. The Allies made a near royal progress through the streets and the rapturous attentions became embarrassing. One kiss was welcome but a score a bit too lavish. Italian, British and American flags were produced. Business came to a complete standstill. The whole moved into a crescendo of wild enthusiasm. *Urrah! Evviva! Viva!*

~ Under the Red Eagle ~

When we entered Rome ourselves the racket was still going on. We abandoned our military role and became tourists for a short while. One of the first buildings that could hardly be overlooked was the enormous and ostentatious monument to King Victor Emmanuel II, of white stone surmounted by bronze eagles and heavy decoration. The monument also housed the tomb of the Italian 'Unknown Soldier'. On to Piazza Colonna and the special balcony from which Mussolini had raved; it now sported an ironic Stars and Stripes and was the Allied Administrative Control for the city. Outside was one huge car park, jammed with Jeeps and Staff Cars. We retired into the maze of small streets bordering the Tiber, which flowed between high stone embankments lined with trees throwing a very welcome shade. The dome of St Peter's was silver against a deep blue sky.

The cathedral was obviously next, up an approach thronged with civilians and uniforms of many kinds. It was at least imposing, with fountains dancing in front of huge grey stone. This was technically neutral territory, the first I had stood upon in all these years. It was something apart, inviolable.

A Swiss Guard passed in his many colours and we entered St Peter's itself. The walls carried immense murals in what we at first thought were oils, but later found to be mosaics, with heavy bronze gateways indicating side chapels. Antaeus-like marble figures by Michelangelo, Bernini and others imposed in a powerful calm. In many Italian religious houses we had received impressions of tinsel and rather tawdry decoration. Not here. The effect was one of a huge artistic creation, evolved over centuries. Two cherubs of marble flanked the pillars at the entrance, seeming to be about four or five feet high, but were in fact four times life size, dwarfed by the proportions of the cathedral interior.

The High Altar, far away, rose over St Peter's tomb below. Four huge bronze pillars, each weighing many tons, supported a wood and bronze canopy and were matched by large marble figures – one by Bernini having a stone drapery that appeared to float in the air.

Smaller things were also impressive:

- the toes of the bronze statue of St Peter, worn away by the lips of the faithful;
- the golden throne;
- the richest chapel of all, to the Holy Sacrament;
- the translucent stained glass carrying a dove seeming to hover in a golden halo;
- people the size of ants in the gallery.

All this was a very different aestheticism to the rubble of the Monastery at Cassino, a relatively few miles away.

We even had an audience with the Pope, although it has to be admitted that there were some 6,000 or so others, all crowding the square before the cathedral. A small white figure on a far-off balcony said something unintelligible and waved a tiny arm in blessing.

I also attended another ceremony in Rome – that of my confirmation into the Church of England. I had no idea who the bishop was but it was at least interesting to adopt a protestant faith, in war, at the very centre of Roman Catholicism.

We went into Rome again, a day or two later, with the 15 cwt and made a more thorough tour, adding the Colosseum, Castle of St Angelo and the Catacombs. In the last, our guide was enthralled with his subject and dragged us through many underground corridors stale from the centuries and cold from the damp air. Here the early martyrs were entombed and occasionally their crumbling bones, now yellow dust, lay exposed to view.

In one of our shortest journeys, we moved into Guidonia just outside Rome. Taking over two sides of the main square we had one for the HQ and canteens and the other for the Officers' Mess. Guidonia was a full-scale aerodrome and we passed relics of aircraft, both experimental and antique. In addition, it was rumoured that there was an Italian jet somewhere around but we never found it. The administrative buildings and hangers no longer existed.

We had hardly been in the place an hour when the local police turned up. When the Italian finally got translated it appeared that there was a pocket of Germans nearby. The police gesticulated wildly and with alarm, so we passed the report to the RAF Regiment "for information and necessary action."

Browsing around, we found some offices full of Fascisti records of local Italians, spread all over the floor and with files upturned. We thought we might do some good to our new Italian allies, and for any unfortunates in the records, and burnt the lot in the centre of the floor. We needed a run back to Caserta Palace, the HQ for the Allies. It had the air of being an attempt to outdo Versailles. Impressive as it was – scores of large staircases, park, gardens, waterfalls and lakes – it failed somehow. It was formerly the palace of the King of Naples and, for the English, the place where Nelson used to meet Lady Hamilton.

It had a striking approach through thickly foliaged trees and one came on the palace suddenly. Every doorway had a heavy guard – American or British MPs and Italian *carabinieri* and military. Its 1,200 rooms were reached off corridors stretching away into the distance and we clattered over marble floors worked in different colours and textures. The ceilings bore oils and delicate paint and plaster. Door after door announced "Finance", "Military Intelligence", "ATS only", "Command Accountant" and a hundred others. Salutes everywhere. I was astonished to find that high-ranking officers were so numerous as to have the messes divided – one for Group Captains and below and another for Air Commodores and above. This was at least unusual and probably unique in the RAF.

Caserta was now so far behind the lines that it had become known jokingly as "Hind Quarters".

While at the palace, I picked up a story that one of these Air ranking officers, a little in his cups, rolled down one of the many staircases flanked by statues of various mythical figures and was attracted to one stone lady who seized his attention. He tickled her under the armpit observing the while "itchycoo" – whereupon she swayed gracefully and crashed down the stairs in fragments. The statue happened to be very valuable and the Italian government was not amused. What then happened to the officer concerned was not available to me. I relayed this anecdote to the Wing on my return, amidst much hilarity. Probably apocryphal.

~ Under the Red Eagle ~

Three domestic points around the camp:

The first was that Italy had cheered up after the grim winter months. The tent flap was open and small white cumulus clouds flitted across an intensely blue sky. Nevertheless, we just had one of the fleeting summer storms and the ground was soggy. Wisps of water vapour rose away from the canvas of the tents and evaporated as they drifted upwards. Around the camp ground staff and aircrew mopped up and removed bedding to dry on the olive trees. The tent skirts were raised to let through the soft breeze, and the occupants sat on the stones and lit fags.

Secondly, I arranged a personal shower for myself, consisting of a petrol tin with a hole punched in the bottom and a plug that could be pulled out for a sluice. I had hung it in one of the olive trees with which we were surrounded. On this morning, I had been well drenched with water – without, of course, having a stitch on – when to my unease I saw two Italian women walking down the avenue between the olives, chatting vociferously. It was too late to duck and my towel was in the tree. They spotted me and merely said *"Buongiorno signor Capitano."* They did not break their chat and passed on. Well… at least they got the sex right.

Thirdly, we came across another form of domestic laundry near the camp. A petrol tin or old oil drum, well scrubbed, was filled with water and the farm fire raked out for some wood ash. This was dropped into a cloth hung over the top of the container drooping just below the water level, so that the ash was submerged. The clothes for washing were already in the container. The whole was left overnight and the clothes wrung out, rinsed, and hung out to dry. Something in the wood ash did the cleaning, it appeared. This seemed to revert to Italian tribal technology, but it got the clothes clean all right.

To complete this chapter in and around the Holy City I have to record an ugly story that reached the 239 Wing Operations Room. If we had any doubts as to why we were here, this report stilled them. It appeared that about 2 months previously an SS police column marching through a street in Rome was attacked by the Italian Resistance. Over 30 of the police were killed and many more injured.

~ Under the Red Eagle ~

The centre of the explosion was a large bomb placed in a refuse truck, parked near the marching route of the police. It savaged them into bloody remnants with body parts lying around the narrow street. It was a murderous blow.

Apparently, a reprisal was ordered by Hitler, at first for 50 Italians to be executed for every dead German, later reduced to 10. The order was carried out by an SS Commandant and his troops shot well over 300 civilians in a quarry south of Rome, leaving the bodies piled in the tunnels with the entrances blown in. There was no indication that the Pope intervened, which one might have expected. The method of execution was brutal. The men were made to kneel, then shot in the back of the head. The subsequent closure of the caves by explosive created a sepulchre. It was the ultimate Nazi perversion. It was small wonder that this did not remain a secret – perhaps the Germans did not want it to, to act as a deterrent. Rome soon knew about the atrocity and it filtered back to us.

The 239 pilots heard this story in a powerful silence. At the next mission, two squadrons took off to wreak a little vengeance on somebody. While it was true that the Italians fought us in the desert and Sicily, they were never regarded as the primary enemy – Hitler and the Nazis were that – and in any case the men butchered in the caves were civilians with only a few military among them.

The squadrons flew to the area north of Rome, through which the Germans were retreating. They found a substantial convoy dragging its way up a mountain slope with recognisable SS emblems on the sides. The CO flew in first and hit the roadside with his bomb, directly beside a truck which promptly overturned and burst into flames. This effectively blocked any convoy attempt to escape and all the vehicles ground to a halt, one behind the other. The squadrons dropped their remaining bombs along this jam and then raked and strafed it from end to end. It was now in a real panic and fires burst out along the column and threw high pillars of black smoke towards the Kittyhawks and Mustangs.

~ Under the Red Eagle ~

This was highly satisfactory psychologically, if not a true revenge on the perpetrators of the massacre in the Ardeatine caves. However, sins of commission had at least been visited on some of the SS.

As Bacon said: "Revenge is a kind of wild justice."

22. The D-Day Dodgers

"It's north you may run to the rime-ringed sun."
Kipling

Alexander had fought this campaign with a minimum of troops, airmen and resources. Now that the Normandy landings had begun, however, the number of German divisions held down here had reached about twenty-six and this would continue throughout this summer of 1944. This was a vital stalemate that could otherwise have engulfed the main effort in Normandy. Kesselring, it appeared, envisaged a steady withdrawal to the Pisa-Rimini Line, named the 'Gothic' and later the 'Green' Line. Hitler had other views, having a low opinion of the Line's resistance capacity, and wanted a stand to bring the Allies to a halt further south. Our assessment was the same as Kesselring's – that the Germans had little choice but to fall back on the 'Gothic'.

This evening had brought a storm after a sultry day, during which we could feel a gale building up. The vines waved in a stiff breeze and I had to chase papers frisking through the tent. Wheat and barley ripened around us, with many poppies, much like the Flanders of the Great War, again. An Italian came over to the tent and handed me some cherries. Why, I had no idea, except that I had been at his farm earlier in the day, paying his wife my dues for the washing. The locals were friendly and I had the impression that the belief that they had been strongly behind Mussolini was nonsense. All this good feeling did not, of course, prevent them giving us a little rooking if possible. But we were a match for them, having dealt with much tougher vendors – the Arabs. The real problem in prices stemmed from the

Americans, who seemed to have so much spare cash that prices soared to about six times what they should have been.

Another move – this time north-east of Rome to a landing strip at Falerium. Our operating sites had certainly varied. In four moves they were beach, mountain valley, airfield, and open country.

I should record the presence of 'Fanny' on the Wing, a bitch Mastiff. She was white, tinted black round the nose, and with drooping but pointed ears. One of the squadrons also had 'Prince', an Alsatian. The result duly arrived – ten puppies, of which Fanny rolled on one. She was very proud, prepared to have visitors, and was housed in a roughly-made kennel. All these pups were 'booked' by prospective owners on the Wing. There would be Alsatian-Mastiffs all over the place. The dogs recognised khaki drill and were amiable but did not approve anyone in civilian clothes. They got very attached to their unit. The Air Ministry actually laid down, would one believe, an 'establishment' for dogs that put them 'on the ration strength'.

While mentioning mascots, I should refer to Italian folklore. They apparently believe in the "evil eye" and touching metal was recommended because that was associated with magnetism, which can absorb evil powers. If no iron were available, then a man grasped his testicles. Hmmm… Garlic was also well approved and a little may be carried in the pocket or strung around the neck. Then there was worth in a piece of onion, a saint's picture, a necklace of pigs' teeth or a goat's horn. What these actually protected against I had no idea. Vampires probably! Finally, if you encounter an evil one with the 'eye', then piss on the ground where he, she or it stood. It was allegedly powerful counter-magic!

We were not long at Falerium and moved quickly to Creti, north of Lake Trasimeno, where Hannibal fought a great battle in 217 AD. Now another two armies, bigger and more ferocious, were locked together over the same ground. Not a road, and hardly a building, had escaped damage. This was very much an "engineer's war" since the Germans blew up everything in order to hinder the Allied advance while our own sappers struggled to reinstate the bridges for the armour to get through. They had plenty to do since the whole country was veined with rivers and streams.

Before we moved here, one of the Wing Officers came in and remarked mysteriously that he had heard some big news that was secret. But he could not contain it and revealed that we were to move to Crete. Crete? What on earth would a "close support" Wing do there? I was grinningly passed a note, at which I laughed.

"You've got the wrong end of the stick. It's an LG near the village of Creti, not the island!"

The rumour-monger looked sheepish and departed. It showed how easily "duff gen" could be created!

The same night I was Guard Commander. There was a continuous roll of artillery and the hum of night fighters. Another barrage was laying down some HE in front of the Guards, so we had a front seat.

A few hours later, I disbanded the guard and we left for Creti. We were to be last away on this occasion since the 15 cwt was on other MT duty and it was not returned until immediately before the move at 06.00. The vehicle was a mess – oil at "danger", no petrol or water, air intake missing and a plug lead detached. So much for MT servicing! I ought to have put someone on a charge except that I had no idea who had been doing the driving. Luckily, I knew the route and after some attention the 15 cwt and I headed towards Viterbo along the eastern side of Lake Trasimeno. The water lay in a saucer in the hills so there was a stiff climb with glorious views to the west. Viterbo turned out to be a litter of burned-out MT and tanks. On into Orvieto, one of the classical Italian towns. Tortured railway lines arched over a broken bridge where coaches had plunged nose first into the river bed. The station was useless – overturned carriages and deep craters making the place look like a honeycomb. Nearby there appeared to be some German MT under the trees. It was transport all right, but the trees had not been adequate camouflage: the vehicles had been swept from end to end with fire and were mere shells. The whole area had suffered a 239 Wing attack. Hoist by our own petard!

Hills and wooded country followed but I could not pay attention to much of it, being more concerned with meeting wild truck drivers, usually Indian or Negro, thundering towards me with the apparent object of sweeping aside all oncoming traffic.

Finally we got to Creti and found ourselves under the German guns. The units around the LG, including 244 Wing, were being heavily shelled so we hurriedly dug slit trenches and camouflaged the tents by slinging green paint over them and draping some artistic netting. It seemed to do little except make them stand out like sore thumbs – from the deck, anyway. Perhaps it was better from the air? We hoped so! The Wing had an enduring tradition of moving well forward, on occasions being so far in advance that we were ahead of the front line. So having shells laid down on us was nothing new.

❖ ❖ ❖

Humour was always rife. This time the Church of England Padre was the butt. He came in early, rather distracted. He had visited an Italian barber and had humorously indicated his thinning crown and said, *"Simile Francescano",* meaning that he was losing so much hair that he was beginning to, look like a Franciscan. "*Si, si?*" said the barber, looking surprised. Padre dozed in the chair while the barber performed and was then passed a mirror. The barber had removed all the crown hair, under the impression that a tonsure was what his customer required. Padre walked the camp under knowing grins and hoped that his hair would grow again soon. The Roman Catholic Padre, already informed, met Padre in the Mess and chuckled.

"I am so pleased, Arthur!"

I was Guard Commander again and wrote a diary note in the small hours, with a bottle of wine. This was eastern Tuscany, so we were very near, if not in, Chianti country, hence the bottle. This red wine matured on the limestone of the hills and came from grapes nourished by the valley heat. The bottle had a black cock on the neck, which made it true Chianti. Anything else was red Tuscan wine – not bad, but not Chianti.

53 Repair and Salvage had ceased to be a separate unit and had been merged into a greatly enlarged Wing HQ. That put them under me. This was apparently in conformity with a general policy to abol-

ish single-engine aircraft RSUs and absorb them into a higher formation. This roughly doubled the Wing personnel, adding 136 airmen. There was much redisposition like this as we approached the Po valley. New Wings were formed, to which we lost experienced men. At the Po, we still didn't know whether we would turn east, west, or go straight on. Hitler, apparently, had no illusions about this threat from south of the Alps. At the worst of the fighting in France he dispatched into Italy no less than seven divisions withdrawn from the west, and even the east, to reinforce his Army Group "C" in front of us. On top of that came a battalion of Tiger tanks and three divisions from Germany itself. A compliment in its way, but clearly things would get rough.

At the beginning of June 1944 Kesselring envisaged withdrawal to the 'Gothic' Line although Hitler had doubts and wanted a stand at the 'Caesar' Line, which ran a little south of Rome across to Pescara on the Adriatic coast. The order was that the former line should be the final defensive boundary, since this was the only point at which the Allies could be prevented from breaking into the Po Valley with, for the Germans, alarming consequences. Hitler further ordered that any idea prevalent in Army Group 'C' that there was a fortified defence system behind them, running across the Appenines, should be eradicated. Therefore the name 'Gothic', which might be misleading, should be changed to 'Green'. Since the most southerly lines had already been overrun, Kesselring had himself to order that the Allies be brought to a halt on the central 'Albert' Line. But this proved to be a false hope and he finally had to fall back on the Gothic Line. All these different lines were confusing unless the airman was concerned with strategy or tactics, but they were critical in their time. From Cassino north they would be:

Gustav	Cassino NNE to Ortona
Caesar	NE to Pescara
Albert	Castiglione ENE to Ancona
Gothic/Green	La Spezia E to Pesaro
Genghis Khan	Bologna to Lake Comachio
Venetian or Blue	Lake Garda ESE to Chioggia

~ Under the Red Eagle ~

There was a notable attack one morning with our squadrons being sent off on a special mission to reduce an enemy HQ. They were led by Lt Col Baker, a South African. Over the target, low cloud obscured it completely, so Baker ordered the squadrons back and decided to risk the cloud base himself. He was able to pinpoint two road junctions through cloud breaks and estimate the target position. He then dived through the murk, passed through its base at 500 feet and released three 500lb bombs. They scored on the target and we awaited Army confirmation with interest. Quite a feat.

On 20th July we heard that von Stauffenberg had planted a bomb under a table near Hitler in the 'Wolf's Lair'. It had failed to kill Hitler, who was only wounded and able to meet Mussolini that same afternoon. Mussolini was elated, it appeared, since this plot against Hitler was much like the way that Italian monarchists had plotted against him. "We no longer have a monopoly of treachery!" he said.

There is a final song to record, which ran to the tune of "Lili Marlene". It had always been believed in Italy that Lady Astor MP had referred to the 8th Army and Desert Air Force as the "D-Day Dodgers." She was also alleged to have said in Parliament that all who had served in the east should wear a yellow arm band on the ground that they might have been infected with unmentionable diseases.

One should have doubts whether this could be true and it may well be unjust. It was hardly the thing that one expected to be vented in the House of Commons. An alternative explanation offered was that some unit had written to her on a service matter and signed themselves in that way. So she replied in the same vein. The "yellow armband" remark seems even more unlikely. Lady A was no fool.

Whatever the truth, this song resounded in the messes of the 8th Army and Desert Air Force;

*"We are the D-Day Dodgers, out in Italy,
Always on the vino, always on the spree,
Eighth Army skivers and their tanks,
We go to war in ties like swanks,
For we are the D-Day Dodgers, in sunny Italy.*

~ Under the Red Eagle ~

Landed at Salerno, a holiday with pay,
Jerry brought his bands out to cheer us on our way...
Showed us the sights and gave us tea,
We all sang songs, the beer was free,
For we are the D-Day Dodgers, the lads that D-Day dodged,

Salerno and Cassino were taken in our stride,
Did not go to fight there, we just went for the ride,
Anzio and Sangro are just names. We only went to look for dames,
For we are the D-Day Dodgers, in sunny Italy.

Our way to Florence we had a lovely time,
We drove a 'bus from Rimini right through the Gothic Line,
Then to Bologna we did go, and went bathing, in the Po,
For we are the D-Day Dodgers, the lads that D-Day dodged,

We hear the boys in Florence are going home on leave,
After six months' service: such a shame they're not relieved,
And we're told to carry on for a few more years,
Because our wives don't shed no tears
For we are the D-Day Dodgers, out in sunny Italy.

Once we had a "blue light" that we were going home,
Back to dear old Blighty, never more to roam,
Then someone whispered "in France we'll fight,"
We said "not that, we'll just sit tight",
For we are the D-Day Dodgers, the lads that D-Day dodged.

Dear Lady Astor, you think you know a lot,
Standing on a platform and talking tommy-rot,
Dear England's sweetheart and her pride,
We think your mouth is much too wide,
From the D-Day Dodgers, out in sunny Italy.

Now, all together.

Look around the hillsides, through the mist and rain,
See the scattered crosses, some that bear no name,
Heartbreak and toil and suffering gone,
The lads beneath, they slumber on,
They are the D-Day Dodgers, who'll stay in Italy.

This was pure irony, of course, expressed by men resentful that their fight in the desert and then up the long mountain trek of Italy, had not received its due. Hence the light reference to what in fact were some of the most savage battles of the war.

This was the final version. Some of the battles mentioned, such as those in France, Bologna, and Florence, had yet to be fought at this time. Verses or lines were just revised or added as the song was repeated. The last verse turned irony into a more bitter sarcasm.

23. Assisi

> *"I like a church; I like a cowl;*
> *I love a prophet of the soul;*
> *And on my heart monastic aisles,*
> *Fall like sweet strains."*
>
> **Emerson**

The Italian sky swept over us in a thin diaphanous veil of heat stretched taut over the mountains as we headed towards Lake Trasimeno and Assisi. That was in the morning, but on this July afternoon the sky had begun to darken and the nimbo-cumulus over us was building to thunder-heads, dark below then piled up into albescent pyramids of white cloud full of ice, hail, and turbulence. It would be no place to fly. Rain streamed towards us in long, falling, cinerous banners.

Our objective was Assisi. My own parish church at home was dedicated to St. Francis and was built in basilica style, so Assisi was a natural destination for me now that I was so near.

We made a steady run round the peace of Lake Trasimeno, with its ancient and more recent battles a memory. The blue of the lake shimmered between a thousand olive trees, with hardly a ripple on its surface but a million raindrops. Then we climbed into the hills, the gradients up which the staff car laboured rising steeply with the road curving round and round on itself in one hairpin bend after another. The drops on either side were precipitous.

Assisi finally appeared in the distance, in a patch of sunlight. It lay on the side of the mountains forming the 'spine' of Italy. The river glinted below it, meandering towards us and our iridescent Appenine road through a hundred vineyards. We ran into the Assisi sun and approached a town with a basilica dominating the skyline and giving a fortified impression. The campanile of the basilica towered over the roofs, the whole a study in sunlit cinnamon stone, with the long sweep of the cloisters curving back towards the cobbled streets of the town. The clouds and laden sky had now passed away to the west but the narrow streets were still shaded under a blazing sun.

We encountered a religious parade, led by a priest carrying a golden cross, closely attended by men in centuries-old dress of bright colours. They twisted and revolved flags and banners in the Sienese style. The girls and women wore equally bright dress and huge circular hats rolled around the head and centred on a tight cap. Long hair fell loosely over their shoulders and dark eyes flashed and danced. They passed closely and flung flowers towards us.

With the procession behind, we entered through an archway into the cloistered quadrangle of the monastery which was also, it appeared, a convent for sisters of the order of Poor Clares. We pulled on a chain and a bell tolled far away. A monk appeared. I could not place the accented English at first, then found out that he was a Dubliner. The long brown/black robe of the Franciscan hung to his ankles, with a white cord girdle and a long rosary carrying a swinging crucifix. He was heavily spectacled, with short hair *en brosse*. He proved to be an enthusiastic and well-informed guide. We should have been there three months later, on October 4th, when pilgrims came to venerate St Francis. But July had to do.

We moved into a scene of colour and splendour. Walls and ceilings were sheathed in many paintings, some six hundred years old. Golden candlesticks swept up towards a curved ceiling. St Francis was born in 1181, died in 1266 and was canonised two years later, when the building of the basilica commenced. Such a short period was unusual then – and would be even more so now – but St Francis was a legend in his own lifetime. His order became a major success and was supported by Pope Innocent III as a mission to promote peace. The legend was that St Francis heard a voice which told him to "go and repair my house" – which he ultimately realised meant the Church, not the buildings. He did so throughout his life, although prior to his death relinquishing the leadership of the order and retiring into the hills to a hermitage above Assisi, buried in the woods. During his life he created some miracles of sainthood and *inter alia* caused water to spout from solid rock.

There were three distinct sections to the basilica – crypt, middle, and upper church. St Francis lay in the first. His tomb seemed to have suffered the depredations of long-dead vandals but was now enclosed by formidable metal grilles. Its dark place in the crypt was relieved by concealed lights glowing over the stonework. The light was much stronger in the two upper churches but all had strong witness of age, veneration, and silence – except for the pad, pad, of dark-robed figures flitting around us.

The Refectory was unusual, being laid out with tables close to the walls. It was claimed to be the largest in Europe. A Spartan meal here would nevertheless be something to remember.

The day waned and the sun dropped in the west as we said *arrivederci* to our friendly guide. What Clough said over a century ago was certainly true of this gem:

"*Mild monastic faces in quiet collegiate cloisters*"

We were not to know that some fifty years later an earthquake would strike…

24. 'General Collingwood' Visits

"Your mystery, your mystery; nay, dispatch."
Shakespeare, *Othello*

We were to have a mysterious visitor, "General Collingwood", who would arrive at 14.25 hours on 27th July 1944. But who exactly was he? No one knew the name. The arrival was obviously going to generate some 'bull'. We of the home brigade could recognise the signs – drill, mentions in DROs, cleaning the kit.

The Commonwealth pilots and airmen spoke freely on the subject, not being enamoured of, nor accustomed to, ceremonial occasions. The Squadron Leader in charge of Admin issued a two-page plan, with sketch map, and issued it to every squadron with two (2) copies to the Wing Adjutant, presumably in case he lost one. This made illuminating reading:

> "All Officers and Airmen will wear clean khaki drill shirts and shorts, stockings, and black boots with anklets. Medal ribbons and decorations will be worn."
>
> "The correct headgear for Officers is caps F.S. but if all Officers are not in possession of this cap, but all are in possession of Caps Ceremonial then the latter should be worn."
>
> "The Officer in charge of each formation will salute the visitor as the car approaches and this will be the signal for all personnel to cheer lustily."
>
> "The cheering should be as spontaneous as possible and personnel must be told that no 'hip hip' will be given and that they may let themselves go as long as they do not break ranks."

"It is NOT repeat NOT permitted to use cameras during the inspection."

Well, well, this visit is being taken seriously. But we still didn't know who could justify this collective carrying on. The red tape continued to unwind. This tended to rattle a rather free and easy Wing, in the middle of hard-fought battles. The day and time arrived. Since they had arranged the parade with taller individuals in front, I found myself promoted to head it. Escorts were everywhere and a fighter patrol overhead.

Who on earth warranted this? General Collingwood alone? The Pope? At 14.25 exactly the DC3 'Freedom', leading a small flight of three, taxied in and out stepped the VIP followed by Air Vice-Marshal Dixon, commanding the Desert Air Force. The visitor had what appeared from the distance to be the Army shoulder rank of wreath, crossed batons and crown; a Field Marshal, no less.

The recognition was instant. The King!

He wore plain khaki drill but no decorations. On his chest he had pilots' wings. His polished black shoes were already picking up Italian dust. He boarded a jeep carrying a huge yellow flag and rather anxiously driven by one "Bones" Jones ("Bones of the Desert" of course!). The jeep and its four occupants disappeared towards Wing Operations, where the King was present at a briefing of 3 Squadron, getting instruction to bomb a petrol dump near Firenze. Twenty-five minutes later, to the programme second, King and assorted escort reappeared and bowled round the various squadron parades.

Now the Wing had something to do except stand around and did their "lusty" bit.

The King had been chatty. Halting in font of an SAAF officer:

"What's that garment you're wearing?"

"Bush jacket, Sir."

"It looks splendid. They dress me up in all these thick clothes because I have to be in correct uniform I'd like a tunic like yours. How do I get one?"

~ Under the Red Eagle ~

"I don't think you'll have much problem in 5 Squadron Stores, sir. They are required South African dress."

It was, of course, coincidence that about six weeks later Air Ministry issued an instruction that RAF personnel might wear bush jackets in hot countries. But there was no mention of suede boots or silk scarves!

This was not the only question the King asked about Desert Air Force dress. Another officer was in desert boots in contrast to the royal highly polished black shoes, now a little scruffy from Italian dust. Enquiring about these boots, the King found that ankle boots in light-brown suede were both comfortable and practical in the desert, and were still worn. Glancing down at his dusty black feet he said:

"Sensible. I'm not allowed to wear things like that."

He shook hands, boarded his jeep again and "Bones" shot swiftly round the squadrons, coming to a halt on the main road outside the camp. A double green Very Light arched over the strip from Flying Control, engines roared, and 3 Squadron tantivied into the air in the general direction of Florence. They had an excellent mission and the petrol dump flared and threw off a large column of black smoke.

Some two hours later, the party returned, boarded their DC3 and vanished south. There was a Parthian shot. One of the airmen happened to have the King's valet as a brother. He vanished with the King and the message came back: "J---- will be away for some time. We'll send him back when we think he should return."

The parades dismissed themselves smartly. Free tea and wads in the Padre's Club. The republicans were well to the fore. We heard later that as Prince Albert the King had served on HMS *Collingwood*, which took part in the Battle of Jutland, hence the pseudonym.

Relating to his own dress, we found that the King was the first sovereign to wear the wings of a qualified pilot.[9]

---

[9] Read more about the history of Royal flying in *A History of The King's Flight and The Queen's Flight*, also published by Woodfield.

25. Rumour, Ever Rumour

> *"Ye shall hear of wars and rumours of wars: see that ye be not troubled: for all these things must come to pass but the end is not yet."*   **St. Matthew ch.24, v.6**

Once again the lapse of a few days had completely changed our situation. One rumour was that the front had advanced; we rarely heard the guns now. The 8th Army had taken Arrezzo and was following up to Florence after an intensive barrage.

Another rumour was of a "gen" talk this evening. At one time these were quite frequent when various battle lines were approached, but they had been less common of late. A large crowd gathered outside Wing Operations enquiringly eyeing a sheet of brown paper pinned over the south of France. The paper was flicked over to show coloured arrows from sea to coast, and then inland. This, it appeared, was to be Operation 'Dragoon', the invasion of southern France tomorrow, the 15th August. We were not to be fully engaged as a Wing but were to detach two squadrons to assist.

More rumours the following day. If the facts were anywhere near right, 7,000 ships had been fully involved in the landings including 5 battleships and 9 escort carriers, 24 cruisers, 122 destroyers and over 400 landing craft. By nightfall, it was alleged that 60,000 men had landed, with 6,000 vehicles and 5,000 tons of materiel. Over 300 killed so far, mainly by stumbling on mines. Seven Divisions had been released from Italy. Hitler ordered a retreat from the French south, so was largely beaten in the West. Despite this, he had despatched seven divisions to reinforce the Italian front, so must be very wary of our attack from his south. We switched 239 Wing offensive – with the remaining four squadrons – to support the 5th and 8th Army attacks and the battle for the Gothic Line commenced by our cutting all 23 bridges over the river.

There had been a massive move of the 8th Army across the mountains to the east coast, which was remarkable since the two main roads over the central heights had both been cut. No fewer than forty Bailey Bridges were constructed by the Engineers and 60,000 vehicles moved. We too had to push closer to the battlefront and this was to be to Iesi west of Ancona. The Po valley began to come to the fore in our operations planning.

Another rumour was that Romania had thrown in its hand with the Allies, which gave rise to sarcastic comments in the Mess.

"Romania? Where's that?"

On our immediate front, Florence fell on 4th August and the Wing flew extensive missions day after day, bombing enemy positions north of the Arno. A SAAF pilot, Lt MacGuire, had been seconded to 250 Squadron. On a sortie he had dropped his bombs on an ammunition dump south of Pesaro when his starboard wing dropped suddenly. An 88mm shell had torn away a third of the wing. The hit was a hard one – the Kittyhawk turned over with its guns misaligned, the trailing edge of the wing shattered and the whole aircraft holed from nose to tail. He managed to get the machine back to the LG, but on the way the ammunition in the wing started to explode. Chaos on chaos! He got down safely, although having to keep above stalling speed of 170mph, and joined his astonished ground crew to view the damage, which was formidable: one of the holes was so big as to allow three ground crew to stand within it. He was lucky; a hit from an 88mm shell usually destroyed an aircraft.

Our "A" Party had already pushed forward and news was scarce since radio silence was being observed, but we gathered that Iesi was a derelict aerodrome rather like Guidonia. Our second party followed, and gave me one of my hardest drives at the wheel.

Reveille was 03.30 hours. O'Mahoney had been celebrating not too wisely but well and was in a near coma when I shook him. No result. So I called his pal the MT Officer to assist, since he also had a thick head and was not in any mind to stand nonsense. O'M was soon up, but cussing and dilatory. The upshot was that we pulled away late again and failed to catch up with the convoy all day. I also found a flat battery, loose leads, and a cracked distributor. Thanks to the MT Section for the second time this year! I effected a running repair with a chunk of wood and we clattered away.

By this time the sun was well up but with the morning mists still low. Although we were on our own, we had a map, luckily, so knew where we were. That didn't help much because we now discovered the reason for the early start by everyone else: the road was packed with 8th Army armour and foul with diesel fumes. We passed tank after tank with little room to spare and were rather too near the churning steel and the ribald commentary from tanks to us and vice versa. We did not lose the tanks for some distance until we overtook their lead jeep with blue flag and large warning "TANKS BEHIND". We were past Perugia and about to cross the Upper Tiber.

The non-armoured traffic added to the congestion and we moved only slowly over the Umbrian Appenines. Hairpin bends curved over and over again until we passed over the crest and down into the saucer of the mountains. The weight of traffic lightened and we followed the Chienti River towards the Adriatic. The scenery was as picturesque as I had seen anywhere in Italy although the road itself was obscured by drifting clouds of dust and flanked with whitened vegetation. One could not step onto the grass verges without stirring up an opaque film of powder, much as it had been in Sicily.

By this time the day was far advanced. We were directed onto lesser roads by Military Police and cut inland towards Iesi. The sun touched the horizon and threw long shadows across the valley. Above us six dots circled raggedly in the clear sky and others landed far below on the new strip; our own aircraft, at last. Another few miles brought us to the Mess, but it was far too late to pitch tents. We bedded down in a stable – no horses present – and took a few glasses of spumante, followed by dreamless exhaustion.

The battle before us was apparently going well, although we noted that the BBC tended to play down this front with, "The 8th Army is leaning steadily on the Gothic Line east of Florence." In fact, this was more than a "lean" – it was a fierce exchange which had already turned the Gothic Line at Pesaro.

An American "Mitchell" came roaring over the airstrip, banking and yawing wildly, with a trail of smoke and flame behind. Someone had certainly "winged" it. The aerobatics were presumably an attempt to keep the flames away from the tanks. It did not land, as we expected, but dropped lower and lower behind the trees. What happened next we had no idea – a crash, probably.

It was 03.00 hours. I was Guard Commander again and light came only from a dirty oil lamp, fluttering and emitting noxious fumes. I dealt with it, mentally criticising the last guard. "Leave the guardhouse as you would wish to find it" was the Service watchword.

The two men on duty returned to don 'mosquito helmets', a contraption that dropped over their steel hats and shoulders and was calculated to give a fit to anyone challenged. The two guards knew this and the one said to the other: "Just the job. Now let's scare the living daylights out of someone!"

The remainder of the guard was stretched out around me, so the night was alive with heavy breathing, crickets, and the occasional hum of a lorry or aircraft. A full moon rode over the valley and visibility ranged for miles. Slowly, the time moved on to dawn, and the sky lightened in the east. Guns rumbled and birds sang above them.

More rumours came in about the recent move of the 8th Army to the Adriatic coast. This had been the direct effect of Operation 'Olive'. Alexander had to concentrate his forces and over 60,000 tanks, vehicles and guns had to be shifted many miles. 239 and other wings moved with the Army. It had not been surprising, therefore, that we had met so much traffic on our own move. The American 5th Army moved also, perhaps to a lesser extent, since they were to attack across the centre of the country on the left flank of the 8th.

The Gothic Line was the objective. It was a natural obstacle and the last German chance of halting the Allied advance. The assault on it dragged on for three weeks before Kesselring withdrew his forces.

The 8th Army met a whole series of ridges and rivers while German reinforcements – which Hitler had transferred from west and east – hurried towards them. Eventually they met over the Coriano ridge, from which the Germans were finally driven, but casualties were high. On top of this the weather broke and reduced the earth to glutinous mud and filth. Rimini was finally entered on 20th September and the attack, this time by the 5th Army, turned towards Bologna.

We flew mission after mission, sortie after sortie, from Iesi and threw all we had got at motor transport, gun emplacements, German concentrations, and bridges. Some 7,000 8th Army infantry were lost in this series of battles over the Gothic Line – a loss relatively higher than in any earlier phase of the Italian campaign and due to the highly unfavourable terrain, and appalling weather.

The Desert Air Force were now not only supporting the British 8th Army but the American 5th as well – in fact, it was more than that because most of the effort was directed at getting the 5th's offensive under way. A Lieutenant Colonel in a forward observation post remarked of 239's continuous operations: "I watched the bombing today. The accuracy is quite unbelievable. The German casualties and damage suffered were devastating."

As opposed to the dust and heat of the desert, we now operated in very different conditions – bitter cold, snow, gales and mud. This was the worst winter in Italian living memory. Flak caused us to lose too many aircraft and too many experienced pilots. Our squadrons dived into and along valleys stiff with guns, a few feet above the ground, and there was little room to avoid the shells and ack-ack thrown up at them. We flew over all battlefields – coast, mountains, plains, beaches and Yugoslavia.

But we were very near outright victory. This was probably the last major campaign push of the Italian war. Peace in sight?

Rimini fell and the 8th headed for the Po valley to bring Hitler's worst fears to reality. The Gothic Line was completely turned but we again had rumours – of another set of defences near Venice – the "Blue Line." The weather began to break up again. Low clouds, rain and mud hampered the Kittyhawks and Mustangs and the remnants of late summer only revealed themselves now and again in a bright morning. At least, the "skeeters" grew fewer.

Sludge and mire was everywhere – on roads, dispersals and even the main strip. Our memory of Italy will not be so much of a romantic and sunny clime but of mud, mud and more mud, from October to March. It was not just an annoyance: it could change the course of battles. Roads were choked, rail transport halted and the military arteries clogged – something like a stroke in the human body. Even in the air, where we were free of mud, cloud and rain hindered the missions badly and reduced our level of air superiority. But when we touched down – mud again. Looking back, Italy had been one river crossing after another for both armies and the names Sangro and Cassino will live long in many memories, and in battle honours as well. By this October we were in the middle of another heavy engagement – the assault on Mount Spaduro.

The Fusiliers were foremost in this. First the Irish Fusiliers scaled an almost impossible cliff to surprise the Germans at the top; but at dawn the enemy made a fierce counter-attack. The Irish ran out of ammunition so used anything else – bare hands, rifle butts and even stones. Every company lost men heavily. Two days later the Lancashire Fusiliers had a go and were up and over the top an hour after midnight. They managed to hold the position despite furious counter-attacks.

The preparation for these assaults left much to be desired since the weather was intensely cold with snow and ice. They launched their assaults in white camouflage from soggy slit trenches calf-deep in water. 239 Wing and others did what they could to assist, but this kind of scaling and climbing of precipitous cliffs was not an action easily supported. It was an infantryman's battle.

Mud again. Our aircraft were usually bogged down in it and had to be hauled out by sheer muscle and some mechanical help. We trudged around with chunks of the stuff adhering to our boots and shoes. We had the odd 'old-stager', capable of recalling the trenches of the Great War, and they thought these conditions were just as bad; the difference being that we were not in trenches and dived into ditches or foxholes only if any strafing or bombing was going on.

It was more than a year since we had left the desert, but there were often precedents that could be used. One of these was at Fortunata Ridge, a powerfully defended site near Rimini. Wing Operations recalled El Hamma and put in hand some lively low-level work over the height. The 8th Army then climbed it, as at El Hamma, fought its way over and down, and suffered few casualties.

Looking forward, we realised that the country beyond Rimini offered more serious water crossings. No less than nine major rivers and some hundreds of minor watercourses lay between the Adriatic coast and Bologna. There was a short spell of reasonable weather in early November and this allowed the 8th to push forward. The 5th had less success and failed to gain a decisive advantage, making the main breakthrough now unlikely before the spring of 1945.

I had recorded so many disasters that a lucky accident was a welcome contribution to the diary. The Mustang was probably one of the best – if not the best – fighter to come out of the war (excepting the Spitfire, of course), so let's say the best fighter-bomber, which was probably true, but it was difficult to 'pancake', since it had a big radiator scoop under the cockpit – not unlike the Kittyhawk – which, dug into the ground during a wheels-up landing and could turn over the aircraft or cause it to break in half. One of the pilots, new to the Mustang, went up for a solo and put the aircraft through its paces. He did a few spins and turns and then dived towards the sea, realising a little too late that the waves were very close. In fact, he was so near that he thudded into them and bounced off again in a cloud of spray. He got back the LG and dismounted at dispersal, where he found his radiator smashed in and the propeller blades bent. It said much for the fitters that they replaced and repaired the damage and put the aircraft back into the air. The squadron leader was not sympathetic:

"Bloody prat! As bad as Prune!" (Prune was, of course, the Pilot Officer well known in cartoons and general humour about the RAF, as the clown who did everything wrong and steadily wrote-off the RAF aircraft strength in a series of avoidable mishaps.)

Well, well, something official about demobilisation at last. This was another area of rumour that had been rife for a long time. The

Government White Paper arrived and was thumbed and studied with some interest. First impressions were rather favourable, except that we were surprised to find no distinction between married and single men. My own 'quota' number was quite high and would be more so before we finished here. Then the Far East? My demobilisation leave seemed to work out at 3-3½ months, if I ever got it!

That last remark turned out to be a little prescient. I was again near sudden demise that night. "Gone for a Burton", as the RAF had it.

The Liberty Gharry was on its way back from Iesi with a group of all ranks who had spent a lively evening in town. We were moving smartly along the main, but narrow, road to camp with a line of poplars on both sides of the road, very close to one another. The road narrowed even more at this point and had a muddy surface from rain. It was as if the road were covered in oil. We began to swing wildly into a massive skid. The driver beside me tried to counteract the slide and regain control – which he failed to do. We flew off at a tangent and a crash was obviously imminent in a vehicle of over five tons, heading straight for the poplars. I gripped the dash and waited for the coming purler. The vehicle rear swung and the headlights jazzed crazily towards the boles of the trees with their black bulk now filling the windscreen. All of five seconds had passed. The near wheels dropped and we plunged down the slope, coming up hard against an iron fence in a shatter of broken glass. Dead silence, then…

"Anyone hurt?"

"No… No … No… Yes, I'm bleeding…"

But it could have been worse. The skid marks were fifty yards long but our luck had held – no approaching traffic, and we had the incredible chance of going off the road over a felled poplar which provided the only gap for a mile. The trunk of the broken tree was a foot above the surface and had taken the main shock, striking the transmission and the chassis. We disembarked and viewed the damage. What were the odds against charging through that single gap with only one injury? The gharry had swung round 180 degrees and was now facing back to Iesi. Both front springs had been ripped from their seatings and the chassis had collapsed onto the transmission. We bandaged up the injured one, who was not badly hurt, with a field dressing and got a message back to camp courtesy of a jeep which had pulled up behind us. The driver viewed our wreckage.

"Lucky bastards," he said.

A three-tonner appeared from the MT Section in some twenty minutes, towed the ruin back onto the road and took the now less lively group on board. The engine of the wreck actually started so I and the driver made a careful way back under our own steam, the whole vehicle shaking and shuddering from the full weight of its body resting on the transmission. But we got there, finally. As one of the pilots who had been in the back said, "I shall be glad to get back into the air. It's safer!"

The aerodrome at Iesi was packed with aircraft of all shapes and sizes. Apart from our Kittyhawks and Mustangs there were Marauders, Dakotas, Fortresses, Mitchells, Baltimores, Thunderbolts, Beaufighters, Liberators and even Mosquitos. Two of the last flew in from the UK and brought the morning papers, which caused some interest. The reason for this variety of aircraft was the concrete runway, now rapidly being lengthened. It was one of the few all-weather strips anywhere near the front line and housed everything from visiting VIPs to shot-up wrecks crashing with blood-wagons in close attendance. A Court of Enquiry was held into one of these accidents, involving a Mustang of 112 Squadron, coming in on a forced landing and pranging two Marauders and one petrol bowser. It turned out to be nothing to do with the pilot but with a nut found in the carburettor – a bit of Lease-Lend that we could have done without.

Yesterday was one of our more disastrous days. 5 SAAF and 3 RAAF Squadrons went out over Yugoslavia ten strong and only four got back. Once they crossed the coast cumulo-nimbus built up behind them and in the valley up which they were flying. None of the flight was very experienced in such cloud flying in loose formation. What happened may never be known. Flying Control guessed that six of them probably flew into the precipitous end of the valley. Much gloom around in the messes: we cannot afford such devastating losses at such a late stage in the game.

~ Under the Red Eagle ~

In a lighter vein, I recorded in Sicily how the Americans displayed winged prowess by returning at zero feet, screaming across the strip, and pulling out into a steep climb before actually landing. We even had one episode when two aircraft were landing one way and a Thunderbolt alighted between them, ignoring the shower of red Very lights being fired towards him. This and similar events led to a forthright exchange.

An American Pilot was standing at the bar when one of his colleagues came in across the strip outside after a steep power dive, then flattened out in a howling crescendo which deafened the mess.

Said the American, "Tha-a-ts what we call buzzin' the drome … what do y'all call it?"

A Desert Air Force pilot, suede boots, 'tache, silk scarf and all, lowered his paper and remarked over the top of it, "Bloody silly."

He resumed his reading. There was no further exchange.

The American presence also led to competition in operations. Yesterday a Thunderbolt squadron was briefed to attack a bridge. They did so, plastering the area and returning to announce complete destruction. 239 Wing Operations said: "Good show. But shouldn't you send over a reccy to confirm?"

Three hours later 239 Wing was asked to bomb the same bridge and did so with confirmed success from the Army. No reccy necessary. Wing humorists seized the chance and the Operations Record read: "112 Squadron successfully attacked the bridge already destroyed by 79th Pursuit."

For Flying Control, life proved to be "One damn crash after another." This remark followed a spectacular blaze. The Iesi strip, lined with the many different planes mentioned earlier, included a number of Marauders. A Liberator taking off had a port wheel collapse, dropped onto a wing tip, and hurled itself into the Marauders. Crash – Wreckage – Flames. The only casualty was one of the Liberator crew who exited smartly, cantered along the wing, ran clean off the end, and broke his leg on landing. The ensuing fire destroyed both aircraft and a huge tower of black smoke slanted above the flames. Estimated cost? Considerable!

~ Under the Red Eagle ~

To change the subject to more domestic matters, we had our ration of dogs around the place, as mentioned already. They tended to follow their owners to their aircraft and gaze dismally after the plane as it pulled away into the sky. The other day, one "Lassie" was taken for a ride by her pilot owner. The cockpit being too small for both owner and hound, the latter went behind the armoured plate of the pilot's seat. Reports were that she enjoyed the flight until the pilot curved in to land, which subjected the dog to multiple gravity and flattened her out like a sheepskin rug. The dog didn't seem to be too bothered at first, but the ground staff noted that it shot out of the plane rather smartly. It did not go near the Kittyhawk again!

Following poor weather, the days had been more kindly and khaki drill reappeared. What we were getting would have been "St Luke's Summer" at home; what the Italians call it we do not know.

After a little sun and warmth we got another foretaste of the winter conditions to come. Torrential downpour deepened the sea of mud into a filthy chocolate sauce. This valley, we found out, had some of the heaviest rainfall in Italy. We would have preferred the colder weather to come, since the ground would at least be hard and vehicles and aircraft would be able to move more easily. Otherwise, things didn't proceed too badly: after all, we were winning, and the Germans must be in far poorer shape.

Christmas was not so far off now, so we fattened a few birds. The official 'Turkey-man' came in to report that one of his fowl was in a bad way. This sparked witty rejoinders and promised an entertaining night – the Turkey-man would be hauled before a Fowl Court Martial. He was. The jinks were high and the accused, advocates and judges, had to be put to bed.

The final rumour of the month was that the Wing would be moving again and replace 244 Wing at Fano, on a coastal strip. 244 regaled us with horror stories about their site and we were threatened with being housed in a convent. Perhaps the nuns would be in residence? That should improve the manners and cut down on the maledictions!

26. Venice

> *"Trailing clouds of glory do we come."*
> **Wordsworth**

The Wing still operated long-range Mustangs in Yugoslavia and over one hundred locomotives were destroyed in a week. The shorter-range Kittyhawks continued to attack Italian targets, and we had even been called on to support the Russians in their sweep towards Vienna. The rumour of the shift to Fano proved to be correct for once, which was to be an advantage since the Iesi strip had become even more like a three-ring circus. At Fano we were only with 244 Wing and that probably would not be for long. The front showed little progress and no great change seemed likely before Spring. The rain and mud had beaten us to the Po Valley by days.

Fano proved to be a considerable change for the better and the rumours from 244 about its inadequacies proved to be incorrect, and we told them so. We were truly in a convent, but no nuns were present and we took over some houses opposite for Administration and Messes.

Almost at once there was a more serious than usual accident. A Mustang returned with a "hung up" 1,000lb bomb which detached itself just at the wrong moment and dropped into the town centre. Unfortunately it was the middle of the day when the square was busy. Four civilians were killed, seven could not be traced and the bomb partly demolished a house used by a South African Signals Unit and killed six men. Even more unfortunately, the Mustang was from 5 SAAF Squadron.

I was Guard Commander one night and received a report that one of the airmen in the convent was in a bad way. I found him with severe chest pain and feverish. It took me some time to find the night orderly in the Sick Quarters and then a Medical Officer, who replied that since it was after midnight he had finished his tour of duty. So I raised rank to the Senior Medical Officer who attended, said the man would be all right, that he would send along some pills, and retired to bed again. Next day I removed the airman to hospital myself, now with a developed case of pneumonia. The medical orderly was the one who came away with the honours because after his first examination he had said: "He's got pneumonia. He ought to be where I can keep an eye on him."

Immediately before Christmas I went on leave to Florence, to an Army Rest Camp. "Leave" is perhaps the wrong word and is not now used officially. More like a change of scene. We left in a 250 Squadron gharry. The battle line was not far away but we saw nothing of it. Snow ploughs stood ready at the top of the passes and the far mountain crests were heavily tipped in white.

Florence gave an impression of austerity and seemed peopled by a 50:50 population of civilians and uniforms. It was a "grey" city at ground level, from the stone of which it was built, but changed completely as we climbed the campanile, where we looked out unexpectedly across a city of red roofs. From this vantage point the surrounding hills soared high and folded back ridge on ridge into the blue mists of a winter morning. Below curved the Arno River, swirling around broken blocks of collapsed bridges in lines of creaming white. The only bridge remaining was the Ponte Vecchio but even here some houses on the top had been demolished.

We could only skim the many buildings of interest. In particular, the chapel of the Palazzo Pitti housed some lovely work, including an exquisite carving of Christ on the Cross, only the size of a hand's span but almost living in its accuracy of detail. It was reputed to have been carved from a staff of St Francis, which we took with a grain of salt. It was typically Italian in being enclosed in a cheap case with what looked like wallpaper lining.

Back to camp on Christmas Eve? Lacking chains for the truck we had a long and tedious journey of eleven hours.

~ *Under the Red Eagle* ~

We moved into the New Year of 1945, which I hoped would be my final year in the RAF. It had become very much colder with some bitter weather. Even if there were a bright sun at midday, which there usually wasn't, I had to light the Valor. We watched reports of Russian push towards Berlin with high interest. Whether Stalin's troops could thrust right through remained to be seen. We were too far south to assist. Looking at the map in Wing Operations, the Russians had created a vast salient between Konigsberg and Elbing, with an apex at Frankfurt. We heard two BBC news flashes – one that von Runstedt's Army was retreating in the West and another that Churchill, Stalin and Roosevelt were meeting in the Black Sea.

Looking back over the Italian campaign so far, the fighting here had not been a sinecure. The real facts were that there had been no tougher fighting front anywhere for the infantryman. The Desert Air Force came off rather better since it had command of the air. Italy had a big proportion of the oldest hands – certainly in the 8th Army and to some extent in the 5th. As a consequence the Germans put in twenty-nine divisions of their Wehrmacht elite to hold the Allied armies advancing up Italy. No quarter was asked or given. During the last winter the Allies, both troops and airmen, were killing relatively more than their counterparts anywhere. The campaign had been slow but a continuous push forward with mud, cold and rain intervening. The central spiked mountains never favoured an attack from the south, but it did for defence. The southern provinces were a poor peasant country – boggy on the coasts and flanking heights which persisted all the way up the country to the Lombardy Plain. Water flooded away from these heights and filled the many streams and rivers which had to be crossed without benefit of barges. Moving from side to side of the country was difficult and on at least two occasions gave Air Force and Army severe transport problems. Military operations were therefore carried out on both coasts without much contact between the armies and either had to thrust up the coast or enter the mountains – a real labour of Sisyphus.

On 29th January 1945 six divisions were switched from Italy to assist Eisenhower's push to the Rhine. This effectively put paid to any

~ Under the Red Eagle ~

question of meeting Churchill's idea of advancing on Vienna. Some might get there, but not the main formations.

Throughout this winter of 1944/5 there were rumours that Hitler intended to make a last stand in the Alps. But the Operations Room picked up the counter information that this could be treated as a deception plan, intended to deflect the Allies from insisting on the total capitulation of Germany by exaggerating the degree of resistance the enemy could establish. Whatever the case, 239 Wing could have operated within the Alpine valleys given their experience in the Italian central mountains and in Yugoslavia.

Wing operations were now more tactical than operational; we were less engaged in close support and were concentrating more on cutting railway lines and road bridges. Through rail traffic was brought to a standstill. But we still did some "Rover" patrolling whenever the aircraft could take off and many times they were directed down from "cab ranks" onto targets only two or three hundred yards ahead of the 8th Army's foremost tanks. But it would still be March before large-scale interdiction could be resumed. To get the Kittys and Mustangs into the air, thick snow over mud had to be removed and "all ranks" – in the usual Desert Air Force way – were out with shovels.

We were to fit rockets onto the Mustangs and to 260 Squadron went the honour of being the first chosen for the tests, and the first squadron in this war to use them in battle. The next move cast its shadow before, and would probably be towards the end of January.

Operations being few, we took a day off and visited the neutral state of San Marino south of Rimini. It was only 30 or so square miles in extent and the tiny capital was perched on top of a precipitous rock. The place has been opened only recently for troops and ours was the first run up from the Wing. The town gave an ancient impression with frowning and fortified towers darkly jutting against the sky, steeply sloping streets, small houses and shops, and occasional cobbles. We wandered round grey battlements under a leaden sky with the surrounding hills lost in mist. From the highest point we gazed through breaks down into valleys falling away towards the Adriatic.

We were actually above cloud level, which swirled up the rock face like steam from an outhouse window on a winter day. The war was as if it had never been. We were forbidden to buy made-up clothing but I bought some pyjama material since my own had given up the ghost long ago. Prices were stiff. It was easy to save here; we didn't buy the goods! I came away feeling that in crossing this 'border' we had dropped back a few hundred years or so. I think they had one policeman and one soldier.

An enquiry came in by air letter from home about how we dealt with laundry. Actually, we either did it ourselves or arranged for a willing signora to do it for us. The older woman to whom I took mine surprised me the other day when I offered her what I thought was a reasonable amount and she replied "Troppo, troppo" (too much) and gave me back about one-third of what I had given her. Colleagues just didn't believe this and promptly sought her services. Perhaps she knew more about marketing than I gave her credit for!

Another courageous act – F/Lt Blumer of the RAAF 3 Squadron, on an anti-barge strike, was hit in the knee by a 20mm shell which failed to explode but shattered his kneecap. He lost a lot of blood before getting back to us but achieved a perfect crash landing and – what's more – did it off the main PSP. Immediate award of the DSO; why this decoration I was not sure – I would have expected DFC or CGM, but some major award was certainly in order, as was the immediacy.

By the end of March the Desert Air Force, since 1st January, had flown 27,000 sorties, claiming over 1,000 German vehicles, 5,000 railway trucks and over 500 locomotives, quite apart from successful attacks on 500 barges and ships. One needed to add imagination to cold statistics like this. It was an incredible achievement. The enemy was being very severely battered and such losses must have formed a high proportion of the resources they actually had available.

Accidents of one sort and another still plagued us. An example was the aircraft of 112 Squadron which returned with an engine spluttering and coughing and bordering on the unserviceable. He was carrying two 1,000 lb bombs which had refused to detach in the air but promptly fell off above the runway as the kite was coming in. Much of the aircraft was blown to bits and caught fire in a mass of flames. Whoof! To the stunned astonishment of all, the pilot actually walked away from the wreckage and flames, carrying his parachute to the ambulance, but with facial and hand burns. If one can walk away like this, it is regarded by pilots as "a good landing".

The runway was out of action for two hours only – despite the fact that the PSP plating had been torn up over its full width. This was thanks to smart work by an American service group who got the Wing back into action in an incredibly short time.

❖ ❖ ❖

We moved again – we were getting very good at this – to Cervia, which had been a Fascist holiday resort amidst sand and palm trees. Chalets were available and promptly occupied by Admin, Sick Quarters, Operations, Flying Control, and me. We were even near a Mobile Field Hospital – 22 MFH – which was a great help in fast blood transfusions for injured pilots. We had never before had such advanced medical attention near us. Wing Sick Quarters had done the job – and very efficiently, usually.

This was actually an unusual site if only because the strip was constructed through the edge of a fir wood and the Squadrons and HQ were strung along a road running parallel to the strip. Pilots do not enthuse about being close to trees. One comment was:

"Landing on this strip is like cycling down tram lines."

We didn't need mosquito nets here yet but we spotted water in and around the wood, so there would be myriads of the insects here later on. Were the Fascists immune? We hoped to have moved again before they swarmed – the skeeters, that is.

All these buildings needed cleaning up. They looked as though the Canadians, here before us, had built fires inside the chalets. Much elbow grease restored the interiors to better condition. The remainder of the Wing came forward and the lone and bare camp resounded with many voices:

"Where's that grey box…?"

"Who's got the guts of the Valor…?"
 "Huh! This place is a bit u/s…?"
"Wizard site, George…"
And so on.

Some airmen had to inveigle a large trailer through a narrow gateway:

"We'll never get this through the gap."
"Go on – shove."
"Eee aahh…"
"Push it, don't stroke it…"
"Eeee aaahh…"
Sounds of tearing and dislodged brickwork:
"You've torn the canvas."
"Well, you said push…"
"Yes, but not flat out. Watch it: here's Flighty…"
The Flight Sergeant Discip appears.
"What do you comedians think you are doing?"
"Moving this trailer to MT, Flight."
"You set of goons! You're all on a fizzer!"

Another bad crash occurred and the proximity of the Field Hospital proved to be vital, if ultimately useless. We had just finished a parade when we heard the clang of ambulances powering towards the beach, closely followed by the CO in his jeep and the crash tenders. Ten feet or so from the Officers' Mess on the beach lay a mass of wreckage, flaming furiously. A flight of 250 Squadron Kittyhawks had just returned, it appeared, and had been circling the LG in close formation when two of them "peeled off" together for some inexplicable reason. The slipstream of the one in front caught the aircraft behind, which reared up and sheared off the leader's tail. The plane dived heavily from 300 feet and created a considerable crater. The pilot was pulled out muttering something about the dance the squadron was holding that night, but died in the ambulance.

The other aircraft was no luckier and buried itself into the sand with colossal force. The fuselage tore away, hurtled on to demolish three trees, and then proceeded into a house where some Army personnel were billeted. When I got there a large civilian crowd had gathered, including women and children, watching the ground crew extricating the pilot's body from the wreckage. It had been an instantaneous death and he was huddled in such a position that the medical orderlies found it difficult to prise him out. They had covered the corpse with a blanket before trying to extract it from the cockpit. This was not usual and showed a proper refinement, given the presence of women and children.

There was nothing to do, and ground and aircrew turned away with regret for the loss of two good men.

Two more write-offs, two more "cash in effects" and two more telegrams: "The Air Ministry regrets to inform you…"

Two odd coincidences. The first was that the Wing postman – known to all as "Tubby" – had become tour-expired and was due to be released to the UK. The new man lived only two doors from "Tubby's" home. Strange that they should live so close, be of the same trade and serve on the same unit, with one replacing the other.

The other coincidence was that in the Wing Library someone picked up a book and said to his pal, "George, this is one of your books. Your name is on the flyleaf!" So it was, and the owner had not seen the book for ten years. The explanation must have been that his mother handed it in to the Post Office at home, who were requesting books for servicemen, and it had travelled here into his hands again.

❖ ❖ ❖

239 Wing Kittyhawks met enemy aircraft on 11th March 1945.

3 Squadron R.A.A.F. encountered four Bf109s, an SM79 and a Ju52. The last two were shot down. Again, 112 Squadron surprised 12 FW190s taking off from Rieti and downed three for the loss of two of their own formation. These could be amongst the last of the fighting missions.

In late March 250 Squadron had the ill-luck to lose F/O Devlin. He had to bale out when his engine failed just west of Marano. His chute was seen to bellow from the cockpit and catch on the tailplane before tearing away. It could not spread and he dropped like a stone.

Devlin was one of the Americans who preferred to remain in the RAF rather than transfer to the USAAF. As was aptly put by one of his colleagues he was "a shining example of Lease-Lend."

A considerable number of high army and air ranks were about today, sporting much red and blue ribbon and tabs. They included Air Vice Marshal Foster, now commanding the Desert Air Force, Major General Cannon, Lt General McCreery, General Anders and others… plus five hundred or so onlookers.

The occasion was a demonstration of close support tactics. The range lay beyond the end of the runway and was "out of bounds" – naturally – to a radius of one thousand yards. The targets were some houses and three unserviceable tanks.

A Mosquito came in and marked the target with flares – this being a supposed night attack – before running in again and strafing, alternating with tracer and explosive shells. Bursts of smoke trailed back from its wings with twinkles of orange on the targets as the shells impacted. A Boston came in with fragmentation bombs, and then 79th Pursuit with rockets. One was not supposed to see rockets in flight, unless they were in front, but I could see them well enough as they swept down in a flat trajectory to the target tanks. There was a fierce swelling hiss as the sound reached us and then a surprisingly loud roar as the 60lb rockets detonated. A salvo of these was, apparently, as powerful as the broadside of a cruiser.

Some dive-bombing followed, by 244 Wing, after our own 260 Squadron had improved on the rocketing, then fire bombs. These were petrol tanks filled with a gelatinous mass of petrol treated into a viscous jelly. They had fearsome results as Spitfires arrived and dropped their tanks in shallow dives. The missiles twisted over and over in the air and exploded on the deck in a huge semicircle of fire and smoke. The imagination was stirred as to what it was like to be on the receiving end of a great surrounding pool of what amounted to flaming jelly. The effect on morale must be grievous.

One pilot raised a loud laugh, senior ranks included, when he forgot where he was and his voice, amplified to giant dimensions, instructed an aircraft pottering around in front of him:

~ Under the Red Eagle ~

"Well get out of the way for Christ's sake, you silly -----!"
This was received with a loud cheer by the assembly.

This kind of operation of course gave rise to the Wing crest – which was a flying eagle gripping a bomb in its claws and with the motto "Close Support" underneath. Before we were to leave the Wing and Italy we were all presented with an enamelled brooch which could be worn above medals and decorations as a record of service with this famous Desert Air Force Wing.

Following this demonstration of close support, what could have been the Desert Air Force's last special mission of the war took place on 21st March 1945. A precision attack on Venice Harbour was ordered, using the whole of 239 Wing and all US 79th Group. This was the only time that Venice was to be attacked, because of its status as a protected city. There was an extremely tight bomb-line for the aircrews – attack harbour only, with no bomb to drop in the city or destroy any houses or places of historical interest. The Air Vice Marshal said openly that if there were any mistake in this, he and the leader of the attack would be "bowler-hatted" – that is, discharged from the air force – hence the codename Operation 'Bowler' for this mission.

The onslaught was successful and no one lost rank or was retired to the UK. In twenty minutes, 800 fragmentation bombs were dropped onto the harbour and ships, over 90 1,000lb bombs, and a clutch of semi armour-piercing bombs. One dockside explosion was so great as to be felt by the aircraft at 20,000 feet.

❖ ❖ ❖

A Special Order of the Day came in from Allied Force Headquarters:

"Final victory is near. The German forces are now very groggy and only need one mighty punch to knock them out for good. The moment has now come for us to take the field for the last battle which will end the war in Europe. You know what our comrades in the West and East are doing on the battlefields. It is

now our turn to play our decisive part. It will not be a walk-over. A mortally wounded beast can still be very dangerous. You must be prepared for a hard and bitter fight; but the end is quite certain – there is not the slightest shadow of doubt about that. You, who have won every battle you have fought, are going to win this last one.

Forward, then, into battle with confidence, faith and determination to see it through to the end. Godspeed and good luck to you all.

H.R. Alexander, Field Marshal,
Supreme Allied Commander Mediterranean Theatre

This order was simply dated April 1945. By 9th all was ready for a new offensive and heavy bombers attacked the German defences. The 8th Army pushed forward. Nearly 750 fighter-bombers contributed, dealing with anything they could find in the forward area. The guns opened in a massive barrage and apart from the 8th Army, three Polish divisions and three American aimed for Bologna. The whole was completely successful, as the Special Order had predicted, and the enemy fell back to the River Po, which for them was the watershed between retreat and rout.

I was promoted again, after three recommendations it appeared, and became the senior man on the Wing. It was a jump of ten places.

27. The End in Italy

> *"There must be a beginning of any great matter, but the continuing unto the end until it be thoroughly finished yields the true glory."*
>
> ***Francis Drake***

A day or two before the cease fire, the 239 Wing CO, G/C Eaton, was shot up while leading a formation. But he was luckier than John Darwen of Chapter 18, his only personal damage being the glass of his wrist watch, "property of the Air Ministry".

The same night there was a disturbance in the small hours when an unduly optimistic unknown raced through the camp shouting: "It's all over! It's all over!" He was probably sozzled, having anticipated the event by four days.

The invasion of Italy had now fulfilled its main purpose. Many German divisions had been held down from the threat presented by the Allied Armies and Air Forces. There had been four amphibious landings and three prepared offensives, while all the Allies had faced tough conditions and a determined foe. Throughout the winter we had been under the impression, helped by German radio, that the last German stand would be in the Alps but the tendency now was to regard this as propaganda to deflect Allied insistence on complete surrender.

Hitler committed suicide, with Eva Braun, on the evening of 30th April. His "victory or death" had resulted in his extinction. Two days earlier on the 28th April, Mussolini and his mistress Clara Petacci had been shot – against specific Allied instructions – by partisans and hung upside down from the roof of a Milan garage.

The Desert Air Force continued its operations until the very last day and no enemy could move between first and last light without being spotted and bombed or strafed.

Poor weather earlier in 1945 had prevented DAF from backing up the Allied Armies as solidly as throughout the previous two years. Nevertheless the troops got to Bologna on 21st April. The Germans backed away northwards with a brief rearguard action at the River Afige. By May the 8th Army had curved round and linked up with Tito's partisans near Trieste. This was at the same time as the German defeat in the West and the loss of Berlin to the Russians. The German Army Group 'C' was utterly defeated and the surrender document was signed at Caserta on 24th April with what was left of the German High Command. The cease fire took effect on 2nd May. Only four German divisions were left. This finally brought to an end the fighting in Italy which had lasted for nearly two years from Sicily to the Alps. It had been one of the harder campaigns of the war, fought up the whole length of Italy and against some elite German divisions. We had held down German forces that would otherwise have appeared on the western and eastern fronts. It was not too wild a claim that if this had not been achieved, the outcome on those fronts might well have been very different.

An abrupt hush fell over the battlefields, over which the Desert Air Force had fought and bombed until last light of 7th May.

For a few days more the Wing flew over northern Italy, dropping leaflets to troops who had not received the order to surrender, then that ceased and that was all. We were all out of a job. 239 Wing as a major operational unit ended with this structure:

112 Squadron*	British
250 Squadron	British
260 Squadron*	British
3 Squadron*	Australian
450 Squadron	Australian
5 Squadron*	South African

✴ These were Mustang squadrons, the other two still flew Kittyhawks

~ Under the Red Eagle ~

An order came in that all Allied aircraft were grounded from 8th May, "Victory in Europe" Day. The Western Desert was now far behind us and the Alps were in front, only a few flying minutes away.

The Desert Air Force retained an identity stronger than any other overseas formation and its cohesion extended right from Commanders down to the most recently joined "Aircraftman, Second Class." Professionally, it had been superb and, amongst other technical flowerings, had evolved a system of Army-Air cooperation taken over by other commands. It had been an extraordinary gathering of different nationalities, especially of the Commonwealth, and, as Montgomery had said, produced a supremely successful partnership with the 8th and other armies. Its Wings were powerful and impressive right up to the end and it had achieved not so much "air superiority" as "air dominance." While the pilots were the fighting tip, they were a relatively small part of the whole and each had to be supported by something like forty or fifty ground staff. The aircrews were well aware of this and that they depended, in the ultimate, on technicians, administrative and general duty men. The "ground" was far from a safe occupation: Nearly 10,000 ground staff were killed on active service, 6,500 wounded and 4,500 taken prisoner of war.

The Italians in Cervia assumed that the war was over some days before the actual event and commenced a *"grande fiesta"*. They seemed to initiate these at the drop of a hat, to couple with their considerable number of Saints' Days. At the same time, the local Fascisti, or quondam Fascisti, were shorn of their hair by amateur barbers and tufts of hair lay in the main street for days, kicked about by casual passers-by. At HQ we received a request from the town for a Union Flag to fly in the main square, but we had to admit that we possessed only an RAF Ensign. So the main balcony in the square failed to announce the British presence and had to make do with red Communist banners and an old Italian monarchical flag.

While this was going on in Cervia we had our own considerable Wing celebration. I attended a party in Operations where we threw an impromptu pyrotechnic display with the aid of red, green, and white Very lights, which national colours were received with great enthusiasm by the Italians. In addition there was a large bonfire to mark the end of the blackout. The locals aspired to testify to the same freedom and light streamed from civilian windows as shutters were thrown back to the night after many years.

We found ourselves recalling many names who did not get this far and had fallen by the way. We had been long used to sudden death but at the time this was not dwelt upon. It could not have been, otherwise some inexperienced pilots would have become nervous wrecks. Now, however, it was different and we drank to many familiar but deceased comrades and colleagues – in short to "absent friends".

The weather began to hot up again and Italy regained its reputation for warm southern nights.

Despite the cessation of hostilities we were to move again – this time to Lavariano near Udine and the Yugoslav/Austrian border. Most of our sister Wings seemed to be doing the same so we assumed that this was the final concentration of forces before dispersal. What would happen then was unknown: Japan had yet to be beaten, of course, so we anticipated that some of us would be travelling to the Far East, some into Germany, and some back home. In fact, we had orders to prepare release papers for groups 1-5 and indent for documents for groups up to 15.

We finally moved off, on our own and ahead of the Wing, on 17 May. As we drove up the Ravenna road I noticed groups of MPs around a sign that this was to be a POW area, which confirmed the rumour that Cervia would become a holding camp for the remnants of the enemy. On seeing these redcaps I wondered what the collective noun for a group of them might be Λ "pinch" perhaps?

Then another notice appeared, courtesy of the 8th Army:

"This is the Argenta Gap – don't block it!"

It was surrounded by all the painful signs of that hard battle.

At the River Po we had to wait in line for an hour to cross by the pontoons. There were two – one up, and one down, built on the pillars of the former bridge and with green waters below, racing down to the Adriatic. Into Padua that evening, which was a clean, attractive place still, with lively young ladies, perhaps descendants of Katharina and Bianca, although they did not look like shrews, and youths with red flashes around their necks, former Blackshirts probably, with a new Communist allegiance.

Darkness fell and we found a spot to spend a warm night under the stars, which were sparkling pinpoints of light in a black sky unpolluted with light. The moon lay on its back and unless I was mistaken, nightingales sang around us. From afar came the strains of an accordion as local Italians danced into the night.

I was up as the sun cast yellow paths across the corn and we headed past Venice onto a long, straight, road driving towards the foothills of the Alps. Silver specks floated against the mountains as various squadrons came in to their landing grounds. We reached Lavariano and pitched a tent against a small row of mulberry trees.

The sun went down in a blaze: to the north and east lowered dark hills and far mountains in Yugoslavia and Austria.

❖ ❖ ❖

The 28th May was the final curtain for the Desert Air Force – the "Fly Past" at Campoformido airfield. A detachment of the RAF Regiment, my former unit when I was at Waddington in Lincolnshire, resplendent in blanco'd gaiters and belts, marched smartly to the saluting base. They did the Regiment credit. Senior Officers took their place, including Air Marshal Garrod, commanding the RAF in the Mediterranean and Middle East, and Air Vice-Marshal Foster, commanding the DAF. An announcer recalled the latter's work since it was first formed in the Delta of Egypt.

Precisely at 18.00 hours the first squadron of the first Wing – which had to be 239 – was led over by the CO in a Mustang at 500 feet. The order of flight was:

250 Squadron RAF in two groups of six
450 and 3 Squadrons RAAF in a long arrowhead
5 Squadron SAAF in two groups of six
112 Squadron RAF twelve in line abreast
260 Squadron RAF in a short arrowhead

To all intents and purposes the flying was perfect – more, remarkable, since ceremonial flying was new to the Wing.

239 completely overshadowed other aircraft who showed little originality in their formations. In all, 43 squadrons and 756 aircraft flew past.

> *"239 Wing has been without question the finest Wing in the Desert Air Force; probably it is the best in the world."*
>
> **Operations Record Book**

The flypast was to be the last big effort. Already, 250 Squadron was to be reduced to "number basis only" and the DAF was much too cosmopolitan to hold together as one unit much longer. Their work was done, and had been executed well, which would be the biggest commendation.

As an individual, it had been a privilege to be associated with a Wing in such an historical passage of arms. Now the moment of victory had passed and was much too transient an event for us to live for that and nothing else. The future beckoned…

> *"The great final battle in Italy will stand out in history as one of the most famous episodes in the Second World War."*
>
> **Winston Churchill**

The whole campaign was commemorated by the "Italy Star" bearing the Italian national colours of red, green and white.

Most of those on the Wing were awarded:
- 1939-45 Star;
- Defence Medal;
- War Medal 1939-45;
- Africa Star;
- Italy Star;
- and the special 'Close Support' shield.

28. Homeward Bounders

> *"As home his footsteps he hath turned*
> *From wandering on a foreign strand."*
> **Scott**

After passing it at speed during the last move we were now able to visit Venice. We made fair running, twenty of us, to Mestre, opposite a city dreaming in its lagoon. It looked as though it had been built on islands and it was uncertain to us which canal was natural and which artificial. The "main street" was the Canale Grande, winding through the heart of the city and carrying heavy water traffic. The ordinary rule of the road did not seem to apply: the heavier craft keeping to the centre of the waterway and the smaller to the sides. Army "ducks" were numerous. The shops carried surprising stocks considering that the cessation of hostilities was so recent. Married servicemen examined all kinds of underwear and the shopgirls were resigned to having flimsy garments held against them:

"Mary will look good in that."

"Me ne pub fare un pacco?"

The parcel is wrapped and borne away with a grin.

The most open space appeared to be the Piazzo San Marco, reminiscent of Trafalgar Square with its pigeons whirling around. They were quite tame and well aware of the seed sold by enterprising Italians. One Palestinian soldier asked me to take a photograph of him and a friend, asking afterwards:

"Are you sure you've got some pigeons?"

I assured him that he was positively ankle-deep in *piccioni* and their droppings.

~ *Under the Red Eagle* ~

I found a gondola and headed for the Bridge of Sighs. The gondolier stood at the back and rowed from an upright position, or, if there were two, the second rowed at the prow. They used either single or double oars and propelled the gondola with a rhythmic swaying movement. None of mine burst into song and about two knots an hour seemed to be the limit unless one waved a large Italian note and said *"Presto, presto."*

It was surprising to see how they could manoeuvre even large gondolas through the narrow back canals and past big craft. They knew their width to the centimetre and edged through seemingly impassable gaps.

On the way, two American GIs had obviously taken too much *vino*. One fell out of his gondola with a clumsy somersault and broke the canal surface, swimming furiously. Some Italians hanging out of windows above tittered immoderately. It then occurred to the GI that he could actually stand up in the canal, and did so. The Italians fell about with even greater hilarity. His colleague still in the gondola doubled up with mirth and himself fell over into the water.

"Imbellici," my gondolier observed, acidly.

Byron said that Venice was, "the revel of the earth, the masque of Italy." There was certainly a backcloth of beauty, if weathered and chipped, in buildings which had water lapping around their walls, while the Canale Grande must be the most unusual street in the world. Canaletto recorded it well, and it appeared to be much the same today.

On our last day the sun drifted down towards evening and the water reflected bridges, palaces, domes, spires and the striped mooring poles of the *gondoleri*. But away from the water, in the back streets, lay a secret world – tortuous alleys, small squares, churches, under eternal shadows. Death seemed to lurk here, as it did in the tall poplars of the countryside.

Now that the war was over, Venice had lit herself again and a thousand lights glittered in the dusk, all multiplied by the water. St Mark's Square glowed and the smell of cappuccino wafted through it towards the most Italian Quarter – the Cannaregio – where walls crumble beneath draped washing and the smoky and sordid bars were usually "out of bounds". I heard that the area contained what remained of the oldest Jewish ghetto in the world.

The city had its troubles – apart from the attention we had given to its harbour a little while ago. It flooded regularly, its stone and marble was discoloured and damaged and it teemed with rats with which not even the hordes of Venetian cats could cope.

Nevertheless, children abounded, with mothers calling after them – "Alberto, Giuseppina, Avanti! Faccia presto!" Men gathered to smoke and women to cradle babies in massive communal affection. Typically Italian.

An informant told me the city was sinking and might one day vanish into the sea. Not while we're there, I hoped.

The heat was oppressive now, July and August being the warmest months, but every so often clouds built up over the mountains and drenched the plain with temporary relief. The daytime shade temperature was about 100 degrees and although this was nowhere near Iraqi heights the humidity was high and the air oppressive. If one drank a glass of water, it appeared on the forehead in seconds.

We had even more severe weather breaks from time to time. One evening a storm of hurricane force swept over the camp. Tents were blown flat and occupants of others strained in mild panic to adjust their ropes and pegs and cope with the violence of wind and rain. Even comparatively stable structures such as trailers and Nissen huts were damaged and the heavy gusts went on into the night to disturb even the soundest sleepers. Very like Cutella all over again.

There was much movement to the UK now, by air and sea. Our final static position also permitted more "rest" allocations and the Wing took full advantage of the greater freedom. One or two bright spirits among the pilots even got as far as Paris and caused much "flap" on being discovered.

Then exciting news came over the radio at breakfast, when a cool voice said: "This is VJ Day, 15th August, and here is the news…"

~ Under the Red Eagle ~

There was complete silence, breakfast forgotten for a moment, then a roar of delight. A Wing and squadron signal came in from the Air Officer Commanding:

> "I have spoken to your squadron personally to thank you for the excellent work you have accomplished while serving in the Desert Air Force. The job is now done and your personnel are being dispersed with a return to civilian life or to other occupations in the Service. This, then, is my final message of thanks to all of you. I wish all ranks the very best of good fortune for the future and I hope you will get the just rewards you so fully deserve for your service in this war."

So did we! We looked out of the soiled tents across all the paraphernalia of war to which we had been long accustomed. It now had no purpose and was prospective junk.

The Wing had partly taken over a rest hotel at Forni Avoltri in the Carnic Alps, below the Austro/German border. It had been a holiday area for Italians and even now there were both civilians and airmen in the hotel, which had created a whole new atmosphere.

The Alps at this point were perhaps 7-8,000 feet high but lost little in grandeur. It was far above the hotel, on a high pass, that I finally walked into Greater Germany with a border stone marked "D" and a former German guardhouse a hundred or so feet below me. I knelt beside the stone, hand resting on it, and looked across the mountains deep into Germany. It had been a long trek to get to this point.

The Fruili area around Fornri Avoltri had been troubled in recent times since Hitler had decided to use Cossacks to subdue partisans in Carnia and had offered them the territory for a new homeland. He had other ideas as well, having decided that Fruili should be part of Austria. About 16,000 Cossacks were in the Val de Torre, as far as Forni Avoltri. All this was right in the middle of the so-called Republic of Carnia which was established in September 1944. Communists uneasily shared power here with other political parties and nominally accepted the authority of the Committee of the National Liberation of Northern Italy in Milan (CLNAI). There were continuous clashes between the partisans and others, and civilians, because Tito's partisans said publicly that they intended to make Carnia, and the whole Fruili area, part of Yugoslavia.

The Free Republic was wiped out and the Garibaldi (Communist) partisans had all dispersed by November 1944. Perhaps this indicates why we, as R.A.F., were so well received when we first got there in August 1945.

Forni was a beautiful place in fine weather and, I suspected, even more so under snow, but that did not commence until later in the year. It was still autumn now and the declining sun threw these mountains, on the edge of the Dolomites, into sharp relief. One could lie in the morning and look straight up a valley clothed in peaceful dark green pines with a huge outcrop of rock jagging against an almost blindingly blue sky. With little imagination, it was possible almost to sense the tremendous surge of energy which had thrust the underlying strata upwards – and it was still occurring as Italy thrust like an arrow into the body of the Continent.

The daughters of the hotel guests were Italian, Croat, Serb, French, and one Anglo-Italian. They added real life every evening when we danced to the mountain music of an accordion and gathered around the huge log fire in the centre of the room. The girls were of another world – Alpina, Mina, Dada, Maria, Anna and a dozen others waltzed, picnicked and rambled with us, and one or two obviously permanent relationships were formed. Even where the girls were of slight build they were nevertheless very "sportivo" and I was set aback on one outing to Cortina to have Dada say that she regularly skied down the massive face of the precipitous rock face looming some thousands of feet above us, over the road.

It was on top of one of these mountains, walking and climbing by myself, that I looked down into the forested valley far below. A small wisp of cloud formed, then slowly thickened into a dense cloud completely blanketing the valley from side to side. Presumably, this had developed where the warm valley air layered against the cold of the heights. It was a dramatic, even inspiring, event.

~ Under the Red Eagle ~

These were my last days in Italy. My posting to 56 PTC in Naples had arrived a few days before I came up to the mountains. So it was from the Alps that I would start the trek back home, from scenes that would provide a lasting memory down the years. England was now less of a myth and more of a coming reality.

One last, strange remnant of war…

One or two on the Forni "rest" included the Senior Medical Officer and others. I joined two of them in a trip by jeep to Auronzo. After a mile or two I began to have reservations about the SMO's driving. He had had a spiritous lunch and was wandering vaguely from side to side of the narrow mountain road. Another vehicle appeared over the crest – an Italian farm truck with over-hanging sides. The SMO swept towards it, still weaving, struck the overhang, and tore away the steel rods of the jeep's canvas hood. Since they were only an inch or two away from me, I was not too thrilled with this event. The Italian stopped and gesticulated wildly behind us.

"That's enough," I said. "Drop me off here and I'll make my own way back." The SMO glowered.

The jeep and its remaining occupants shot off up the hill, still swinging left and right. I regarded its departure with some relief and turned to walk to Forni, perhaps ten miles back. A second vehicle appeared over the crest behind me. 'Good – I'll hitch'. I waved a thumb. As it came closer I realised that the vehicle I was thumbing was an open German staff car! Not only that, it contained three well-armed Wehrmacht officers in field grey. They halted.

"Guten Tag. Kann ich Sie mitnehmen?"

This was ridiculous. After chasing the Hun thousands of miles, shooting and being shot at, I was being offered a lift by the enemy – or, at least, the recent enemy. No weapons, nothing! I hoped they knew the war was over. I wondered if the POW camps were still operating!

"Ja, bitte. Forni Avoltri," I tried, and clambered into the back, rather thoughtfully.

The driver had some English.

"You have leave at Forni?"

~ *Under the Red Eagle* ~

"*Ja. Sieben tag.*" That virtually exhausted my German.

I wondered whether this constituted "fraternising with the enemy?" Should I requisition them? But what the hell was 'requisition' in German? My Deutsch was inadequate and the driver seemed to have expended his English. The other two remained silent except for some short exchanges in German.

The staff car racketed along the road, seemingly bereft of springs. The engine could have used some attention as well. Then an uneasy thought crossed my mind. There were many partisans around in these mountains, and they might still be fighting without knowledge of the cease fire. And even if they did know, they might well regard a German staff car as a juicy target. Which included me. Hmmm…

This was about as near to the German Army as any on the Wing had achieved. Field grey and khaki, with Africa Star? Not exactly the common passengers in one German staff car. They looked affable enough but, then, there were still the partisan boys.

This story should have had the benefit of a striking conclusion. Perhaps an attack by a Wing Kittyhawk, an interview with the Gestapo across the near border with the Greater Reich, or more simply, an arrival at the hotel in splendid form. However, this denouement was going to be lacking.

It did not take long, perhaps twenty minutes, to arrive at Forni.

"*Danke*," said I, squandering the rest of my German.

"*Auf wiedersehen*," said they, and accelerated away down the valley. I watched them go with a feeling of deliverance and the grey car disappeared round a bend in the road. I was about round the bend, too. I walked up the hill to the hotel and encountered the drinkers under the vines. Few believed me.

"Gerraway! Hitching with Jerry? Pull the other one."

I left the wing on 31st August 1945 and moved to the main 38 PTC at Treviso. It had not changed much in efficiency since I last saw it at Sfax in Tunisia. I was "not expected", so spent a night on the deck again. At least, the ground was dry.

I thought so – after two days we had not yet started for Naples. Now it was 3rd September, six years to the day since the war started.

~ Under the Red Eagle ~

Once we got moving by lorry, however, we did so at speed – perhaps the fastest I had ever travelled in service transport. It was also hot, very hot. The cab of the lorry had a temperature 30 degrees hotter than that of the outside world, having had a new engine fitted and a pushy driver, so I was slowly baked. We hurtled through well-known names, now in reverse order – Padua, Po, Ferrara, Argenta Gap and Ravenna. The towns had brushed away their layer of white dust but the rubble was still piled – although in more orderly heaps. At the PTC we were informed that we could board a train to Naples the following morning. Mutters of "that's too good to be true" were prophetic. The train failed to arrive.

One pulled in, all right, the following morning but was packed from end to end. Our seat allocation had gone missing at Bologna. So we fumed and watched the last carriage disappear south with cheerful hands showing "V" signs (reversed) from the windows. Some hot exchange with the Railway Transport Officer brought the offer of a box car in a goods train carrying corpses but that – luckily – did not appear either.

The following day we tried again. This time there was a coach reserved for us – although we were not told of it and had to detrain again, humping our kit, and perspire up to the front carriage. No meals, so we were apparently to starve our way home – or at least, fast it. We ran over familiar country with the Adriatic near the line and sighing around a few lucky bathers. On to Iesi, changing from steam to electric. Darkness reduced the outer scene to isolated lights in a black night. Some airmen or army assumed contortionist positions and slept. I hung out of the window and watched the dark shapes of the hills slide past. Rome at 01.30, across many rail points silvered by the station lights, with railwaymen escorts waving red lamps and voicing stentorian shouts: "*Avanti*" "*Tardivo*".

I shoved away some army legs and laid a groundsheet for the night. Unfortunately, in the darkness, I laid it over some unseen grapes with a morning complaint from the owner.

"Who squashed my grapes?"

"Why leave them on the floor, you Charlie?"

~ Under the Red Eagle ~

I fell into an uneasy doze until full light, when I found that we were passing Cassino with its double hill and savage scars partly obscured by the early morning mist. There was a coach in the sidings with much graffiti in white paint:

"Yes, this is Cassino. You can have it."

"Boo Hoo. The ghost town."

Then Naples at last with its attendant smells and dark-eyed filthy children.

"Souvenir of Napoli, George."

"Nice sister."

The city had not changed much, except for the Vesuvian outline, somewhat altered after the recent eruption. We detrained after twenty-eight hours, tired, grimy, perspiring and ready for a bath and a meal – preferably at once. The PTC coped with us well and seemed to have been maligned by our forerunners. We were billeted, showered, and fed within the hour. Things were looking up.

If overseas service could be treated by analogy, the last grains of sand had almost trickled into the bottom of the hourglass.

I think back now that I was on the way home. 24 Wireless Unit was not a fighting detachment but got very near the German front line in the Caucasus and also encountered Russian troops. Its real purpose was to guard the oil pipeline in Iraq, which was absolutely essential to Montgomery and the success of the North African campaign. Then we performed guard duty in the mountain passes of northern Persia, and so helped block Hitler's route to India and a potential link-up with the Japanese. In that sense we backed the 8th Army and should have been entitled to the Africa Star. In the event, I was awarded it after joining the Desert Air Force, but others of 24 WU might have claimed the medal as well. On joining 239 Wing I moved directly into the battlefronts of Western Libya, Tunisia, Sicily, and Italy. The Wing successes on these fronts were undeniable. Those not inclined to be modest, whether in the air or on the ground – and why should they be with their combat ascendancy over Luftwaffe and Wehrmacht? – thought this Commonwealth Wing to be the best fighter and fighter-bomber unit in the Desert Air Force, and that meant the best in the world. For well over two years we fought our way north over what was admitted to be one of the most difficult battle terrains against a defending army of roughly the same size and perhaps even bigger in the last stages of the campaign. The casualties were therefore heavy – 500,000 for the Germans and 300,000 for the Allies. There were two extended and savage battles – for the Gustav Line from late 1943 to the summer of 1944, and for the Gothic Line from August 1944 until early 1945. It is not too much to claim that this campaign drew off vital divisions from the western wall and the Russian east and turned out to be crucial to the success of the Normandy invasion. A hard war, hardily fought.

We were scheduled to fly on an aircraft from Naples airfield and "briefed" with the crew. Reveille was at 04.00 hours and take-off at 08.00 on 9th September 1945. Our aircraft, twenty-five Lancaster bombers carrying twenty men each, were lined up impressively, if grimly, against the dark outline of Vesuvius. At the side of each lay a neat row of "Mae Wests" – lifejackets – since we would be flying over the Tyrrhenian and Ligurian Seas and then the English Channel.

We crammed our kit into the bomb bays and observed that most of the aircraft were carrying army – only two were for the RAF. I looked at the aircraft with some interest. They seemed familiar from when I had served at RAF Waddington in Lincolnshire early in the war. I had seen those squadron markings before.

It turned out to be so. From 5th September 15 Waddington-based Lancasters flew an airlift home from Italy under Operation 'Dodger'.[10]

Aircrew and ground crew milled about on last checks, and we fitted one another with the lifejackets while backchat reigned. The aircraft lumbered off at two-minute intervals with a blare and a din that deafened the ear. We watched the first fifteen into their single

---

[10] Some wit in the Air Ministry had obviously been at large. The RAF had a habit of identifying its operations with humour and it was not hard to realise that this light reference probably referred to us as the "D-Day Dodgers" – the Lady Astor soubriquet mentioned earlier.

circuit of the field before turning north. Time to board our own machine and we clambered into the Lancaster past a notice that instructed "Only one man allowed rear of this notice at a time." I presumed that had something to do with the loo being in the tail. The accommodation was as bare and stark as one would expect from a bomber, and we sat side by side along the fuselage like a set of paratroopers. The amber light came on – we lifted – touched down – lifted again twice … and were airborne. Italy dropped away behind us into the years; our overseas service terminated the moment we lifted into the sky. The light flicked out and we resigned ourselves to a dull journey of seven hours – Corsica – the French coast and then the Channel. The pilot passed back a message to reassure us that the navigator knew where he was:

"Over English Channel. About one hour to landing."

The destination turned out to be a Cambridgeshire airfield, RAF Glatton. The amber light came on again and the Lancaster's engines were cut, apparently well above the deck, since we dropped onto it with a heavy thud, then drummed dully along the grass.

We stepped out of the machine under a low cloud. England spotted on us with heavy drops of rain. Customs checked the aircraft and crew and we boarded vehicles for the reception hanger. Customs again, this time for us, currency exchange, and the inevitable FFI medical.

That night we adjourned for a station dance with the local girls – who actually spoke English – and Cambridgeshire beer. A grey morning broke. Train to London and King's Cross. A long gaggle of airmen humped their kit to the station entrance, with daylight streaming into the gloom from the curved roof.

The 'tour' was over, but we remained 'in' for 'the duration of the present emergency.'

I broke my journey to Paddington and sat under Eros again at Piccadilly Circus. Familiar red buses shot past and the flower girls sold their wares to those in many uniforms. Two RAF Special Police, one a girl, advanced on me, presumably attracted by my khaki battledress carrying RAF Wings:

"ID card please…"
They viewed my tattered 1250 with interest.
"Ah, Desert Air Force we presume?"
Then the female SP surprised me.
"Welcome back home. Would you like to come to our dance at the 'Falcon' tonight?"
Well, well… and an SP too!
I went to the dance; it was a lively occasion. The following day I boarded the train at Paddington. It was 11th September 1945.

POSTSCRIPT

Some years later, Harold Macmillan met Field Marshal Alexander shortly before the latter's death. Alexander had, of course, commanded the Allied Forces in Italy. They were going into the theatre together:

MACMILLAN: Alex, wouldn't it be lovely to have it to do all over again?

ALEXANDER: "Oh no. We might not do *nearly* so well."

~ END ~

Kittyhawk fighter-bombers of 239 Wing strafing German motor transport in northern Italy.

Kittyhawks of 239 Wing 'bridge-busting' on the northern Italian front at Rovigo, south of Padua, 7.4.45.

King George VI as 'General Collingwood' visits 239 Wing on the northern Italian battlefront, 27.6.44.

The end of the war in Italy. Desert Air Force ceremonial flypast [here No.5 (SAAF) Squadron] Mustangs at Campoformido airfield, 28.5.45.

Curtis Kittyhawk in flight – similar to those flown by 112 Squadron.